God Walks into a Bar . . .

"Whether you're a curious skeptic or a seasoned apologist, this remarkable book challenges you to examine the evidence for God and Christianity with both depth and intellectual honesty. Kent's writing is as engaging as it is substantive—witty, insightful, and refreshingly fair. Rather than cherry-picking arguments to support his view, he thoughtfully presents a comprehensive case for belief, engaging with leading thinkers from both sides of the debate. He invites you to wrestle with the ideas that shape our understanding of the universe, ourselves, and truth itself and make a decision for yourself. Highly recommended!"

—**JANA HARMON**, Senior Fellow, C.S. Lewis Institute

"This insightful book, conversational in tone, invites the reader into an exploration of life's most important questions. With gentle humor it moves you along. Is it likely God exists? What explanations can there be for our finely tuned Universe? How do we explain consciousness or our desire for moral guidance? What should we make of suffering? or of the empty tomb of Jesus? The tone is fresh, generous, and convincing. It makes complex arguments accessible. It is a book that will spark many rich discussions and is a wonderful contribution to apologetics."

—**BRIAN HARRIS**, author of *Why Christianity is Probably True*

"This is a wonderful book. Grenville Kent is one of our most creative and skillful apologists. Every chapter is engaging and equips and encourages a follower of Christ as well as being a most helpful and challenging read for the seeker. This is Acts 17 at its best."

—**ROSS CLIFFORD**, Past Principal, Morling Theological College

"Is believing in God madder than Nietzsche's moustache? In *God Walks into a Bar . . .* Grenville Kent pulls up a barstool beside atheists, agnostics, and believers alike, waxing theological about primordial soup, pink elephants and the Pearly Gates. If you've ever wondered which would win in a (metaphorical) barfight between faith and skepticism, then stay for a round with this book."

—**ERIN MARTINE HUTTON**, Moderation and Inclusion Manager, Australian University of Theology

God Walks into a Bar . . .

Evidence For (and Against) Faith

Grenville Kent

RESOURCE *Publications* • Eugene, Oregon

GOD WALKS INTO A BAR...
Evidence For (and Against) Faith

Copyright © 2025 Grenville Kent. All rights reserved. Except for brief quotations in critical publications or reviews, no part of this book may be reproduced in any manner without prior written permission from the publisher. Write: Permissions, Wipf and Stock Publishers, 199 W. 8th Ave., Suite 3, Eugene, OR 97401.

Resource Publications
An Imprint of Wipf and Stock Publishers
199 W. 8th Ave., Suite 3
Eugene, OR 97401

www.wipfandstock.com

PAPERBACK ISBN: 979-8-3852-5051-6
HARDCOVER ISBN: 979-8-3852-5052-3
EBOOK ISBN: 979-8-3852-5053-0
VERSION NUMBER 09/24/25

For Zoe

חסד

always and forever

Contents

Acknowledgements | ix
Introduction | xi

1. Nothing really matters... | 1
   Evidence from Atheism & Nihilism

2. The First Domino | 14
   Evidence from Cosmology

3. The Good Earth | 29
   Evidence from Cosmic Fine Tuning / Teleology

4. This is Mental! | 43
   Evidence from Consciousness

5. Are You Just Physical? | 61
   Evidence from Consciousness & Reason

6. Choose Your Own Morality? | 76
   Evidence from Morality / Axiology

7. Does Suffering Disprove God? | 96
   Suffering as Evidence Against God; and a Free Will Defence

8. Hitler's moustache | 109
   Evidence from Religious Experience

9. So far, so God | 119
   Is Evidence Enough?

10. Jesus and the Non-Christian Historians | 125
    Historical Evidence of Jesus

Contents

11 Jesus & predictions: can you find a hole in this? | 138
    Evidence from Fulfilled Prophecies

12 Jesus and Afterlife: four agreed facts | 153
    Evidence for the Historical Resurrection of Jesus, Part I

13 Jesus and Afterlife: conclusions | 166
    Evidence for the Historical Resurrection of Jesus, Part II

14 Ruby | 179
    A Curious Conclusion

Endnotes | 185

Acknowledgements

HUGE APPRECIATION TO THE Cambridge Scholars Network and European Leadership Forum for opportunities to learn and teach, and to Dr Ross Clifford, Dr Jason Hinze, Pr Norman Hurlow, Philip Johnson, Dr Philip Rodionoff and Dr Mark Stephens, who have taught Apologetics with me in various places.

Thanks to the following people—whether atheists, agnostics or theists—for catalytic interviews: Phillip Adams, Bishop Mar Aprem, Professor Peter Atkins, Dr Darrel Bock, Dr Rostislav Bogdashevski, Dr Ben Carson, Dr Gemma Christian, Dr Paul Copan, Dr William Lane Craig, Professor Bumbein Dashnyam, Professor Daniel Dennett, Dr Jacques Doukhan, Dr Liliana Endo-Muñoz, Professor Bart Ehrmann, Dr Kevin Fong, Dr Connie Gane, Professor Henk Gertsema, Dr Oliver Glanz, Clifford Goldstein, A/Professor Ross Grant, Dr Sam Harris, Dr Michael Hasel, Dr David Instone-Brewer, Professor Hiroshi Ishiguro, Dr Dirk Jongkind, Professor Laurence Krauss, Professor Hiroshi Kobayashi, Professor John Lennox, Dr Jonathan Loose, Professor Alister McGrath, Professor Andy MacIntosh, Professor George Menachery, Rev Dr Finny Philip, Geoffrey Robertson KC, Rabbi Dr David Rosen, Dr Hugh Ross, Professor John Sanford, Professor Tim Standish, Natalya Talanova, Professor Mike Tarburton, Dr Leslie Wickman, Dr Peter J. Williams, Peter S. Williams and Dr John Wyatt.

For critical feedback on (parts of) this book, thanks to Jacob Carson, Gary Christian, Dr Glen Cousins, Dr John Cox, Dr Mart de Groot, Miroslav Doncevic, Dr Bernadene Erasmus, Philip Johnson, Dr Sally Kemp, Dr Jacqueline Kent, Dr Aleta King, Adelle Magus, Letitia Meany, Dr Nada Millen, Dr Sven Östring, Isabelle Papadopoulos, Dr Andrew Pennington, Dr

Acknowledgements

Lynden Rogers, Tony Stephens and Sherwin Titus. Any mistakes are due to my own effulgent genius.

Thanks to students who have questioned and challenged me at campus talks, and to my Apologetics students at Australian College of Ministry, Avondale University, Morling College and Wesley Institute.

Introduction

You might have heard of the Babel fish. . .

In *The Hitchhiker's Guide to the Galaxy*, the Babel fish can translate every language in the known universe. Since it's so improbable that something so useful could have appeared by chance, it is seen as the final proof of the *non*-existence of God.

"'I refuse to prove that I exist,' says God, 'for proof denies faith, and without faith, I am nothing.'

'But,' says Man, 'the Babel fish is a dead giveaway, isn't it? It could not have evolved by chance. It proves you exist, and so, by your own arguments, you don't. QED.'

'Oh dear,' says God, 'I hadn't thought of that,' and vanishes in a puff of logic.

'Oh, that was easy,' says Man, and for an encore goes on to prove that black is white and gets himself killed on the next zebra crossing."[1]

I'm having lunch with Professor Peter Atkins, author of my university Chemistry textbook and 70 other books on science. He has told me on camera that God is a silly idea, life arose by "happenchance" and studying philosophy or theology is a waste of a good mind. I've just hosted his debate with his Oxford colleague, Professor John Lennox, a Christian.

Over dessert I ask, "Peter, what if you're wrong?"

---

1. Douglas Adams, *The Hitchhiker's Guide to the Galaxy: The Trilogy of Five* (Pan Macmillan, 2012), 47.

Introduction

He says, "You mean if I die and find there is a loving Father wanting to welcome me into an eternity of joy and love? Of course I'd be happy. But I would be intellectually embarrassed."

I ask the obvious. "Would you rather be intellectually embarrassed and alive or be right and dead?"

"Of course, but I would ask this God, 'Why didn't you give us evidence of your existence?'"

I've often heard that question.

A lot of people say atheism is a bit bleak and sad, but they're not convinced by religious talk. So they stay in the middle ground, hoping for a better place when they die, wondering if Someone might be watching over them, but unsure Who—or whether science explains everything without needing a God. They're agnostics—meaning they just don't know. Some are open to evidence, some are closed.

I'm a lapsed agnostic myself. Through school and university, I was a pretty closed agnostic, bordering on atheism. But then I was surprised to find myself getting curious, partly because I found scant meaning in the belief that I was just a collection of chemical particles together for a while, and partly because of hard evidence offered by people whose intellects I respected. If an eternity of happiness and the love of a kind father were on offer, I didn't want to miss out—but only if it was real. I wasn't interested in fairy stories. Over time I accumulated evidence for and against God. Mostly for. This book sums it up for you, making a cumulative case argument.

If you don't want to believe, you can find reasons. But if you're curious, or if you might like the encouragement of faith, then this little book could give you a logical launch-ramp, some intellectual permission for faith, some reasons to hope.

Quite simply, I find deep happiness from my faith in God. In life's depressing, confusing times, it has kept me from jumping under the Number 5 bus. So I always enjoy seeing other people open up to the possibility that

> There are more things in heaven and earth, Horatio
> Than are dreamt of in your philosophy.
> (*Hamlet*, I, v, 165–67)

Grenville Kent
Sydney, Pesach / Easter 2025

1

Nothing really matters . . .

Evidence from Atheism & Nihilism

I WAS ATTRACTED TO atheism when I was at university. I had Christian parents, but I wanted to do what I wanted to do without religious guilt or finger-wagging about morals. I read more about atheism and tried to practise it, but I was surprised to find that it had serious problems, and that atheists had been writing about them for a long time. Here's a sample:

1. No redemption

The philosopher and journalist Julian Baggini[1] says atheists may try to make their atheism look "positive, warm [and] cheerful" to others, but that's trying too hard. He says, "life without God can be meaningful, moral and happy. But that's 'can' not 'is' or even 'should usually be'. And that means it can just as easily be meaningless, nihilistic and miserable." Nihilism (Latin *nihil* = nothing) is the belief that life has no meaning or purpose, and faith and morals have no value.

Baggini says, "Atheists have to live with the knowledge that there is no salvation, no redemption, no second chances. Lives can go terribly wrong in ways that can never be put right. . . Sometimes life is sh** and that's all there is to it."

So why be an atheist? His reason is "not that it makes us feel better or gives us a more rewarding life [but because] there is no God and we would rather live in full recognition of that, accepting the consequences, even if it makes us less happy. The more brutal facts of life are harsher for us than they are for those who have a story to tell in which it all works out right in the end".

Baggini says we should stoically "detach ourselves from the ups and downs of life", but he admits the ancient Stoics could do this because they believed in divine reason, which was God by another name.

He admits it's difficult for atheists to find a foundation for morality, while religious people have "some bedrock belief that gives us a reason to believe morality is real" and good will win in the end. Atheists can reject morality without any fear of punishment, and atheism gives no "clear, compelling reason to believe" morality is real, so people often ignore it.

I respect his honesty, but his atheism seems a depressing view of life. Of course, that doesn't mean it's wrong. If there's enough evidence, we'd have to accept it and try not to be gloomy. But everything in me hopes there's better news.

When I discuss this with atheist friends, they seem a bit surprised that other atheists make atheism sound so depressing. They've managed to build lives with love and purpose and joy in them. Yet I wonder if they've done that because of their atheism, or in spite of it.

2. Embracing the Black Hole

I've always enjoyed the film-maker and broadcaster Phillip Adams. His book *Adams vs God* had a huge impact on me as a student. He says:

> To me, God is the great redundancy, the wrong answer to the incorrect question . . .
> God is the word we use for what we don't understand, and as knowledge advances, He, She or It recedes. God is an anthropomorphic projection onto a meaningless universe. He is also the starting point for the biggest, cruellest bureaucracies on earth, not to mention thousands of years of pogroms, wars, cruelties and inquisitions. All things considered, it really is an enormous relief to be an atheist.[2]

That sounds compelling. Yet in fairness, atheist dictators like Stalin, Mao and Pol Pot murdered around 148 million people in the 20th century (which is fifteen times the kill rate of the Crusades and the European wars of religion put together). So, does atheism really help?

"I believe and always have believed that life is totally meaningless", says Adams, "and that we have no destiny, no purpose, no author. We just are. For a while, anyway. Then we aren't."[3]

Hang on, *meaningless*? Nihilism can sound cool in a Philosophy class, but if you say that to a struggling teenager, they might stick a needle in their arm or jump under a train.

He says, "The only meaning life has is subjective, what we care to assign to it as individuals or communities. Rather like people seeing shapes in a Rorschach blot. We cling to these meanings like drowning people to straws."

It is important to do things we find meaningful, but why do we search for meaning if our brains evolved for basic survival on the African savannah? Could our desire to search be a clue that life is meant to be meaningful and we are made for a purpose? Adams says, "I believe, I *know*, that we live on a minor planet in an off-Broadway solar system on the edge of the Milky Way and that, in the final analysis, we're as significant as the eight billionth grain of sand beyond the final palm trees in the most distant oasis in the Sahara". But the universe seems fine-tuned in a lot of ways. And how do you live a good life if you think you're insignificant?

Adams says, "I believe it's absurdly vain to see ourselves as echoing God's image and just as silly to anthropomorphise, to Disneyfy, the concept of God into anything vaguely human. Like the hippopotamus or the hedgehog, humans are simply an evanescent expression of the life force, as destined for oblivion as dodos and dinosaurs." Yet the idea of human rights was first stated by people who believe humans bear God's image. The life force—is that God by another name? And how can we live well if we think we're destined for oblivion?

Adams thinks morals "are simply expedients, rules that we set up like traffic lights to sort things out. . . . Clearly, if you live in a universe where there's no meaning, there is, finally, no absolute morality." If that's true, what is there to stop people terribly mistreating others?

I enjoyed interviewing Adams and learning the story behind his atheism. His father was a Christian minister who went off as a chaplain for troops in WWII. His mother had an affair with a "smooth and unpleasant businessman" with a big car, who gave her a fur coat. The young Adams missed his father. He lived with his grandparents and, when they died, he moved in with his mother and her new husband, who turned out to be

3

a violent schizophrenic. Then Adams' father married again, and his new step-mother tried to stab Phillip with scissors.

> So that was my childhood... Living under great tension at home and not being able to rely on my natural father for support... But from about the age of six, I guess because I felt lost and alienated... I began to doubt the paternalism of the universe... I'd lie in bed at night, five or six years old, and terrified by the thought of death... I knew intuitively that the universe is completely senseless... that there's no paternal figure in the sky.

I'd much rather tell children they are loved and looked after, and can live happily forever. They seem to need that comforting belief, even if they are secular: Adams says he found "surrogate fathers" in "great big macho guys" like Superman, Captain Marvel and Batman.

People say their parents influence their view of God. Those of us who were lucky enough to experience steady, wise, unselfish, proud love from our parents– and to know the feeling of that unstoppable, visceral, bigger-than-the-world love of our own children—seem more likely to believe in a God, and the Bible often compares God to a mother or father. The alternative seems a bit sad as Adams puts it: "Most atheists... don't come to this conclusion happily... I can assure you that most atheists, in my experience, do not happily embrace that black hole. They'd rather like there to be a father and a purpose and a meaning and a destiny."[4]

I would too—but only if the evidence convinces me that it's true.

3. Still An Atheist, Thank God

In 1929, Salvador Dali and his Surrealist atheist friend Luis Buñuel made one of the strangest films ever. A woman's eye is slit by a razor... pubic hair attaches to a man's face... a man walks towards a woman but finds he is dragging grand pianos containing rotting donkeys, the Ten Commandments on stone tables, and two priests—perhaps symbolising that love and human progress are held back by religion and society. Nothing causes anything—a rebellion against normal stories where each event causes the next. Time doesn't flow: the story jumps back and forward. The film's title, *Un Chien Andalou* ("An Andalusian Dog"), makes no sense either. Nothing makes sense—and that's the point.

Buñuel and Dali had read Sigmund Freud, and saw the subconscious mind as full of sexual desire, murder and chaos. They rejected any "idea or image that might lend itself to a rational explanation of any kind . . . We had to open all the doors to the irrational".[5] This art fits the belief that "Chance governs all things", which is the first sentence of a chapter called "Still An Atheist. . . Thank God." Buñuel says, "We are the children of accident. . . deep down inside, we all have a penchant for chaos." He says his atheism means he cannot explain much at all, and has to "live in a kind of shadowy confusion."[6]

Buñuel was raised Catholic, but lost faith after rejecting the Church's teaching on sex, its behaviour during the Spanish Civil War, and "the problem of hell".[7] He was expelled from his Jesuit school after getting drunk on communion wine. Having binned the idea of God, he tries to make sense of things: "All my life I've been harassed by questions. . . This rage to understand, to fill in the blanks, only makes life more banal. If only we could find the courage to leave our destiny to chance, to accept the fundamental mystery of our lives."[8]

Yet he admits he can't realistically live by chance, and chance offers no real future:

> I foresee only catastrophe and chaos . . . Evil seems victorious at last; the forces of destruction have carried the day; the human mind hasn't made any progress whatsoever toward clarity. Perhaps it's even regressed. We live in an age of frailty, fear, and morbidity. Where will the kindness and intelligence come from that will save us? Even chance seems impotent.[9]

Without any kindness or intelligence behind the universe, is there any reason to hope for a happy ending?

> The thought of death has been familiar to me for a long time . . . but there's not much to say about it when you're an atheist. When all is said and done, there's nothing, nothing but decay and the sweetish smell of eternity. Only one regret. I hate to leave while there's so much going on. It's like quitting in the middle of a serial.[10]

It sounds like Buñuel hankered for immortality, for mental clarity and for kindness and intelligence in the world, but couldn't find these things in his brand of atheism.

4. "God is Dead"

Thus spoke Friedrich Nietzsche, son of a Christian minister.

Nietzsche was brilliant—a professor by 24—but had mental problems from early in life. Some say they were caused by syphilis he caught in a Cologne brothel as a student[11], though he said he left without touching more than the leg of a piano.

He compared Christian faith to alcohol, because both could dull the pain of life, a pain that Nietzsche said we should embrace. Christian faith was for those too weak to take revenge, too scared and humble and cowardly to get up and live a life and tolerate the type of pain that it takes to get what you really want. To be a Christian, he would have to believe "an absurdity."

Nietzsche was blunt about the implications of atheism. His story "The Madman" exposes the atheism that he saw becoming fashionable in Europe. It was written in 1882, when Rationalism was turning Europe's universities secular. Charles Darwin's theory of evolution was replacing God as an explanation for the origin and diversity of life on Earth. God wasn't needed to explain why chemicals react in a certain way. History could now be explained as the survival of the fittest or Marx's class struggle, rather than looking for God's providential influence or any moral principles that bring success to people or nations. Psychology would replace the confessional and prayer for many people, and the soul would be explained away by Freud as the subconscious. God would even be ejected from theology, making Jesus into a miracle-free human teacher in a fictional, man-made Bible. Then Nietzsche's mad-brilliant character appears:

> Have you not heard of that madman who lit a lantern in the bright morning hours, ran to the market place, and cried incessantly: "I seek God! I seek God!" As many of those who did not believe in God were standing around just then, he provoked much laughter. Has he got lost? asked one. Did he lose his way like a child? asked another. Or is he hiding? Is he afraid of us? Has he gone on a voyage? emigrated?—- Thus they yelled and laughed.
>
> The madman jumped into their midst and pierced them with his eyes. "Whither is God?" he cried; "I will tell you. We have killed him—-you and I. All of us are his murderers. But how did we do this? How could we drink up the sea? Who gave us the sponge to wipe away the entire horizon? What were we doing when we unchained this earth from its sun? Whither is it moving now? Whither are we moving? Away from all suns? Are we not plunging continually? Backward, sideward, forward, in all directions? Is there still any up or down? Are we not straying, as through an infinite nothing? Do we not feel the breath of empty space? Has it

> not become colder? Is not night continually closing in on us? Do we not need to light lanterns in the morning? Do we hear nothing as yet of the noise of the gravediggers who are burying God? Do we smell nothing as yet of the divine decomposition? Gods, too, decompose. God is dead. God remains dead. And we have killed him.
>
> How shall we comfort ourselves, the murderers of all murderers? What was holiest and mightiest of all that the world has yet owned has bled to death under our knives: who will wipe this blood off us? What water is there for us to clean ourselves? What festivals of atonement, what sacred games shall we have to invent? Is not the greatness of this deed too great for us? Must we ourselves not become gods simply to appear worthy of it? There has never been a greater deed; and whoever is born after us—-for the sake of this deed he will belong to a higher history than all history hitherto.[12]

Here the madman stops, and realises his listeners don't understand what he is talking about, because he has come too early. He throws his lantern down and smashes it. Later he pushes into churches with his Requiem to the Eternal God, telling people their churches are now just tombs.

The Madman's predictions came true in the 20th century, which saw human attempts to "become gods". Nazism wanted humans to evolve into the Superman. Communism gave us "Soviet Man", who would master himself and his world and "create a higher social biologic type, or, if you please, a superman", an idea which is "entirely in accord with evolution".[13]

The line "God is Dead" is famous, but less well known is Nietzsche's brutally honest comments about what it means. If we abolish God, we cannot really keep meaning, purpose, hope, moral progress, forgiveness from guilt, or hope of after-life. Instead, we are left alone in a dark and random universe.

I wouldn't call that great news, would you?

5. Albert Camus

Following Nietzsche, many famous atheists like Albert Camus, Martin Heidegger and Jean-Paul Sartre[14] take it as fact that human existence is absurd and pointless, full of anguish and despair. Camus was an Absurdist, believing that the universe is meaningless and irrational, and that a rational person looking for meaning can only be frustrated.

In an interesting twist, he used that as proof of atheism: if God existed, he would have given us meaning and purpose, but since we lack those things, there is no God. This is called the Atheist-Existentialist Argument, but I find it a textbook case of circular reasoning: God doesn't exist, so life must be meaningless, so God mustn't exist. It's easy to flip that logic: if we do find things in life that give us meaning and purpose (like loving, generous relationships or great causes that help others), then God does exist.

Camus sought solace in pleasure—his numerous affairs caused his wife Francine Fauré a nervous breakdown. His famously gloomy novels won him a Nobel Prize. Yet few knew that one of the most famous atheists of the 20th century was secretly searching for God. Camus went to hear a famous organist in a Paris church and ended up talking deeply with the pastor, "seeking something to fill the void that I am experiencing", and "searching for something that the world is not giving me". He kept quiet about their meetings over several years, writing:

> no one else knows. Certainly the public and the readers of my novels, while they see that void, are not finding the answers in what they are reading...
> Since I have been coming to church, I have been thinking a great deal about the idea of a transcendent, something that is other than this world. It is something that you do not hear much about today but I am finding it...
> there is something that can bring meaning to my life. I certainly don't have it, but it is there... We may not hear the voice, but there is some way in which we can become aware that we are not the only ones in the world and that there is help for all of us.[15]

Camus and the pastor discussed God, spiritual growth and being born again. The pastor explained Christian baptism as a symbol of forgiveness and a clean slate without guilt, and Camus looked at him with tears and said, "I want this. This is what I want to commit my life to."

We don't know what might have happened next, because Camus rode home from holidays in his publisher's luxury car and was killed in an accident.

I felt more fortunate than Camus. I was relatively young when I realised that I didn't want to accept despair and lack of meaning as all that I can hope for in life. Seriously, what are your odds of finding *jouissance* if you don't think meaning and purpose even exist?

6. Unyielding despair

My exit from the Church of Agnosticism was inspired by a quote from the mathematician-philosopher Bertrand Russell, who said that all we are is chemicals randomly connecting, and we're doomed. He spelled out his beliefs:

> That man is the product of causes which had no prevision of the end they were achieving;
> that his origin, his growth, his hopes and fears, his loves and his beliefs, are but the outcome of accidental collocations of atoms;
> that no fire, no heroism, no intensity of thought and feeling can preserve an individual life beyond the grave;
> that all the labours of the ages, all the devotion, all the inspiration, all the noonday brightness of human genius, are destined to extinction in the vast death of the solar system, and that the whole temple of Man's achievement must inevitably be buried beneath the debris of a universe in ruins...
> Only within the scaffolding of these truths, only on the firm foundation of unyielding despair, can the soul's habitation henceforth be safely built.[16]

How did Russell himself cope with this despair? Like many, he turned to pleasure, to hedonism. He was an early advocate of "free love", yet his affairs left a long line of broken hearts and damaged people behind, and at least one lover suicided.[17] Russell wrote:

> What else is there to make life tolerable? We stand on the shore of an ocean, crying to the night and the emptiness; sometimes a voice answers out of the darkness. But it is a voice of one drowning; and in a moment the silence returns. The world seems to me quite dreadful, the unhappiness of many people is very great, and I often wonder how they all endure it... The life of man is a long march through the night... tortured by weariness and pain, towards a goal that few can hope to reach, and where none may tarry long.[18]

What a view of life! It sounds like clinical depression. His atheism would make me an inmate on death row. Ditto for the universe. What meaning would that leave? Would it make any difference if I had ever lived at all? I'd be a cosmic accident, a poor unwanted bastard in the giant unplanned human family. And so would everyone else. On Russell's view, how was the human race any more significant than the dodo?

Death would smash everything. Even if you became a doctor who cured poor children of loathsome diseases, or a civil rights lawyer who brought democratic freedoms to a whole country, or a general who freed citizens from some vile dictator, none of it would matter ultimately because, in 100 years, all the people you helped are dead and forgotten. Then in time the entire human race would die and be forgotten because the universe never wanted us or knew us or cared about us at all. It all comes to nothing. In the end, it makes no difference. You had some happy moments and some sad moments but it's all over.

In the end, nothing really mattered. Anyone can see that, in an atheist worldview, ultimately it makes no difference whether you put a gun against a man's head and pull the trigger or entertain millions with music. Baggini said he couldn't find a foundation for morality. Adams said a universe with no meaning ultimately had no morality. And Nietzsche's madman said there was no up or down any more.

If a person is just molecules—like earthworms and dirt—why would we ultimately have more objective value? Russian Communism, which banned religion and enforced atheism, put this into practice by killing 120 million of their own people. (Stalin was quoted as saying, "If only one man dies of hunger, that is a tragedy. If millions die, that's only statistics.") Richard Wurmbrand, who was locked up and tortured for his stubborn faith, wrote: "The communist torturers often said, "There is no God, no Hereafter, no punishment for evil. We can do what we wish."[19]

Later I interviewed the *New York Times* bestselling author Dr Bart Ehrman, who started as a Christian theologian, became an agnostic and ended up as an atheist, partly because of all the suffering he saw in the world. I asked him if he missed God. He laughed at first, then said he actually had missed God terribly, but decided there was no point missing someone who did not exist. He said, "People who have a kind of de-conversion experience find it emotionally quite wrenching. It took me a number of years actually to get over it. I have a good friend who said that I went from being born again to being dead again." He added that now he enjoys good wine, food and friends, and values these moments even more because one day they will be over. "I suppose my happiness is rooted in the understanding that life is to be cherished, because I think this life is all that we have."

That's about the best you could say if you don't have eternity. But to me the logic seems wrong: if moments are precious because they are rare, then why wouldn't you kill yourself at 40 to make your life twice as precious?

Emotionally I couldn't enjoy those moments as much if I realised that each one was gone as soon as it came.

For me, atheism didn't make sense. Why would we have a brain and a rage to understand and find meaning and purpose in life if there was actually none in the universe? Atheism couldn't give me value, purpose, love or eternity.

Those three old questions prodded me: What am I? Why am I here? Where am I going? Atheism answered, "Dunno. No reason. To your death, but try to enjoy the trip."

By contrast, my parents' Christianity said there was a purpose to life. Happiness was in loving and being loved. Caring for others would lead to the greatest satisfaction, contrary to what our culture advertised, and God could inspire a life worth living and then an afterlife with "pleasures forevermore."[20] Centuries of Christian thinkers[21] made a simple claim: God made humans for love and happiness, the ultimate good. Happiness is possible—even in this life, though it can be hit-and-miss, but there is an eternity of bliss waiting for us.

Great, but was there any evidence for that? I started looking.

One night about 3am I was driving home from a friend's party. I was nineteen, and everything in my life was going as I hoped. I was near the top of my class in the best Law school in my country. I had a small business rolling. I had a stunner of a girlfriend (if you're reading this, hello) and fantastic friends. My night had just gone perfectly but I couldn't quieten an annoying voice in my head that said, "Is that it? Is this all there is?" For months I had been unable to shake a feeling of hollowness and lack of satisfaction that I couldn't understand. My mother quoted philosopher Blaise Pascal about a God-shaped gap in the human heart which only God can fill. I loved her and respected her formidable brain, but surely that was superstitious nonsense. Yet what if Mum and Pascal were right? I said in the general direction of the sky, "If you're really out there, can you please show me?" Then I turned the music up louder and tried to content myself.

I watched Fellini's classic film *La Dolce Vita*. Marcello the likeable but jaded journalist tries to find something to lift his ho-hum hollowness and *ennui*. He meets celebrities in glittering clubs on the Via Veneto but finds them shallow and lost. He hob-nobs with aristocrats in stately homes, and notices how odd and self-indulgent the very wealthy can be. He experiences religion as irrelevant, fake, superstitious, or dangerously fanatical—a sick little girl is trampled by a crowd waiting for an appearance of the Virgin, and dies. His intellectual friend spins impressive words but then suicides after murdering his own children. His fiancé Emma *Emma* EMMA! overdoses. He seeks love and family connection with his father when he comes to town, but the old man is more interested in chasing a young dancer. In seven scenes across seven nights, Marcello tries every materialistic pleasure on offer, but happiness eludes him. In the final scene, he turns a party into a wild orgy, manipulating and humiliating people. At dawn he staggers out onto a beach where a large sea creature stares at him with dead eyes. A teenage girl called Paola calls to him. We have met Paola before, a young waitress who seems the only happy, centred person in the film. She has encouraged Marcello to do something worthwhile with all his talent. Marcello has told Paola she looks like an angel in paintings, and she might even be his guardian angel, always radiating joy and love, wisdom and simple goodness. Now she is calling out to him to cross a small stream to come over to her, perhaps to *la dolce vita*, the sweet life, to redemption, but her words are lost on the wind and Marcello doesn't go to her. She smiles and gestures to him but he shrugs and walks back to his party crowd, with the same bored, dead-eyed expression and the film ends.

If Paola was calling to me, I didn't want to walk away.

I read *Ecclesiastes*, the 3,000-year-old diary of a king who experiments with everything under the sun—wealth, a harem of beautiful women, learning, music, entertainment, achievement, great building projects—and finds it all pointless and surreal, as temporary as a breath. After this experience, his conclusion is that knowing God can bring satisfaction and joy to ordinary life like nothing else can. Despite myself, I was beginning to wonder if he was right. If material things can't satisfy us without spirituality, maybe we're more than just physical ourselves, and our spiritual needs should be taken seriously.

With so many professors and media pundits promoting atheism, I thought it was logical and intellectual. I nearly accepted that these authority figures were right and got on with my hedonism—partying in the teeth of meaninglessness and nihilism and my impending death, and trying to ignore the God-shaped gap widening in my chest.

But for some reason I went looking for evidence for myself, and I was surprised by how much there was—not just fluffy feelings and pixie dust, but evidence and logic. Faith has had a massive, positive impact on me, so I've summarised a range of evidence in this book so you can see what you think.

Summary: atheism

1. Many atheists say that atheism doesn't offer many of the really significant things we long for—like meaning, hope, purpose, life after death, redemption, or objective morality.
2. Humans desire those things—perhaps more than anything else. This desire in us suggests these things are real.
3. If these things we long for are real, then atheism is not true.
4. This is not hard evidence, but it can be emotionally compelling, and can drive people to search for hard evidence.

2

The First Domino

Evidence from Cosmology

[The universe] does perform a version of the ultimate bootstrapping trick; it creates itself *ex nihilo*. Or at any rate out of something that is well-nigh indistinguishable from nothing at all.

—ATHEIST PHILOSOPHER DANIEL DENNETT[22]

Astronomy leads us to a unique event, a universe which was created out of nothing, one with the very delicate balance needed to provide exactly the right conditions required to permit life, and one which has an underlying (one might say 'supernatural') plan.

—JEWISH NOBEL PRIZE-WINNING PHYSICIST ARNO PENZIAS[23]

As I FOUND MY seat on a Sydney-London flight, my seatmate spotted the religious book I was reading, and groaned, "You believe in God?"

"Is that allowed? Or is this the non-smoking, non-believing section?" He snorted, so I continued, "Are you a believer?"

"Hell, no! I'm an engineer", he said. "I'm trained to analyse reality."

"Great!" I said. "Maybe you can answer my four questions about the universe."

"What questions?"

"One, does the universe really exist?"

The First Domino

"Of course." He didn't even bother to look out the window and check. But I didn't expect him to be an Idealist who thought it was all in our minds.

"Two, did the universe always exist or did it have a beginning?"

"It had a beginning—the Big Bang", he said. "If the universe was eternal, we'd be in entropy before now. Do you know what entropy is?"

"It's randomness, the lack of useful energy and organisation described by the Second Law of Thermodynamics. So, if the universe had been here forever, its batteries would be flat and its coffee would have gone cold long ago."

"Yep", he said, seeming surprised that a religious person had any clue at all.

"Third question: Was the beginning of the universe caused or uncaused?"

"Caused", he said. "Science is all about finding causes."

"Agreed so far. Question four: Was the first cause of the universe personal or non-personal?" There was a pause and he looked puzzled, so I added, "By 'personal' I simply mean it had the ability to decide whether to cause the universe or not."

He frowned, so I said, "Imagine a line of falling dominoes, with each event caused by the one before. Now stop the film and rewind, right back to the first domino. Why did the first domino fall? Did it cause itself to fall? If it did, then it has mind and is not a mere domino, not a mere physical thing. If something else caused it to fall, then the domino is not the first cause, and we need to look further back. Because the first physical event can't have a physical cause, can it?"

He thought a bit more and said quietly, "By definition, the first cause has to be personal." Then he must have realised how wide a door he had opened, because he swore and said, "Wait, let me think about that."

People have been thinking about that since at least Aristotle in 350 BC. It's called the cosmological argument for God's existence.[24] Here are some of its different forms:

1. Biiiiiig things movIng

Anyone who has flown around the world knows it is big. But our sun is a million times bigger, and a star called Betelgeuse is a *billion* times bigger *again*. There are 100 million. . . no, wait, the James Webb telescope estimates maybe 500 billion stars in our Milky Way galaxy. And there are maybe 200 billion galaxies—no, hang on, new research suggests 2 trillion galaxies—with 200 billion stars *each*. Crossing our solar system at airliner speed would take 1280 years. It's 9,000,000,000 kilometres or 0.0009 light years. The Milky Way is 100,000 light years, while the known universe is 93 B-for-billion light years across.

Are you sitting still? No, you're moving at about 1,000,000 km/h as you read this—1600 km/h with Earth's rotation, 107,000 km/h as it orbits the sun and 720,000 km/h as our solar system waltzes round the Milky Way.[25]

And that made thinkers like Aristotle ask the obvious questions: How much energy would it take to get these enormous objects moving so fast? And how much skill to get them moving so precisely?

Thomas Aquinas says "some cause must clearly be posited for this... motion".[26]

The standard answer is the Big Bang, but it's not the first domino: where did all its matter, energy and precise organisation come from?

It makes no sense to say that movement was caused by a force which was caused by another force before it, and so on, back and back forever. That's called an "infinite regression", and it's logically impossible. Why? Imagine you're riding in a train carriage. You look out the window and see your carriage is being pulled along by the carriage in front, which is being pulled by the carriage in front of it, and so on as far as you can see. Would you think the carriages stretched on forever and there was no locomotive? Of course not. If that were the case, there would be an infinite regression of carriages, and you wouldn't start moving.[27]

A guru[28] goes to an astronomy lecture and says it's all wrong, because Earth is on the back of a giant tiger that's standing on an elephant that's standing on a turtle. The astronomer asks, "But what is the turtle standing on?" "Ah", says the guru, "you're clever, young man, but you can't fool me. It's turtles all the way down."

I told that story to my nine-year-old daughter Zara and she asked, "All the way down to *what*?" Exactly! Where does the regression stop? It can't be infinite.

There must be a first force with enormous power, or else none of the later motion would have happened. Aristotle and the Christian philosopher Aquinas reasoned that there must be an Unmoved Mover, an Uncaused Cause of Motion, and they called this God.

2. Why is there anything at all?

Have you ever come home and asked, "Why isn't there a walrus in my lounge-room?"? No? Me either. But if you did find a two-tonne Pacific walrus on your (smashed) lounge listening to Beatles songs, I bet you'd ask why—especially if it had appeared out of thin air. Something that starts to exist needs an explanation for its existence.[29] Plato said "it is impossible for anything to come into existence without a cause."

So why is there a universe? Atheist chemistry professor Peter Atkins claims, "Space-time generates its own dust in the process of its own self-assembly."[30] Atheist philosopher Daniel Dennett says it pulls itself up by its own bootlaces, and "creates itself *ex nihilo* ["out of nothing"] or almost nothing."[31] Do you see the logical holes in those statements? Let me suggest why they're about as sensible as "I am the egg man / They are the egg men / I am the walrus / goo-goo-g'joob" (a song John Lennon wrote on LSD).[32]

First, how can anything create itself? A walrus would need to exist before it existed so it could make itself exist. That's laughable. Worse, it would need to know that it didn't exist and have the intention and ability to create itself *before it even existed*. And if we're talking about the universe, it would need resources to create itself before *anything* existed. Self-assembly? That's a giggle.

Time, space and matter had to be created by something (or someone) timeless, spaceless and immaterial. Most theists say the universe was created *ex nihilo* because God had infinite resources of energy. By the way, ever since Einstein's famous formula $e = mc^2$, we know energy (e) can be turned into matter (m), and their relationship is neatly defined by the speed of light (c). (It's interesting that early in the Genesis creation story, God says, "Let there be light...")

The second problem with a self-creating universe theory is that, with great affection for Professor Dennett, there's a huge difference between nothing and almost nothing. *Almost* nothing is actually something. If there's something there at the beginning of the universe, then

a. that's not really the beginning of the universe and
b. we'd have to explain how the something appeared.

Dennett doesn't want to bother thinking much about the universe's origin, calling it "arcane" and "nitpicking", not "compelling, or even fathomable".[33] Move on, nothing to see here!

Yet this is a huge walrus and it needs explanation. Thinkers like Aristotle and Gottfried Leibniz go deep, asking: Why does *anything* exist? It needs sufficient reason for its existence, either in a cause or in its own nature.

Everything that exists is either[34]

- *Dependent*, i.e. it owes its existence to something else. (Also called contingent.)
- *Independent*, i.e. it exists in and of itself.

You're a dependent thing. (I know you're more than just a thing, but we'll talk about that later.). You exist because of your parents, oxygen, vitamin B12, carrots, the sun and so on. There's a long chain of dependent things that you depend on. But can dependent things exist because of a chain of other dependent things stretching back forever? Logic says no—again, an infinite regress is impossible. There must be at least one independent thing back there somewhere to cause all the dependent things.

Now let's apply this logic to the universe. Big Bang theory says the universe came into existence. So, the universe is a dependent thing[35] and there must be an independent thing behind it. But what? Some suggest mathematics or physical laws are the independent thing[36]—but they couldn't cause themselves. Others, like David Hume, suggested that, "the material universe" was "the necessarily existent being".[37] But Hume wrote back when scientists thought matter was eternal. If scientists today are correct that it all had a beginning at the Big Bang, then his logic doesn't work.

Some argue that an eternal multiverse might be the independent thing—but where did that come from? If you think of the multiverse as a blob of everything, then what caused that blob? It can't logically be something inside the blob. It has to be outside. But the blob by definition includes every material thing. So, the first cause has to be non-physical and outside of time.

To summarise[38]:

1. Dependent things (also called contingent things) exist.
2. Dependent things can't be caused by an infinite regress of dependent things.
3. So, there must be at least one independent thing (also called "metaphysically necessary or self-existent"), an uncaused cause of things that exist.

4. You could call it "a Mind or... a more abstract Creative Principle" but it "can reasonably be called God."[39]

3. The first cause

Stuff happens.

There must be sufficient cause.

So says this version of the cosmological argument.[40]

You can't trace causes backwards forever in an "infinite regress of causes", says Aquinas. (Think of the train carriages or the turtles.) There must be an originating cause, or else none of the later events would have happened. "One is therefore forced to suppose some first cause, to which everyone gives the name God."[41]

OK, not *every*one nowadays. And there are some counter-arguments[42]:

a. Who says there must be sufficient reason for everything?[43]

   Well, science! And logic. Would we really be happy to say things appear for no reason? Isn't that anti-scientific, as anti-intellectual as the "close-your-eyes-and-just-believe" style of religious fundamentalism?

b. "Why does the universe exist?" is a silly question, since the universe includes everything there is, and there is nothing else to explain it.[44]

   Yet the universe cannot cause itself—that's illogical—so the First Cause must be beyond it. It must be beyond the *physical* universe, but not beyond reality. (We'll see later that a few real things are beyond the physical universe.)

4. The Kalām cosmological argument

This argument came from Al-Kindi, a brilliant Arab philosopher, mathematician, musician and medico in the 800s, and his *kalām* school of Muslim thinkers. Here's the logic:

1. Whatever begins to exist has a cause.
2. The universe began to exist.
3. So the universe has a cause.

It sounds simple, but deserves careful thought. It shows "that transcending the entire universe there exists a cause which brought the universe into being."[45]

The standard Big Bang model says the universe had a beginning, when "space and time came into existence; literally nothing existed before this singularity", so there really was "creation *ex nihilo*."[46] This was first suggested by the astronomer Georges Lemaitre, who was also a Roman Catholic priest, and the editor of the prestigious science journal *Nature* said the idea was "unacceptable" because it suggested an "ultimate origin of our world" and gave creationists "ample justification" for believing in a creator God.[47] Stephen Hawking explained, "Many people do not like the idea that time has a beginning, probably because it smacks of divine intervention."[48] But later he wrote, "Almost everyone now believes that the universe and time itself had a beginning at the Big Bang."[49]

What can logic tell us about the First Cause?

First, it must be beyond the universe since the universe couldn't cause itself.

Second, it must be immaterial, existing before matter. As cosmologist Paul Davies says, "We can attribute no *physical* cause to the Big Bang."[50]

Third, it must be outside time, unchanging, eternal. There is no time when it doesn't exist, or else it never would have existed.

Fourth, it must be uncaused, non-contingent, philosophically necessary in and of itself.

Fifth, it must have enormous power and not be limited, since it caused everything.[51] And either that power came into existence from nothing, which is impossible, or it didn't come into existence because it is eternal.

Sixth, it must be personal. This sounds strange and yet, as my engineer seatmate realised, the first domino in the line can't cause itself to drop, but a person can choose to cause things. A personal explanation and a scientific explanation can go together. Imagine we're having a beach picnic, and a watermelon peel hits me on the back of the head. You laugh and wonder why. You could calculate its mass, velocity and air resistance and plot its trajectory, and there's a scientific explanation. You could also see my twelve-year-old son Tom laughing nearby, and there's a personal explanation. Scientific explanations involve laws and initial conditions, while personal explanations involve agents and their choices. With my watermelon, the personal explanation doesn't deny the scientific explanation[52]—in fact it includes and completes it. Things don't intend things, but persons do. This is called agent causation.

There are other reasons the first cause must be personal:

a. If the first cause is just a thing, then we should include it as part of the universe—and the universe can't cause itself.

b. If the First Cause is eternal but the universe had a beginning, then there must have been a time before the First Cause began the universe. So the First Cause must have chosen when to initiate things, rather than doing it automatically as an impersonal cause would.

A transcendent God is the logical fit. Astronomer Alan Sandage, who discovered quasars, wrote, "God to me is a mystery but is the explanation for. . . why there is something rather than nothing."[53]

5. Probability

A complex, fine-tuned universe is significantly more *likely* if there's a God than if there isn't.

Consider two options. In one, the universe is "an ultimate, unconditioned, irreducible, uncaused, inexplicable (i.e. 'brute') fact"[54] that bootstrapped itself into existence (which is logically impossible). In the second, it was caused by God. The second seems a simpler hypothesis.[55] Atheists respond that an all-powerful, all-knowing, infinite, immaterial God is hardly simple.[56] That is true—God himself would be infinitely complex, but the God hypothesis is simpler than the chance hypothesis.

6. Why do the laws of physics exist?

Let's say you're staring up at the night sky and you start thinking about how gravity makes it all work. You remember that every mass attracts every other mass in the universe, and the force of that attraction increases as the masses increase, and decreases with the distance between them squared. That's called Newton's Law of Universal Gravitation

$$F = \frac{G m_1 m_2}{d^2}$$

But why is it like that? Why isn't it different? Who set big G, the gravitational constant, at the level it is? Why isn't the force inversely proportional to the distance, rather than the distance squared? That would change everything!

Then you wonder if this law is a thing. (Or in nerd-speak, does it have ontological status?) And what kind of thing it is? It's immaterial and abstract, yet it seems to govern everything from the path of a kicked football to the orbit of the satellite that beams the World Cup to your screen. It governs *every particle*, and *all physical reality* in the universe.[57] But how could it? You know Sir Isaac Newton didn't write it—he just observed it after seeing an apple fall. Then who did write this law? And where is it written anyway? And what makes it *govern* or influence anything?

This is called the Argument to God from Physical Laws, or the "nomological contingency" (Greek *nomos* = law). It says the laws of physics seem to depend on a lawmaker wise enough to write them, powerful enough to make them govern reality and kind enough to bother. You'd expect laws like this if there is an Intelligence governing the universe, but not if it's governed by random chance.[58] Einstein was surprised by this. He wrote:

> one should expect a chaotic world, which cannot be grasped by the mind in any way... [but] the kind of order created by Newton's theory of gravitation, for example, is wholly different... [It] presupposes a high degree of ordering of the objective world, and this could not be expected *a priori*. That is the 'miracle' which is being constantly reinforced as our knowledge expands.[59]

7. Pop! A Universe from Nothing?

Let's look at one best-selling atheist's explanation for the origin of everything. Lawrence Krauss wrote *A Universe From Nothing: Why There Is Something Rather Than Nothing* to show that science (not religion) can answer the question. He claims the universe "could and plausibly did arise from a deeper nothing—involving the absence of space itself", and it was "created by quantum fluctuations from nothing"—"the ultimate free lunch".

I found Professor Krauss enormously entertaining company when I interviewed him at the Sydney Observatory. It was the morning after I had watched him and Professor Richard Dawkins in a sell-out performance at the Sydney Opera House. He told the audience we are made of "star stuff", since all the chemicals in our bodies came from 200 million exploding stars. His famous line is, "Forget Jesus, the stars died so you could be born."

The First Domino

He was just as witty the next time I interviewed him, at Australian National University. He claims science "does not make it impossible to believe in God, but rather makes it possible to not believe in God", and he finds this "oddly satisfying".[60]

New Atheists love it. Dawkins crowed that Charles Darwin's *Origin of Species* was "biology's deadliest blow to supernaturalism" and Krauss' book is "the equivalent from cosmology".[61]

Yet the argument has serious holes, as other atheists have seen.[62]

First, the book's major problem is, well, nothing. Krauss defines a "quantum vacuum" as "nothing". Physics professor David Z. Albert, also an atheist[63], wrote, "that's just not right. Relativistic-quantum-field-theoretical vacuum states—no less than giraffes or refrigerators or solar systems—are particular arrangements of *elementary physical stuff*."[64]

Krauss replied by calling Albert a "moronic philosopher"[65]—wrongly, since his PhD is actually in Physics. Krauss loathes philosophers and theologians (like me), and says we are experts on nothing. But I think it's worth making much ado about how he misuses the word "nothing". He smuggles in a bagful of complex quantum mechanics, field theory, particle physics, etc, and says the bag contains nothing. He says, "I don't really give a damn about what 'nothing' means to philosophers... [I]f the 'nothing' of reality is full of stuff, then I'll go with that."[66] I'd say that bends logic and word meanings.

Two, Krauss doesn't explain where the quantum vacuum came from: he's "more or less upfront... about not having a clue about that." He admits (in brackets, just a few pages before the end of his book) that he "simply takes the basic principles of quantum mechanics for granted." Yet the complex laws of quantum mechanics are not nothing. And quantum field theory doesn't do magic. Albert says particles popping in and out of existence as fields rearrange themselves is no more magical than your fists popping in and out of existence as your fingers rearrange themselves. Quantum theory says which fields are possible and how they behave, but has "nothing whatsoever to say on the subject of where those fields came from, or why the world should have consisted of the particular kinds of fields it does, or of why it should have consisted of fields at all, or of why there should have been a world in the first place. Period. Case closed. End of story."[67]

Physics professor George Ellis agrees: "Krauss does not address why the laws of physics exist, why they have the form they have, or in what kind of manifestation they existed before the universe existed (which he must believe if he believes they brought the universe into existence)."[68]

But the problems don't end there. Krauss goes on to say that the multiverse may be eternal, which "addresses one of these questions about a prime mover and a creator. Even if there is a creator you might say, 'Well, if there's a beginning, what happened before the beginning?' And that's why some people have been driven to this sort of semantic cop-out which is God, which is someone or something that exists outside of time. Well, it could be that the multi-verse fulfils that role."

Whoa! Krauss admits that *something* had to be eternal and outside of time to start the universe! I like where that could go! He claims the external eternal thing is the multiverse, but I know of no mathematical modelling that extends the multiverse into the infinite past. All the models give it a beginning. And again, Krauss doesn't say why there is a multiverse in the first place, so he tries to sweep the problem further back under the carpet.

Even if Krauss had exciting new research showing that these fields and laws came from another property of the universe, I would still ask: Where did *that* come from? Why is it like that and not different? And what is beneath *that*? Another turtle? Krauss can't escape infinite regress.

The atheist physicist Sean Carrol wrote the following:

> Do advances in modern physics and cosmology help us address these underlying questions, of why there is something called the universe at all, and why there are things called 'the laws of physics', and why those laws seem to take the form of quantum mechanics [instead of something else]? In a word: no. I don't see how they could. Sometimes physicists pretend that they are addressing these questions, which is too bad, because they are... not thinking carefully about the problem.[69]

If you want a final explanation of why there is a universe at all, and why it's fine-tuned[70], the only non-contingent and necessary explanation is an omnipotent, eternal Being—or, in other words, God.

8. What caused God?

My airline seatmate said, "I have a question for you."

"Let me guess", I said. "What caused God?"

"Yes. If the universe needs a cause, then God does too. You said, 'Whatever exists must have a cause.'"

"Close but not quite", I said. "Leading atheists like Dawkins and Dennett misquote the Kalām argument that way,[71] but in fact it says 'Whatever *begins to exist* has a cause.' If something has no beginning—if it's timeless and independent or necessary—then it needs no cause because it is the first cause.[72] Remember, there must be a first cause, because an infinite train of causes won't move—you need a locomotive. Infinite regress is impossible."

What then is the first cause? Paul Davies said we "don't have much choice", either the Big Bang was "an event without a cause" (which makes no scientific sense) or it was caused by "something outside of the physical world". He doesn't believe in God, but he said, "One might consider some supernatural force, some agency beyond space and time as being responsible."[73]

If all matter, space and time came into existence at the Big Bang, then the first cause must be outside of matter, space and time.

So logically we're looking for a First Cause that's timeless, non-spatial, self-existent, powerful enough to make a huge universe, intelligent enough to fine-tune it, and personal so that it can decide to do so. That's how theists since Moses and Plato have defined God. The First Cause was uncaused, so asking who made God is a category error, something like asking "How does a jazz chord taste?" It's illogical as a Surrealist joke:

Q: What's the difference between a fish?
A: One of its legs is both the same.

9. The Ultimate Futility of Nothing—or not

Krauss's chapter "Our Miserable Future" says galaxies will recede "at faster-than-light speed, which means they will become invisible to us." Eventually, our universe will "return to nothing". Krauss says that its "both remarkable and exciting to find ourselves in a universe dominated by nothing" but doesn't explain why he thinks that. His advice is to enjoy it while you can, because "we live in perhaps the worst of all universes. . ., at least as far as the future of life is concerned", and this "underscores what some may view as the ultimate futility of our brief moment in the sun."[74]

. . .and suddenly we're back to the bleakness of atheism.

Personally, it makes me happy to know Krauss's logical basis for these claims is very weak.

We've seen good reasons to think there's a First Cause, an Unmoved Mover, a Non-Contingent, Necessary Being, nature's Lawgiver, a transcendent personal cause who chose to make a space-time universe without anything requiring that. The universe has oxygen and strawberries and countless other things that allow us to live and even to enjoy life, and that suggests benevolence. There is no shortage of physicists who think this.

For example, Werner Heisenberg won the Nobel Prize for creating quantum mechanics. The Nazis threatened him and called him a White Jew (whatever that might be) for quoting Jewish physicists like Albert Einstein and Niels Bohr, rather than the "Aryan Physics" of the Nazis. He survived only because his mother happened to be friends with Reichsfuhrer Heinrich Himmler's mother. Heisenberg gave us the uncertainty principle, a key idea in quantum mechanics, which says that the more we know about the location of a sub-atomic particle, the less we can know about its velocity, and vice-versa. Albert Einstein didn't like this at first, but Heisenberg wrote to him, "We can comfort ourselves that the good Lord God would know the position of the particles".[75] A devout Christian, he saw nature as "God's second book" after the Bible. He said, "Physics is a reflection on the divine ideas of Creation", and humans can understand because we are "created as the spiritual image of God". He saw science and religion as compatible ways of seeing the world.[76]

Or there's Arno Penzias, a practicing Jew who won a Nobel Prize for Physics. (He also narrowly escaped the Nazis as a child). He thought the universe showed "an underlying (one might say 'supernatural') plan."[77]

Astrophysicist Robert Jastrow, who ran NASA's Lunar Exploration program, was "agnostic, and not a believer" in God, yet he said:

> Astronomers now find they have painted themselves into a corner because they have proven, by their own methods, that the world began abruptly in an act of creation to which you can trace the seeds of... every living thing in this cosmos...
> That there are what I or anyone would call supernatural forces at work is now, I think, a scientifically proven fact.[78]

Personally, I find it encouraging that science points in this direction.

I'll never forget stepping out of my teenage son's hospital ward to get some air, trying to cope with what the doctor had just told me about his low chances of survival. I was on the dark side of the moon. Why would the sun bother shining next morning, or earth keep schlepping around and around it in pointless circles? Through the city smog and my tears, I saw a few stars, and started remembering things from the Astronomy unit I taught. There was stunning precision and beauty in the gigantic ballet occurring so far above me. Our golden sun would rise next morning to shine on the leaves of plants and cause photosynthesis that would turn human waste into food for the whole world, and would drive evaporation in the water cycle, and do a myriad other things on which all our lives depend, even if we never think of them. The whole brilliant system silently spoke to me of astronomical power and care. If it was running to plan, maybe there was a plan for my son as well, in this life or the next, and a kind face looking down in love.

Seems there was. Today he's a strong, happy, decent young man with some impressive scars, and a faith that he is loved and cared for, whether in life or death.

Summary: The Cosmological Argument(s).

1. It isn't possible for everything to be caused, because an infinite regress of causes is illogical. There must be a first uncaused cause.

2. The precise motion of huge objects in space cannot be explained by an infinite regression of forces, but requires an Unmoved Mover, a First Uncaused Cause of Motion.

3. Non-existence requires no explanation, but existence does. Existence requires sufficient reason.

4. Contingent things depend on other things for their existence. There cannot be an eternal chain of contingent things. There must be a non-contingent or philosophically necessary thing that anchors the chain. Without that, nothing would have started. This cannot be matter or mathematics. The only logical option is God.

5. The Kalām Cosmological Argument states:

    a. Whatever begins to exist has a cause.

    b. The universe began to exist.

    c. So the universe has a cause.

    This cause can't logically be the universe itself.

6. The existence of a complex, finely-tuned universe is significantly more likely if there is a God than if there isn't.

7. The many complex, elegant laws of nature suggest a Lawgiver.

This argument points towards the existence of God, though it does not describe which God.

Further reading:

Geraint F. Lewis and Luke A. Barnes, *A Fortunate Universe: Life in a Finely-Tuned Cosmos* (Cambridge University Press, 2016)
William Lane Craig, "The Cosmological Argument", in *Reasonable Faith: Christian Truth and Apologetics* (Wheaton: Crossway Books, 2008), 96–156.
Richard Swinburne, 'The Cosmological Argument', in *The Existence of God* (Oxford: Clarendon Press, 2004), 133–52.
John C. Lennox, *Cosmic Chemistry: Do God and Science Mix?* (London: Lion, 2021), ch 7.

3

The Good Earth

Evidence from Cosmic Fine Tuning / Teleology

The human race is just a chemical scum on a moderate-sized planet, orbiting around a very average star in the outer suburb of one among a hundred billion galaxies. We are so insignificant that I can't believe the whole universe exists for our benefit.

—ATHEIST COSMOLOGIST STEPHEN HAWKING[79]

It's as if there are a large number of dials that have to be tuned to within extremely narrow limits for life to be possible in our universe. It is extremely unlikely that this should happen by chance, but much more likely. . . if there is such a person as God.

—CHRISTIAN PHILOSOPHER ALVIN PLANTINGA[80]

NEIL ARMSTRONG LANDED ON the moon with only 40 seconds worth of fuel to spare, after having to reboot a crashed computer. He and Buzz Aldrin had six hours to wait before they could take "one small step", but NASA didn't publicise what happened next. Aldrin poured wine, watching its edges curl up the sides of the cup in the moon's weak gravity. He read from the Bible:

> When I consider thy heavens, the work of thy fingers,
> The moon and the stars, which thou hast ordained;
> What is man that thou art mindful of him?

Then Aldrin ate bread, completing a Christian communion service. He had asked Houston Mission Control for a moment's silence so everyone could give thanks in their own way for a safe mission. Armstrong just watched: he was a Deist, believing a god had created the universe long ago but wasn't active in it any more.

Earlier, the Apollo 8 crew had orbited the moon, finding it was not "a very inviting place to live", and saying "it makes you realise just what you have back there on Earth". A quarter of the Earth's population watched their Christmas broadcast from orbit, as they read, "In the beginning, God created the heavens and the earth. . . And God saw that it was good." Just before igniting a booster and scorching home at 40,000 km/h, they said: "Good night. . . God bless all of you. . . on the good Earth."[81]

Back on Earth, Madalyn Murray of American Atheists bristled at the mention of God, and sued the government. She lost, but NASA were scared to broadcast Aldrin's communion.

On the Soviet side, Yuri Gagarin, the first man in space, was quoted as saying, "I don't see any god up here." Yet his mission recordings and later interviews don't contain that line. I checked with his former next-door neighbour, Natalya Talanova, who is now the historian at the Museum of Cosmonautics named in his honour. Contrary to the rumour, she said, "I think he did feel the presence of something higher than himself." Gagarin and his wife Valentina baptised their daughters, often prayed, and celebrated Christmas and Easter. The no-god quote was probably made up by President Khrushchev during his anti-religion campaign that closed churches, killed 50,000 priests, and took away parents' right to talk about their faith with their children.[82]

Ever since Gagarin, space science has shown just how good and delicately balanced Earth is, and revealed many ways in which the universe and even the laws and constants of Physics are friendly to us.[83] And that raises the question: were we astronomically just lucky or did a great Mind plan all this?

Living on a knife-edge

Russian Alexei Leonov was the first to step outside the space capsule. He said, "Only out there can you feel the greatness—the huge size of all that surrounds us." Awesome—until he couldn't get back inside his spacecraft. His suit had ballooned up in size in the vacuum of space, no longer pressed in by Earth's atmosphere. He could loosen a valve to let air pressure out of his suit, but doctors had warned he'd be conscious for only twelve seconds before unoxygenated blood reached his brain and he blacked out. Digestive gases would over-inflate his stomach, pressuring his lungs and Vagus nerve and causing cardiovascular depression. And if he held his breath during this decompression, it could cause lung rupture and ebullism, which is when body fluids turn into vapour and can cause rapid loss of consciousness, bleeding and brain tissue damage. He had seconds to decide as his spacecraft hurtled towards darkness. Staying outside meant death. Leonov loosened the valve and, now slim again, jumped into the airlock doorway headfirst. He somehow managed to turn around in there with 2cm of room on each side—and he survived. I had the privilege of interviewing Leonov's psychiatrist, Dr Rostislav Bogdashevski, who told me, "Alexei understood pretty good he was walking on a knife edge."

We only really appreciated Earth when we started leaving it. Space science shows us that so many things we take for granted on Earth are actually crucial to our survival and, if they were slightly different, we'd die. Here are some examples:

- The Sun is a thermo-nuclear reaction blasting out a trillion Hiroshima-size explosions per *second*. Heavy particles would shotgun through our DNA causing cancer, but we just happen to be protected by our atmosphere and by a magnetic field which just happens to exist because Earth just happens to have iron in its core. (But not too much. More iron would mean a stronger magnetic field and severe electromagnetic storms.[84]) The Northern or Southern Lights are pretty, but what you're seeing is deadly radiation slamming into our magnetosphere at 70,000 km/h and being batted away. Earth dodges trillions of these bullets every hour—and we stay alive.

- This radiation threatens astronauts outside Earth's protection.[85] It damages their eyes: ask Valentin Lebedev, who became blind after 221 days in orbit. A metal space capsule stops some particles, but astronauts suffer radiation sickness—nausea, anaemia, headaches, fatigue and possible death, even at normal levels, let alone when a solar storm causes a radiation spike. (The 1972 moon landings luckily just missed one that would have killed the crew.)

- Our sun blasts out unthinkable heat—its core is a million degrees—but we are just the right distance away. A 1% change either way could wipe us all out.[86] Venus is one planet closer and can be 460° Celsius. Mars is one planet further away, and it's freezing. We're in the Goldilocks zone, which is "just right", like Baby Bear's porridge.

- And a planet's temperature depends not only on its distance from the Sun, but also on its albedo (basically how much of the sun's heat its surface reflects) and its greenhouse effect (how much its atmosphere traps heat, which depends on the gases in it). The interaction of these three factors has to be fine-tuned as well.

- Our orbit is a near-perfect circle. A long elliptical one could freeze and boil our oceans and we'd be as dead as a reheated chicken dinner.

- Mercury spins 59 times more slowly than Earth, and one side reaches 465° C while the dark side is—185°. By contrast, Earth's rotation rate keeps our temperatures fairly even (and most of us get a dark night for sleeping!).

- Earth's spin axis is tilted 23.5 degrees, giving us seasons. When the Northern Hemisphere leans away from the Sun, it's winter there. If we had no tilt, we'd have no seasons—and how would plants live and give us food and oxygen? Yet a bigger tilt would make seasons too severe. Again, the setup is just right.

- The Moon's gravitational pull causes the ocean tides crucial to marine life. And marine plants give us half our oxygen—we owe them every second breath we take.

- Earth has a great address in the galaxy. If we were much closer to the centre[87], X-rays and Gamma rays from the black hole could fry us, exploding supernovae could threaten us, and thick traffic would risk fatal collisions and gravity disturbances. A spiral arm protects us from radiation but we're far enough away for a great view, without the constant clouds that Venus, Jupiter and Saturn have.

- We're near enough for big brother Jupiter to protect us from asteroid strikes, but far enough to avoid gravity disturbances.

- Our sun is a main-sequence star, which is the only kind that supports life. A red giant or white dwarf wouldn't support life, and red dwarfs can only make a tiny habitable zone.[88]

- Earth's gravity is fine-tuned to chemistry. It is just right to hold water, which weighs 18 g/mol, but not to hold much poisonous methane and ammonia, which weigh 16 and 17 g/mol. Oh, and our gravity is set just right to hold an atmosphere we can breathe. The Moon has 1/6 of our gravity, and no atmosphere.

- Jupiter's gravity is 2.4 times ours, so if you weigh 80kg here, you'd weigh 192kg there. Physicists estimate that gravity four times stronger would crack our leg bones and make our blood too heavy for our hearts to pump up from our legs, and we couldn't get up.[89]

I took a Zero Gravity flight with my son Marcus. He did flips and ate water drops that were hanging in the air, but I lost my breakfast. I was happy to hear that about half of astronauts find zero gravity disturbs the balance system in their ears, resulting in airsickness—they practice in an aircraft nicknamed the Vomit Comet. And space medicine[90] reveals other major problems with living in microgravity:

- Heart. You don't have to pump blood uphill against gravity, so your heart muscle quickly deconditions, seriously reducing aerobic fitness and risking arrythmia.[91]
- Muscles. You don't have to lift anything, so you quickly get weaker—in fact, your muscle mass decreases as much as 20% on an eleven-day mission. Special exercise equipment only helps a bit.
- Blood. Astronauts lose 20% of their red blood cells. The body doesn't work as hard and needs less oxygen, so it retires some of the cells that carry it.
- Skeleton. Bones need load-bearing exercise and mechanical stress to keep rebuilding themselves. (Ask someone with osteoporosis.) With no gravity, bones waste away rapidly. A year on the Space Station could cost 20% of your bone mass, and all that calcium goes into the blood and you pee it out, risking constipation, painful kidney stones and even psychotic depression.
- Bacteria. Bugs thrive in microgravity, and sneezes hang in the air.[92]
- Body waste. Um, well, other things also hang in microgravity. In one NASA recording, astronauts shout, "We have a floater!", so NASA spent a million dollars designing a zero-G toilet that uses suction.
- Eyes. Body mechanisms keep fluid up in our heads, but without gravity, too much fluid accumulates. Extra pressure in the head can puff up faces, distort eyeballs and pressure optic nerves.[93]

Who knew gravity was so important to so many technologies in our bodies? Earth's gravity is just right.

The gravity of all this

Gravity bonds planets to stars, stars into galaxies, and galaxies into clusters and super-clusters, working across ginormous distances—and also within atoms. It's one of the four basic forces of nature, and the way they all balance is crucial.[94]

Inside a tiny atom, forces known as the strong nuclear force and the weak force help bind the atom's nucleus together, while the "electromagnetic force" keeps protons in the nucleus apart. If you could change the electromagnetic force by one in a hundred thousand million million, then all atoms bigger than Hydrogen would break up. No chemistry. No us. Imagine those odds as a pack of 100,000,000,000,000,000 cards and if, Physics pulls the wrong card, we die.

The force of gravity follows the gravitational constant G, described by Sir Isaac Newton and Albert Einstein. G is set exactly right. Make G smaller and everything flies apart—your burrito, you, the planet. Make G bigger and the orbits of atoms and solar systems contract, and stars burn faster, making our sun 1000 times hotter.[95] So our lives depend on physics constants being infinitesimally correct. Astrophysicist Martin Rees names six constants that make the universe possible.[96] Stephen Hawking said, "The laws of science. . . contain many fundamental numbers. . . The remarkable fact is that the values of these numbers seem to have been very finely adjusted to make possible the development of life."[97]

Astronomy, cosmology and physics keep finding more of these fine-tuned constants, relevant not only to Earth but to the universe.[98] Physicist Paul Davies suggested 20 factors from physics and ten from cosmology in *The Goldilocks Enigma: Why is the Universe Just Right for Life?*[99] Astrophysicist Hugh Ross lists 140 factors required for the *possibility* of advanced life, then 402 factors to do with a planetary system and its galaxy.[100] (Of course we're not the only advanced life-form that could have appeared—science fiction can dream up all kinds—but we are the only one known.)

These are numbers that describe the universe, but immaterial mathematics cannot influence physical reality. What does? These constants can hardly "somehow exist outside of physical reality and command its

The Good Earth

obedience".[101] Where are they written or stored? How were they set? Why are they there at all—why isn't the universe random? Why don't they change?

Some thinkers say numbers don't really exist except in our minds. But Maths doesn't depend on our minds: triangles have three sides whether I know it or not. Maths is much bigger than our minds: Galois Theory and Teichmüller Theory work even if your Maths teacher doesn't know about them. Two plus two equalled four before Pythagoras was born, and it always will. And everyone who has ever gotten a Maths question wrong knows that Maths shows a true and a false.

So we just found something non-physical that is real, true, beyond our minds, and timeless. Plato said numbers were real, eternal and unchanging, but not part of the physical world and not able to cause anything. That's a major threat to materialism (the belief that matter is all there is). Maths is made of abstract concepts and theories. It is thought-like, but what are thoughts made of? They can only be made of other thoughts, concepts, ideas, theories. . . so thought and Mind seem to exist in a non-physical reality of their own. Materialism cannot recognise this, so it is not fully describing reality.

If we define the universe as all existing matter, then Maths is *outside the universe* but still real. Materialism cannot imagine anything non-physical or existing outside space-time, so perhaps materialism is not telling us the full story. What then would be the foundation for the existence of Maths outside the physical universe? A mental foundation to all reality.[102] A great Mind thinking of it.

So where could these abstract things exist? What if Maths exists in a great Mind? What if that great Mind designed the universe using Maths? (And also the laws of logic, which are also non-physical but real.). As Keith Ward put it:

> The continued conformity of physical particles to precise mathematical relationships is. . . much more likely to exist if there is an ordering cosmic mathematician who sets up the correlation. . . The existence of laws of physics. . . strongly implies there is a God who formulates such laws and ensures that the physical realm conforms to them.[103]

Real Maths geniuses see beauty and elegance there. Take Paul Erdős, who saw Maths as pure, deep, artistic and aesthetic:

Why are numbers beautiful? It's like asking why is Beethoven's Ninth Symphony beautiful. If you don't see why, someone can't tell you. I *know* numbers are beautiful. If they aren't beautiful, nothing is.[104]

Erdős doubted whether God existed—most of his Jewish family had been murdered in WWII—but he joked that God had a book with the most "elegant and perfect" mathematical proofs in it.[105]

Johannes Kepler, who discovered the laws of planetary motion among many other things, said, "Those laws [of nature] are within the grasp of the human mind; God wanted us to recognize them by creating us after his own image so that we could share in his own thoughts."[106]

The bottom line: so many things (huge and tiny) went right, or we wouldn't be here. What are the odds of that? Minute. Teeny-weeny. Nanoscopically low.

So the obvious question is. . .

Why is the universe so fine-tuned for life?

Here are the main answers[107] scientists give:

1. Don't ask

Mathematician-philosopher Bertrand Russell was asked why the universe exists, and said, "I should say that the universe is just there, and that's all."[108] Not exactly a scientific explanation, is it? But Russell said this in 1948, when scientists thought matter had always been there in a steady state, before Big Bang theory suggested that the universe had a beginning was created in a one-off event or singularity.

2. Chance

If there's no God, we're left with chance driving everything. But Hugh Ross calculated the probability of getting all the complex, inter-connected factors for life on earth was 1 in 10^{311}.

That's 1 in 100,000,000,000,000,000,000,000,000,000,000,000,000,000,000,000,000,000,000,000,000,000,000,000,000,000,000,000,000,000,000,000,000,000,000,000,000,000,000,000,000,000,000,000,000,000,0

00,000,000,000,000,000,000,000,000,000,000,000,000,000,000,00
0,000,000,000,000,000,000,000,000,000,000,000,000,000,000,000,
000,000,000,000,000,000,000,000,000,000,000,000,000,000,000,0
00,000,000,000.

That's a lot of zeroes, but what does 1 in 10^{311} actually mean? Well, there are 10^{80} atoms in the known universe, and so the chances of getting the right conditions for life on earth are (take a deep breath) the number of atoms in the universe *times* the number of atoms in the universe *times* the number of atoms in the universe *times* one hundred million billion billion billion billion billion billion billion.

And Ross told me that as he reads new scientific research, these odds get about a million times worse each month. So multiply all that by 1,000,000 every month, then all that by 1,000,000 next month...

Worse, those are just the chances of getting a planet ready for humans. We'd have to multiply them by the odds of everything that happened since, for example the chances of chemicals getting together to form the first cell, then multi-cellular animals appearing and evolving into us—entirely by chance.

How do atheists account for those odds? Astrophysicist (and New Atheist) Lawrence Krauss told me, "The universe is big and old and accidents happen all the time... In a universe as complex as ours, very, very strange things can happen. And in fact the laws of physics are such that if it isn't impossible, it's inevitable."

The problem with that claim is that I could use it to argue there must be a God. If God is not impossible, then he's inevitable. But this logic would mean *anything* is inevitable—there must be a purple crocodile who burps German stock market results in Mongolian while playing Beethoven's Nineteenth Symphony backwards on a glockenspiel. In other words, Krauss's comment would destroy probability theory. Unlikely things do happen, but mathematicians talk about the lower probability bound, below which things are functionally impossible. The argument might have worked in the old days when scientists assumed matter and the universe were eternal. Given eternity, literally anything could happen. But now Big Bang theory says the universe is only 13.8 billion years old. (Yes, that's a long time, but not long enough for blind chance to work.)

If it's all by chance, then humans are an unwanted accident in a mindless, absurd universe—"chemical scum"—but instead we have Hawking doing brilliant physics and coming up with funny lines about chemical scum, and all of us capable of curiosity and logic, empathy and love, creativity and kindness. How would an irrational universe produce all that?

Even the Nobel-winning physicist Roger Penrose, while saying he has no religion[109], said,

> I think I would say that the universe has a purpose, it's not somehow just there by chance. . . some people, I think, take the view that the universe is just there and it runs along—it's a bit like it just sort of computes, and we happen somehow by accident to find ourselves in this thing. But I don't think that's a very fruitful or helpful way of looking at the universe. I think that there is something much deeper about it.[110]

Respect to an atheist for looking for purpose and something deeper than just chance, even if he doesn't quite know where to look.

3. Laws of nature

Hawking wrote that "the beginning of the universe was governed by the laws of science and doesn't need to be set in motion by some god."[111] He thought we may find a "Theory of Everything" that pulled all the laws together.

There's no doubt that the constants of physics and cosmology happen to be exactly right for a life-permitting universe and the laws are complex and elegant. Yet that's a description, not an explanation of a universe fine-tuned for life. We have to ask: Why are the laws like this when they could be different? Did they just happen, with no thought behind them? And where are these laws stored?

Laws might logically suggest a law-maker.

4. Multiple universes

Multiverse theory seems to give us more chances to fluke all that fine-tuning. With depressingly low odds of winning a lottery, you could buy more tickets in more lotteries to up your chances. Multiverse theory buys us a ticket in more universes. With a very large number—even an infinite number—then *of course* one of them would have everything go right for life. And *of course* we'd be in that universe or we wouldn't be around to see it. Multiverse theory says you shouldn't be surprised by that, or you're making a logic error called survivor bias or observation bias.[112] Krauss wrote, "it is not too surprising to find that we live in a universe in which we can live!"[113]

But imagine you survived execution by a firing squad. Would you think, "It's not surprising that I survived: if I didn't, I wouldn't be thinking about it"? Or would you be very surprised that you survived against high odds?[114]

Krauss says religious people imagine "that each fundamental constant is significant because God presumably chose each one to have the value it does as part of a divine plan for our universe. In this case, nothing is an accident, but by the same token, nothing is predicted or actually explained."[115]

I'd say that God fine-tuning constants could explain everything.

Krauss told me that there only *seems* to be fine-tuning, and maybe the constants could have other values in other universes. "Could life be possible? We just don't know the answer."[116] And yet we don't actually know whether other universes exist—they would not be observable by us—so multiverse theories are science fiction. Even if they existed, the chances of getting one more universe with another combination of constants fine-tuned for life could be as low as Ross's 1 in 10^{311}. Two universes would demand *more* fine-tuning and *more* explanation than one, and so on. And all these universes would have a beginning, and would need resources to create them. Multiverse theory is a guess intended to make fine-tuning seem less amazing, but it actually creates more problems.[117]

5. Designer

The astronomer Sir Fred Hoyle, who made up the term "Big Bang", was an atheist. He came up with the theory that chemical elements were created when smaller elements were joined together by nuclear fusion inside stars at temperatures of billions of degrees. When these stars died, the elements blew out into the universe. Some then joined together in other stars to form even larger elements. This theory is called stellar nucleosynthesis, and is widely accepted today. To put it very simply, Hoyle noticed that Carbon was formed when two Helium atoms collided to form a Beryllium atom, and then another Helium atom attached before the Beryllium decayed. The Carbon atom formed only because three factors were exactly right:

- The Beryllium atom's rate of decay was slow enough that there was time for the Helium atom to join the party before it ended.

- There happens to be an excited state of the Carbon atom with exactly the right energy level and spin to allow the Beryllium and Helium atoms to fuse into it. Then the Carbon calms down to a stable ground state.
- There is another process where adding another Helium atom to a Carbon atom can produce an Oxygen atom, and if Oxygen had a slightly more excited state, this process would happen more easily and most of the Carbon in the universe would have turned into Oxygen.

(There's so much more detail! Google the Triple-alpha process if you're interested.)

When you think that all known life is Carbon-based, it's lucky that all these things went right. Or was it lucky? Hoyle found it very unlikely that Carbon would have exactly the right energy level by chance. He wrote:

> Some super-calculating intellect must have designed the properties of the carbon atom, otherwise the chance of my finding such an atom through the blind forces of nature would be utterly minuscule. A common sense interpretation of the facts suggests that a superintellect has monkeyed with physics, as well as with chemistry and biology, and that there are no blind forces worth speaking about in nature. The numbers one calculates from the facts seem to me so overwhelming as to put this conclusion almost beyond question.[118]

Hoyle thought that "any scientist who examined the evidence" would infer that "the laws of nuclear physics have been deliberately designed with regard to the consequences they produce inside stars."[119]

Hoyle started searching for the "superintellect", and spent his later life studying religion.

Many scientists have also been open and curious about a big Mind. For example, physicist Freeman Dyson wrote, "As we look out into the universe and identify the many accidents of physics and astronomy that have worked together to our benefit, it almost seems as if the universe must in some sense have known we were coming."[120]

The odds of us existing by chance are one in a number much greater than the number of atoms in this huge universe, so is chance really our best, most scientific explanation?

How fragile we are! Tweak any one of many delicately interdependent factors and we vanish like a soap bubble. We're highly improbable and almost impossible—yet here we are.

Some argue that one planet would have been enough for a God to create life, and that a vast, mostly empty, mostly hostile universe looks more like a place where chemicals could have enough chances to mix randomly and make everything.[121] But probability destroys that claim. And what if God is lavish rather than stingy and boring? We see violent detonations of unimaginable amounts of matter at a safe distance, and an elegant ballet with dancers a million billion times bigger than Earth, some icy, some in nuclear furnaces at millions of degrees. It demands our attention—from children to Nobel laureates. Could God be hoping we'll react with curiosity and wonder about the power and genius on display?

It's fair to say that this line of reasoning suggests a God but says nothing about which God or gods are involved. But I'm with Sir Isaac Newton: "This most beautiful system of the sun, planets, and comets could only proceed from the counsel and dominion of an intelligent and powerful Being."[122]

Summary: evidence from cosmic fine-tuning/teleology

1. Astronomy and cosmology reveal many, many factors that had to be incredibly precise to allow complex life such as humans to exist.

2. The chance occurrence of this seems to be beyond the probability bound.

3. It is much more likely that these factors would be right if there is a Designer.

See:

Luke Barnes, "The Fine-Tuning of the Universe for Intelligent Life", *Publications of the Astronomical Society of Australia* 29.4(2012):529–64

John Hawthorne and Yoaav Isaacs, "Fine-Tuning Fine-Tuning", in Matthew A. Benton, John Hawthorne and Dani Rabinowitz (eds), *Knowledge, Belief and God: New Insights in Religious Epistemology* (Oxford University Press, 2018)

John C. Lennox, *God and Stephen Hawking: Whose Design Is It Anyway?* (Oxford: Lion, 2011)

———, "Designer universe?", in *God's Undertaker: Has Science Buried God?* (Oxford: Lion, 2009)

J. Warner Wallace, *God's Crime Scene: A Cold-Case Detective Examines the Evidence for a Divinely Created Universe* (Colorado Springs: David C. Cook, 2016)

Guillermo Gonzalez and Jay W. Richards, *The Privileged Planet: How Our Place in the Cosmos is Designed for Discovery* (2004)

William Lane Craig, "Fine Tuning", www.reasonablefaith.org/finetuning

Alister McGrath, "In The Beginning: The Constants of the Universe", *A Fine-Tuned Universe: The Quest for God in Science and Theology* (Louisville: Westminster John Knox Press, 2009).

Richard Swinburne, "Argument from the fine-tuning of the Universe", in John Leslie (ed), *Physical Cosmology and Philosophy* (New York: Collier Macmillan, 1990), 154–73.

4

This is Mental!

Evidence from Consciousness

. . .we'll see how deeply wrong consciousness is when it comes to the self, free will, human purpose, and the meanings of our actions, our lives, and our creations. It's all because of the illusion that thought is about stuff.
—ATHEIST PHILOSOPHER ALEX ROSENBERG[123]

"Consciousness is not physical: it helps us understand physics. Science made immense progress in a time. . . when everyone was familiar with the concepts of soul and spirit."
—CHRISTIAN PHYSICIAN / NEUROPHILOSOPHER ARIE BOS[124]

I COULD BARELY BELIEVE it when I read what leading atheist philosophers say about our minds.

- They think you can't think about things.
- They tell you you have no identity.
- They've decided you don't have free will.

Huh? Why would such brilliant thinkers be consciousness-deniers.[125] Let's start at the beginning.

In the Beginning were the Particles...

Imagine the Big Bang blasts out particles of matter which randomly combine to form everything—planets, seas, the first cell, people. The particles act like billiard balls, randomly bumping each other, and every event is physically caused by the event before. Imagine there is no God, and thus no plan or mind to guide the billiard balls, just the laws of physics. (For now, don't worry about where the laws came from, or the particles or the energy.)

Who are you in that story? Physicist Brian Greene says

> you and I are nothing but constellations of particles whose behaviour is fully governed by physical law. Our choices are the result of particles coursing one way or another through our brains. Our actions are the result of our particles moving this way or that through our bodies. And all particle motion—whether in a brain, a body, or a baseball—is controlled by physics and so is fully dictated by mathematical decree... [and] by the non-negotiable and insensate laws of physics, which determine the structure and function of everything that exists. We are no more than playthings knocked to and fro by the dispassionate rules of the cosmos.[126]

If your brain is influenced only by physical events and in turn can only influence other physical objects, then you don't have a non-physical mind or self with the volition to choose or to cause anything.[127] You are an accidental collection of billiard balls in a physical universe which is mindless, purposeless and valueless, and there is "neither need, nor room, to fit any non-physical substances or properties into our theoretical account of ourselves."[128] There's nothing but matter and "natural forces", and "what happens in the world is never the result of the agency of independent spiritual or mental powers".[129] There's only physics, not metaphysics.

In this materialist story, minds arrive late in the history of the universe as an afterthought—no, not even that, because the universe had no thoughts about us or anything else. Only physical things (and effects they cause) can be real.

Beliefs explained:

- materialism: matter is all there is in the universe
- determinism: every event since the Big Bang has inevitably been physically caused only by the physical events before it

- scientism: science can explain everything (eventually)
- reductionism: every explanation eventually boils down to physics
- naturalism: physical nature is everything; there is nothing supernatural; "nature is a self-contained system of physical causes and effects"[130]
- dualism: you are physical and you also have a non-physical part, which can be called mind, consciousness, spirit or soul
- supernaturalism: (opposite of naturalism) there is a force or agent outside the natural world
- theism: God or gods exist
- atheism: no God or gods exist

The Problem

There's a serious problem with the materialist story: your brain, the most complex object in the known universe. You have 100,000 braincells—if you're a fruit fly. Humans have 100 billion, each one more complex than a Porsche factory, but the truly staggering complexity is in the million-billion connections between them.[131]

The problem for materialism is that all of this has to happen by sheer blind chance, and that's simply not believable: the atheist philosopher Thomas Nagel sees that probability theory destroys that story and we need to find a new one.[132] But wait, there's more.

The "Hard Problem"

If materialism can't explain your brain, it has an even harder problem with your mind. Matthew Lieberman says:

> Given a materialist view of the universe, it makes no sense to talk about consciousness or experience at all. We have absolutely no idea what it is about the three pounds of mush between our ears that allows it to perform this trick of being conscious. . . I am a neuroscientist and so 99% of the time I behave like a materialist,

acknowledging that the mind is real but fully dependent on the brain. But we don't actually know this. We really don't.[133]

Atheist philosopher Jerry Fodor says, "Nobody has the slightest idea how anything material could be conscious".[134] If the universe contains only unconscious particles, those billiard balls can bump forever and they won't develop thoughts, free will or experiences like how it feels to taste a mango.

Scientists in the 20th century were confident they would crack the problem, but the more they learned about the brain, the more obvious it became that a brain wasn't enough to produce consciousness. Atheist neuroscientist Raymond Tallis said, "The attempt to fit consciousness into the material world. . . has failed dismally."[135] Some still have faith that science will eventually explain the mind, but "it's open to you to doubt whether the explanation ever will be forthcoming", says atheist biologist Richard Dawkins. "That's a perfectly reasonable doubt."[136]

Thomas Nagel thinks physical science is fine as far as it goes, but we need to find another explanation that includes mind not as "an accident or an add-on, but a basic aspect of nature."[137]

Neurobiologist Dick Swaab, an atheist, says: "Just as the kidneys produce urine, the brain produces consciousness."[138] But he's joking. Physical science can analyse what urine is and how it is produced, but can't do that with thoughts, so saying "Brain creates mind" is about as clear as saying "Kidney writes novel".[139]

Atheist philosopher Colin McGinn says, "Consciousness seems like a radical novelty in the universe, not. . . [predicted by] the Big Bang" and there is nothing "that might explain how ever-expanding lumps of matter might have developed an inner conscious life." He writes, "The brain is just the wrong kind of thing to give birth to consciousness. You might as well assert that numbers emerge from biscuits or ethics from rhubarb."[140]

I could quote many more admissions by leading scientists. This is what atheist philosopher David Chalmers called "the hard problem"[141] of neuroscience, and many think we'll never crack it, perhaps because objective, third-person, physical science can't touch consciousness, which is subjective and first-person, and seems beyond the reach of the physical sciences. But if that's true, then there are things materialism cannot ever explain.

Materialists can't say that mind or reason could be foundational in the universe. That would be bringing in something like God, a resource they refuse to use to explain things. So some materialists go the other way and try to minimise what consciousness is, hoping it might fit within materialism. And the comedy begins...

The Consciousness-Deniers

1. They think you can't think about things

You can't think about Paris, says philosopher Alex Rosenberg in *The Atheist's Guide To Reality*. In case you think I'm making this up, here's the quote:

> Thinking about things can't happen at all. The brain can't have thoughts about Paris, or about France... or about anything else for that matter. When consciousness convinces you that you, or your mind, or your brain has thoughts about things, it is wrong.[142]

I'd argue with that, but I have no thoughts. Help me, doctor, I only *think* I'm thinking!

Can you think about Paris? Hmm, Eiffel Tower, Arc de Triomphe... Easy! Could Rosenberg even write the word Paris without thinking about it? Yet he says his *own* thoughts aren't about anything:

> That goes for every sentence in this book. It's not about anything. Why are we bothering to read it?
> Look, if I am going to get scientism into your skull I have to use the only tools we've got for moving information from one head to another . . . Treat the illusion that goes with them like... optical illusions ... This book isn't conveying statements. It's rearranging neural circuits, removing inaccurate disinformation and replacing it with accurate information.[143]

So he states that he's not making statements. His book is altering your braincells but not passing into your mind, even though it's non-physical "information". Why would a professional thinker talk such nonsense about thinking? He says "it's got to be an illusion, since nothing physical can be about anything."

Ah! There it is. We just found the bug.

He's right that a physical thing can't be *about* another thing. If you say, "My plain grey sock is about Paris", that makes no sense. (Of course, my sock might have a picture of Paris or the word "Paris", but that would be semiotics or language, not just a sock.) A plain physical thing can't be *about* anything or *refer to* anything beyond itself. It can't have what philosophers call "aboutness" or "ofness". But it makes sense to say "My thoughts are about Paris"—and that means your thoughts can't be only physical. Brain science knows plenty about the electro-chemical firing of neurones, but thoughts must have a real, non-physical part because they can be *about* things.

Rosenberg denies that. He insists, "All the processes in the universe, from atomic to bodily to mental, are purely physical processes ... Eventually, science will have to show the details of how the basic physical processes bring about us, our brain, and our behaviour." (That's called scientism, remember?) He claims your first-person view is an illusion:

> Even after scientism convinces us, we'll continue to stick with the first person. But at least we'll know that it's another illusion of introspection and we'll stop taking it seriously. We'll give up all the answers to the persistent questions about free will, the self, the soul, and the meaning of life that the illusion generates.[144]

If you use your introspection to think about that for a minute, you know that Rosenberg doesn't actually know about your introspection, your first-person view—because you're the only expert on that. And I find it funny that he keeps using first-person language while denying any first-person view is real.

Rosenberg bends logic rather than accept that non-physical things might be real. He can't let anything non-physical into the universe because—God forbid! –it would be consistent with a belief in the soul and thus in God. He'd rather say we can't think! But think about that for a second and you'll know that a) you can think, so you just disproved it, and b) it blows a giant hole in materialism.

Here's a summary for you to, er, think about:

1. Physical things are not *about* other things.
2. Thoughts are *about* other things.
3. So thoughts are not (only) physical things.
4. So there are real, non-physical things in the universe.

By the way, Rosenberg adds:

> *What is the purpose of the universe?* There is none.
> *What is the meaning of life?* Ditto.
> *Why am I here?* Just dumb luck...
> *Is there a soul? Is it immortal?* Are you kidding me?

What happens when we die? Everything pretty much goes on as before, except us.[145]

If you find that depressing, he suggests you use drugs to change your brain chemistry, but don't bother with psychology because *your thoughts aren't real*, remember? He says, "what is so valuable about the illusion your thoughts have authenticity anyway?"

But he expects us to accept his thoughts about that.

Rosenberg's book gave me some great laughs, especially because I bought it at an Atheist Convention called A Celebration of Reason.

2. They tell you that you have no identity

Materialism says "you" are nothing but an aggregate of particles. Rosenberg says, "The self, as conveyed to us by introspection, is a fiction. It doesn't exist."[146] But if that's true, who is "us"? And who made up the fiction? And how could we do introspection? And how can he say your thoughts about yourself are wrong and his are right?

Atheist philosopher Daniel Dennett says similar. He told me in interview that the self we commonly understand is an illusion. He writes that "we build up a defining story about ourselves, organised around a sort of basic blip of self-representation. The blip isn't a self, of course, it's a representation of a self".[147] But did you see the contradictions? He says "we" "ourselves" don't have selves. If that's true, then who is having the illusion? Who tells the story? To whom?

He also writes that we can't get closer than some kind of "user interface" with our brains.[148] But if that's true, then who is the user?

It's like the story of the philosophy student who tells a rabbi, "Sometimes I doubt if I even exist." The rabbi replies, "Then who is doing the doubting?"[149]

Or it's like the psychiatric patient panicking that he's a vase of flowers.
Doctor: But vases don't panic...
Patient: Oh, OK. Well... [panicking] I'm just a bag of chemicals!
Doctor: Why didn't you think you were a vase?
Patient: Because I didn't like that idea.[150]

Wait, *who* didn't like that idea? *I*? That's a self that can think and talk, not a vase, and not just a bag of chemicals. To deny that is truly nutty.

The philosopher Rene Descartes (pronounced *day-cart*) tried doubting everything, but the one thing he couldn't doubt was his own existence, because he knew he was thinking. In 1637 he wrote the famous line "I think, therefore I am." *Cogito ergo sum*. That's the first principle of his philosophy. If you're thinking, you must exist. It's impossible to doubt that.

A horse walks into a bar and the bar-tender asks if he'd like a beer. The horse says, "I think not", and *pouf!*—he vanishes out of existence. A philosophy student sitting at the bar starts laughing, and you might not get why if I hadn't written this chapter in the right order, putting Descartes before the horse.

3. They've decided you have no free will

Rosenberg says you can't make choices or have plans or intentions—"human behaviours aren't really driven by purposes, ends or goals".

He applies this to every person in history. When kings and leaders went to the Congress of Vienna in 1815, aiming to negotiate peace after Napoleon's wars, Rosenberg says, "It had no purpose, and neither did the machinations of any of its participants. In fact, none of them... came to the Congress with any purpose. There weren't and indeed aren't any purposes... [just] the appearance of purpose."[151]

Historians say the French diplomat Talleyrand was the most cunning and devious person there, but Rosenberg says he had no purpose in mind. So where did his words come from?

> firings in his hippocampus ... sending sharp wave ripples out across his neocortex, where they stimulated one neural circuit after another, until combined with firings from the pre-frontal cortex and ventral striatum, and doubtless a half dozen or more other regions of Talleyrand's brain, causing his throat, tongue, and lips to move and him to speak.

So sly old Talleyrand had no purpose, "just one damn electrochemical process after another."

Yet in a hilarious contradiction, he writes, "Mother Nature built our minds for other purposes than understanding reality."[152] Huh? So nature had purposes in building our minds, but our minds don't themselves have purposes and Rosenberg writes with the purpose of convincing you of that. I love the comic contradictions.

This is Mental!

What do you think of Rosenberg's view that people have no intentions? Do you now intend to study history that way? I intend not to, because dualism allows me to think a person can have complex neurochemical processes *and* a mind intending things. My worldview includes neuroscience *and* psychology *and* spirituality.

Philosopher Sam Harris's book *Free Willy*... no, sorry, that's a story of a whale and a boy who prize freedom... Ahem. Sam Harris's book *Free Will*[153] says we don't have it: free will is an illusion.

I like Sam Harris and enjoyed interviewing him at an Atheist Convention, but this book has comical contradictions. The publishers are Free Press. The cover says, "Read it: you have no choice"—but that can't be true or they wouldn't need to tell you. And when Harris promoted the book to the Sceptics' Society, his opening sentence shot two holes in his argument. He said, "I hope to convince you that free will is an illusion."[154] But hang on... if he can "convince" you, then you must be free to decide. And if he can "hope", then he has a free will too.

If Harris is right that we have no free choice, then he wrote what something *made* him write—he didn't decide which ideas are true using reason. So why believe him? His wife Annaka thinks about this problem in her book, when she writes, "Did I decide to write this book? In some sense, the answer is yes, but the 'I' in question is not my conscious experience. In actuality, my brain, in conjunction with its history and the outside world, decided. I (my consciousness) simply witness decisions unfolding."[155]

I can't speak for the Harrises, but I can say I wrote this book! I wish I could have just watched the particles do it while I went surfing, but I read, weighed ideas in my mind, argued issues out with friends, and chose what seemed logical and right. And I can write whatever I *wubba-dubba flerpity baf*! (If I just swore in Latvian, I apologise.) Nothing *made* me write that. And I can stop writing and go for a swim...

Splash!

... and play the piano *ponka ponka*...

You can stop reading. If you're still with me, it's by choice. (Thank-you, gentle reader!)

And *you're free to disagree with me!*

In fact, please try disagreeing with me about that last sentence, because you'll prove my point. "No, I'm not free to disagree with you... oops, I just did."

It's all harmless comedy until Sam Harris describes burglars who bash and sexually abuse a mother and young daughter before burning their house. Harris says the burglars are malfunctioning machines, "nothing more than poorly calibrated clockwork". "Whatever their conscious motives, these men cannot know why they are as they are." Wouldn't that mean that the criminals *had* to rape and burn people because the billiard balls in their brains bounced wrong? So they're not responsible. . .? That's insulting to victims. And it's unrealistic: criminal courts are very clear about choice and responsibility, even though they consider a person's background. Human choice and accountability are fundamental assumption of every legal system in the world, for good reason.

But Harris's fellow New Atheist Richard Dawkins says we shouldn't punish crime any more than we punish a car for breaking down. Our brains are "governed by the law of physics" and are not "intentional agents". (Did he intend to say that?) He says "a truly scientific, mechanistic view of the nervous system" will "make nonsense of the very idea of responsibility. . . Any crime, however heinous, is in principle to be blamed on antecedent conditions acting through. . . physiology, heredity and environment."[156]

I'm shocked when Sam Harris says that, if he taught a self-defence class, it would be

> counterproductive to emphasize that all human behaviour, including a woman's response to physical attack, is determined by a prior state of the universe, and that all rapists are, at bottom, unlucky—being themselves victims of prior causes that they did not create.[157]

Wait. . . the *rapist* is the unlucky *victim*? Words fail me. That idea shreds human responsibility and ethics. And if a woman's response to a rapist is already programmed by the universe, then she can't choose how to respond, and can't learn to fight any better, so why bother to teach her self-defence? For that matter, why teach anyone *anything*? Educating a mind couldn't change what the billiard balls do. So why does Harris have a doctorate? Our education system might as well disappear out the window along with our justice system. (See where stupid ideas can lead intelligent people?)

Harris sees this idea that women can't learn self-defence may be "counter-productive". Ya' think? I'd say part of him knows how offensive and ridiculous it is. (Which part of him? His soul, perhaps?)

Yet Harris claims, "My mental life is simply given to me by the cosmos." "There is *no extra part of me* that could decide to see the world differently or to resist the impulse" to horrible crime.[158]

He says, "You are not in control of your mind . . ." Imagine the carnage if people took that seriously.

Don't we know intuitively that we can choose? Our choice can be limited by our genes, habits, education, addictions etc, but we can still set goals, develop self-discipline, make ourselves push on in the gym, avoid crimes, improve ourselves by study and work and refuse to give up under opposition.

We do have a subconscious mind, and our brain makes some decisions on autopilot without conscious thought, e.g. how fast our heart will beat. Some media reports claimed the brain makes *all* decisions before the conscious mind even knows about them, citing Dr Benjamin Libet's experiments from 1983, but the neuroscience of free will is very complex, and there's no consensus that free will is disproven. You can block a punch on reflex without thought, but you make bigger decisions thoughtfully and with deliberate choice.

This suggests we humans have a non-physical part.

Determinism is a joke. A philosopher walks into a bar and the bartender says, "What'll you have?" The philosopher replies, "Dunno. I'm a determinist. We'll have to wait and see what happens."

How free are we?

- hard determinism: our choices are completely pre-determined by our genes, culture, etc and our braincells, which are machines running on the laws of physics. There is no non-physical part of us making decisions.
- soft determinism: our choices are mainly pre-determined by the factors above, but we are sometimes capable of over-riding that and making free, conscious choices.
- libertarianism: we are dealt cards—genes, braincells, culture—but we can usually decide how to play them, i.e. we are mainly in control of our decision-making.

The last two views suggest humans are not merely physical.

You can decide whether or not you have free will—and that itself is evidence. I respect the materialist neuroscientist Matthew Lieberman for his honesty in saying:

> We assume our sense of will is a causal result of the neurochemical processes in our brain, but this is a leap of faith. Perhaps the brain is something like a complex radio receiver that integrates consciousness signals that float around in some form.[159]

Here's a scientist looking for a worldview that takes mind and consciousness seriously. If you have free will, you can't be made of cells alone. Cells can only respond to stimuli. They can't decide to initiate anything. So there must be more to you than cells.

The logic goes like this:

1. No physical system has free will. (e.g. A gun can't decide to kill anyone.)
2. So commonsense says no physical system has moral responsibility. (We don't try a gun for murder.)
3. We think humans do have moral responsibility. (We try a murderer.)
4. So humans are not only a physical system.
5. So there are real, non-physical things in the universe.

Final (non-) thoughts...

The view that we can't really think, decide or have identity is called reductionist or eliminative materialism because it eliminates so many common-sense things that people experience. It calls them folk psychology or mythology, and ignores them. It cannot explain consciousness, so it explains it away. Some major thinkers have bought it.[160] Yet others see that our thoughts, choices and sense of self are

- the very things that make us human, and
- the only things we know with certainty ("I think, therefore I am"), and
- our only way of knowing anything else—including science itself[161]—so that eliminative materialism dynamites its own foundations.

As George Orwell said, "There are some ideas so absurd that only an intellectual could believe them."

Materialism is absurd comedy, and some materialists see it is. They cannot honestly use their minds to deny how awesome and important our minds are. They can't dumb down the all-singing, all-dancing wondrousness of consciousness to make it small enough to hide under the rug of materialism. So they come up with other theories. Let's take a look at those.

Alternatives to Consciousness-Denial

Here are some of their attempts to explain how thought can arise from mere matter.

1. It's a mystery

Because matter and mind are so different, the atheist philosopher Colin McGinn[162] calls consciousness a mystery. He is definite that evolution cannot cause it, and thinks that matter must have some features that make it capable of becoming conscious in a brain, which also has some unknown natural ability he calls C*. He says these features and abilities must be natural and ordinary, not requiring a theistic explanation. And since matter is spatial and mind is non-spatial, these features linking matter and mind must be pre-spatial, or spatial in a way that our senses can't perceive. But McGinn says we can never know what they are, because evolution has not given us that ability.

Then how can he be so confident that all matter has these features? If they are unknowable, this can only really be a guess without any evidence. C* sounds impressive, but it only names the mystery, it doesn't explain it. These features don't naturally fit with the scientific materialist story of billiard balls.

2. Thought "emerges"

John Searle[163] says mind somehow emerges from matter that is complex enough. To put it simply, a certain arrangement of chemicals in your brain produces a mental state—a thought, feeling, experience, desire or intention.

Consciousness emerges like liquidity emerges when you put enough H_2O molecules together.

But how would one particular arrangement of chemicals produce one particular mental state every time in every person's brain? Is there some kind of dictionary that says Brain Chemistry Arrangement A produces Mental State A, and Brain Chemistry B produces Thought B, and so on? Why would these physical and mental states always correlate—why wouldn't chemistry A produce thought B sometimes? And when you think how many subtle thoughts and feelings you are capable of, that dictionary would have to be almost infinite. Who wrote it? And what makes it work? Searle suggests there are natural laws that say which brain states will correlate with each mental states. If so, these laws would need to be extremely complex, and would be like no other laws we know of. (This would suggest an intelligent, powerful lawmaker.)

Some materialists expect future science will find how mental states correlate with brain states. That shows great faith in science, because no one can know what it will discover—our mental processes may remain "closed" to us.[164] And, unless someone invents objective, physical ways to read subjective, non-physical thoughts—which seems logically impossible—then correlating these states would rely on people telling us with great precision what their mental states are while scientists analyse their brains. This would rely on their word. And even if we could one day *describe how* these physical and mental states correlate, and slowly compile a huge dictionary of them, this would not *explain why* they correlate or what causes them to do that. And it wouldn't prove that "consciousness is (nothing but) brain states"[165] because correlation is not causation. As materialist philosopher Jaegwon Kim put it, "How could a series of physical events, like particles jostling against each other... blossom into conscious experience?... Why shouldn't pain and itch be switched around?... Why should *any* experience emerge when these neurons fire?"[166]

One possible explanation could be "God's direct activity and stable activity that things be so."[167]

Further, there is no other example of consciousness emerging from complex matter. Certainly not supercomputers or the Beijing telephone system or even the Internet—they're unimaginably complex, but not conscious. Complexity can improve something that already exists, but in the story that we appeared after "4.5 billion years of purely chemical and biological evolution"[168], why and how would something non-physical appear?

Emergence theory requires that braincells must create something qualitatively different out of nothing.[169]

Water is physical, and science can easily explain how its molecules form various structures. Consciousness is non-physical, so liquidity is a poor comparison. And molecules are in the physical world while the wetness is felt only in your mind.

Emergence seems a vague and hand-waving theory. It's another name for the problem, not a solution. It tries to get something for nothing, and is "a case of magic without a Magician."[170]

3. Conscious particles? Pan-psychism

Some thinkers[171] imagine matter might be conscious or "proto-conscious", with "special properties that are precursors to consciousness and that can collectively constitute consciousness in larger systems"[172]. This theory is called panpsychism (*pan* = all, *psyche* = mind/ soul) or proto-panpsychism.

If matter is all you have to work with, I guess you'd *have* to say matter contains all the ingredients required for mind. But the evidence for this is zero.

And the theory of panpsychism raises some serious questions. If our consciousness is assembled from tiny parts, why is it unified? What's the consciousness of, say, an electron? "Wheee, round the nucleus again!"

Will future chemistry books list consciousness as a property of matter alongside mass and conductivity?

What is proto-consciousness? "Hnnnhhh, I've got 1/64 of a thought on the tip of my tongue, and if I can just find 63 friends, I'll think it." What is a proto-belief that 1 + 1 = 2?[173]

What other complex matter has ever become conscious? Some say AI will become conscious, while others say it never will, since assembling data is not the same as experiencing things.[174]

Could matter ever make something immaterial emerge from it?

Can you really solve the mind-matter problem simply by defining matter as *both*? That doesn't tell us how. As Geoffrey Madell put it, "The sense that the mental and the physical are just inexplicably and gratuitously slapped together is hardly allayed by adopting a pan-psychist view of the mind, for [it has no] explanation to offer as to why or how mental properties cohere with physical."[175]

But let's say I'm wrong. Let's imagine AI becomes truly conscious. Let's say this shows that panpsychism is correct and all matter contains consciousness (or the potential for it). In that case, that potential must have been there from the beginning of the universe. So I'd be asking who or what gave matter these magical properties from the beginning. That's sounding dangerously like a creation story.[176]

4. Laws

Some say there must be "fundamental laws governing the universe" which ensure that "conscious experiences occur" when certain physical things happen.[177] Atheist philosopher Peter Cave writes, "No convincing explanation yet exists of how our experiences relate to the physical world and their evolutionary value. It may be that the development of psychological features—of consciousness, desires, beliefs, sensations—cannot be accounted for in concepts of current scientific and causal laws, but require teleological laws of some kind."[178]

Teleology means having a purpose or goal (Greek, *telos*) in mind. But the First Commandment of materialism is that there is no purpose—just matter. Teleological laws would have to be brilliant and staggeringly complex, so they could hardly appear without a cause. They would suggest a lawmaker—a Mind.

Conclusion:

If the facts don't fit your theory, you can try to deny the facts or you can find a new theory.

We've seen that many materialists end up denying that we can think or choose or have real identity. This is the opposite of "A Celebration of Reason", because it throws individual thought in the bin. If you follow materialism to its logical conclusion, you must believe that there are no logical conclusions.

Others see the brilliance of consciousness and openly admit that a material explanation of what it is, let alone how we got it, is out of reach. And this is not just a temporary gap in science: the more we learn about the brain, the harder the hard problem gets.

Why defend a theory with such a huge logical hole? Biologist Richard Lewontin once said, "Our willingness to accept scientific claims that are against common sense is the key to an understanding of the real struggle between science and the supernatural." He admits a "prior commitment... to materialism", not because science demands it but because he has chosen, "material explanations, no matter how counter-intuitive, no matter how mystifying to the uninitiated. Moreover, that materialism is absolute, for we cannot allow a Divine Foot in the door."[179]

At least he's honest that he's defending a pre-conceived conclusion, rather than really being scientific by searching for truth without fear or favour. Deny that our minds work, sticking with the billiard balls, or else you might see that Mind could be the base layer of reality, and then God might knock on your door.

Yet a number of philosophers are moving away from off-the-rack materialism and thinking of Mind as more fundamental in the universe, perhaps even primary to matter. Some are considering dualism of one kind or another.[180]

Atheist philosopher John Searle sees the problem: a universe "that consists entirely of mindless, meaningless, unfree, nonrational, brute physical particles" would hardly produce humans that are "mindful, meaning-creating, free, rational, etc".[181]

But if humans were made in the likeness of a God who has consciousness, reason, self-determination, freedom, personality, relational ability and objective value, then we'd expect to have these characteristics too.[182] To state the obvious, we do! So it's reasonable to posit a Mind as the cause of other minds, creating simpler versions of itself. (For a roundworm with 302 braincells, much simpler—but enough.) This is called the "foundational mind" hypothesis, and it makes mind the foundation of everything else in the universe.[183]

Materialism is beyond depressing since it says mind "arrived through random processes" and so mind "will slowly decay and die and any meaning to it is an illusion."[184] But theism sees mind as potentially eternal.

If something as important as consciousness doesn't fit into materialist theory, then we need a better theory. As Arie Bos puts it, "Consciousness is not physical: it helps us understand physics. Science made immense progress in a time... when everyone was familiar with the concepts of soul and spirit."[185]

Here are two other ways to state the Argument from Consciousness:

1. Non-physical mental states really exist.
2. They do not fit with materialism.
3. They fit with dualism.
4. Therefore, dualism explains reality better than materialism.
5. Dualism is compatible with the existence of God.

Or:

1. Materialism reduces reasoning to a "closed, mechanistic, deterministic system of physical cause and effect."
2. This cannot explain human consciousness and reasoning (including the reasoning that materialists use themselves).
3. So materialism is self-contradictory.
4. So the alternative explanation—a Mind behind the universe—seems logical.[186]

Recommended:

Arie Bos, *Thinking Outside the Brain Box: Why Humans Are Not Biological Computers* (Edinburgh: Floris Books, 2018)

J.P. Moreland, "The Argument from Consciousness", in J.P. Moreland (ed), *Debating Christian Theism* (Oxford University Press, 2013)

Peter S. Williams, "The Mind-Body Problem", "The Mind and Its Creator" and "Freedom and Responsibility", in *A Faithful Guide to Philosophy: A Christian Introduction to the Love of Wisdom* (Milton Keynes: Paternoster, 2013).

5

Are You Just Physical?

Evidence from Consciousness & Reason

It seems to me immensely unlikely that mind is a mere by-product of matter. For if my mental processes are determined wholly by the motions of atoms in my brain I have no reason to suppose my beliefs are true. That may be sound chemically, but that does not make sense logically.

—ATHEIST SCIENTIST J.B.S. "PRIMORDIAL SOUP" HALDANE[187]

...how can we be certain that our reason is perfectly rational? Only a God could guarantee us that.

—ATHEIST PHILOSOPHER ANDRÉ COMTE-SPONVILLE[188]

SHERLOCK HOLMES EXAMINES A watch for a few seconds and blurts out his deductions. Its owner was careless, took to drink, wasted a good inheritance, suffered periods of poverty and died.

Dr Watson is offended because the watch belonged to his brother, but stunned that Sherlock could deduce all of that from a watch.

Sherlock explains that the dents came from being carried in a pocket with keys, suggesting carelessness. The watch is expensive but has marks from pawnbrokers, showing financial instability. Scratches suggest that whoever wound it up was drunk every night. He says, "What seems strange to you is only because you do not follow my train of thought or observe the small facts upon which large inferences may depend."[189]

Deductions are Sherlock's genius, but they only work because of things about our minds that might sound strange or obvious when I mention them. You may think I've taken to drink, but if you follow my train of thought in this chapter, you'll see why I started seriously questioning materialism and saw the logic of dualism.[190] Let's quickly remind ourselves of those terms:

- Materialism: the view that nothing exists except matter and forces. The Big Bang started particles moving like billiard balls and randomly assembling into larger structures, and each event caused the next, making an unbroken chain of physical events and physical causes for *everything* that has happened since. This would mean consciousness and all mental states are merely by-products caused by "particles coursing one way or another" through a brain "fully controlled by physical law", and that thoughts cannot move the particles in your brain or anywhere else.[191]
- Dualism: mind-body dualism is the view that body and mind are distinct, separate things, and your thoughts and other mental phenomena are not (only) physical phenomena.[192] This would mean that mind is just as much a part of reality as matter is, but the two are completely different categories. This view says Mind is foundational to reality, which fits with a belief in some kind of God.

The game's afoot! Here are some lines of evidence that help us deduce which theory is correct:

1. Sherlock's not on drugs

In the original story from 1887, Watson knows Sherlock is a cocaine addict, and shows him the watch to distract him so he doesn't use.

Would you trust the deductions of a drugged detective? I'd say no, because a thought caused by altering brain chemistry probably won't match reality or logic. We don't fully trust our own thoughts if we know they were caused by vodka shots, a fever, an uppercut or anything other than reason. And that's a big problem for materialism, which says *all* thoughts have physical causes—basically particles obeying the laws of physics. That would mean all our beliefs are caused, not proved.

Agnostic philosopher Karl Popper saw this problem: he said materialism is not a logical belief because "it must explain all our reactions... as due to purely physical conditions", not beliefs "based on arguments".[193]

To summarise:

1. A non-rational cause (e.g. drugs) is highly unlikely to produce a rational thought.
2. Materialism says all causes of thought are non-rational (i.e. chemical particles moving).
3. So if materialism is true, then our thoughts are highly unlikely to be rational.
4. So we cannot rationally claim that materialism is rational.

2. Sherlock's thoughts are reliable

Holmes says, "It is my business to know what other people do not know." People depend on his observations and deductions. But is it rational to trust his thoughts—or ours?

Imagine we're on a train and we see "Welcome to Wales" written in white stones on a mountainside. Then someone shows us their phone footage of a rockslide that they saw there yesterday, and we see hundreds of white stones tumbling down the mountain and forming the words "Welcome to Wales" completely at random. Now where are we? We don't know. At first we believed the stones were arranged by an intelligent person "for the purpose of conveying a certain message having nothing to do with the stones themselves." But now we see their origins are natural and "non-purposive", so it would be irrational to believe them. Yet what if our mental faculties have a "natural, non-purposive" origin?[194] Why would we believe them? If your brain is the result of a completely non-rational process of molecules bumping together, would you trust its thoughts?

Materialism, then, cannot explain Sherlock's deductions and logical inferences—or ours. Processes as random as a spilled bag of lollies wouldn't give you reliable thoughts. You're much more likely to have a (mainly) trustworthy mind if it came from a rational Mind.

C.S. Lewis said it like this:

> Supposing there was no intelligence behind the universe, no creative mind. In that case, nobody designed my brain for the purpose of thinking. It is merely that when the atoms inside my skull happen, for physical or chemical reasons, to arrange themselves in a certain way, this gives me, as a by-product, the sensation I call thought. But, if so, how can I trust my own thinking to be true? It's like upsetting a milk jug and hoping that the way it splashes itself will give you a map of London. But if I can't trust my own thinking, of course I can't trust the arguments leading to Atheism, and therefore have no reason to be an Atheist, or anything else. Unless I believe in God, I cannot believe in thought: so I can never use thought to disbelieve in God.

Rational people should not believe materialism because, if it's true, there are no rational people.

And Lewis[195] built an even larger case here:

1. If everything in nature can be explained by non-rational causes, then human reason (the ability to draw conclusions based on logic alone) must have its source outside nature.

2. If human reason came from non-reason, it would lose all reliability.

3. So the source of human reason must be rational (from 2) and outside nature (from 1), i.e. supernatural.

4. This supernatural source of human reason could be caused by another supernatural source of reason before it, but that chain of causes can't go back forever. Eventually we will get back to an eternal, uncaused source of reason. That can be called God.

3. Sherlock's train of thought runs on content

He observes facts (The watch is dented) and logically infers things from them (...so the owner was careless).

What moves him from the first thought to the second? Is it the arrangement of chemicals in his brain during brain state 1 ("dented watch") causing the arrangement of chemicals in brain state 2 ("careless owner")?

No, it's the content of one thought that causes the content of the next by logic, and his physical brain accommodates that. It's logic, not brain chemistry, that moves Sherlock's train of thought. The atheist philosopher

Are You Just Physical?

Thomas Nagel says "if we can reason, it is because our thoughts can obey the order of logical relations among propositions."[196]

So the logic of his mind drives the chemistry of his brain, not the other way around. That's called mental causation: it means that one idea causes the next idea, and maybe causes a physical action as well, e.g. moving his mouth to talk to Watson.

But mental causation does not fit with materialism, which says all causes are physical and minds cause nothing—the physical world is causally closed.[197] If matter is all there is, then ideas about a watch could not change the movement of the billiard balls, the atoms in his head.

Here's a summary of the argument from mental causation:

1. If materialism completely describes reality, then the content of one thought could not cause the content of the next thought.
2. We can make rational inferences in which the content of one thought causes the content of the next.
3. So materialism is an incomplete description of reality.

You might say, "Hang on, what about a calculator or a computer? It's a physical object obeying the laws of physics and the laws of logic at the same time. Aren't our brains like that?"

Great question. To ask it, you just used some impressive abstract reasoning, way beyond what a computer can do, because a computer just manipulates symbols without actually understanding.

To grasp this, let's imagine you only speak English but you're locked in a room as Mandarin symbols are passed in through a slot, and you have instructions telling you (in English) what to pass back out: If you get this symbol, pass out that symbol, etc. You don't know that people outside the room are handing in questions and you are handing out answers. If your instructions are good enough, the people outside will think that you understand Mandarin and their questions, but you don't—you're just relying on instructions from someone who does.[198] Similarly, computers look like they understand logic but they're really just shuffling symbols and following instructions in algorithms written by people who do understand. They are not thinking. They're like this book, which contains knowledge but knows nothing itself. But you're different from that. You can reason, understand ideas and their implications, and can have experiences. You *know*.

A computer doesn't think or feel. A thermostat chip turns your air conditioning up or down but doesn't feel hot or cold like you do. A computer understands nothing. It doesn't follow mental causation. It follows algorithms—a series of commands. These commands may be extremely sophisticated in an AI, and may have access to vast amounts of knowledge, but the machine is still not thinking like you are.

Computers are designed and created by intelligent beings, who have programmed their own logic into machines. The machines are the result of minds, not physical causation (unless you try to say that the human programmers are only physical, which would be assuming the very thing we're debating.)

4. Sherlock's logic is real but not physical

The watch's owner cannot be both dead and alive. Even a child knows that, and doesn't need a philosopher to recite the Law of Non-Contradiction, "Something cannot be both A and non-A."

The laws of logic apply always and everywhere. Just for fun, try to argue that they don't exist. You'll soon realise that everything you say is illogical.[199]

The laws of logic are elementary, my dear Watson, yet they are not part of the material world. They're outside space and time. They seem to float above physical reality, yet they are real—in fact they govern *all valid thinking!* And there is no logical limit to them—they're about everything in the known universe. This is a huge challenge to materialism, which says the physical is all there is. It cannot tell us how these laws can exist without a material foundation, or where they could have come from.

Yet there's a bigger problem—these immaterial laws of logic don't govern Sherlock's brain chemistry or the movement of particles in his skull, yet his mind follows them exactly. And materialism cannot tell us why a physical brain would be guided by non-physical laws. But dualism recognises that our non-physical mind can follow non-physical laws, and suggests that these laws had their origin in a great Mind, and that there is a foundational mental layer to reality. Without a Mind like that, the universe would not have the principles of reason in it, or any reason to produce other minds, or the resources to do that, since building mental things from physical things alone seems impossible.

I like how Joshua Rasmussen put it: "Without these things, there is, then, no reason for reason to be anywhere, ever. Yet we can see, by reason itself, that reason is real. From here we can see—by reason—that reason does not spring from non-reason. Only one options remains: reason exists at the foundation of everything."[200]

5. Sherlock has one mind

A human brain is a collection of specialised areas and processes, so one part of Sherlock's brain would have to notice the watch is expensive, another part would see the marks, another would find a memory of a pawnbroker's mark, another would match them, and so on. Yet what co-ordinates all this? There must be a Central Processing Unit, a conductor directing this 100-billion-member braincell orchestra, knowing the laws of logic, choosing which to apply, and creating Sherlock's deductions. Yet neuroscience knows of no physical part like that in the brain. That's called "the binding problem": what binds all areas into the unified whole that we experience? The best solution seems to be that all this activity and information is "not combined by the brain but by consciousness".[201] So who is binding all the brain's activities? Sherlock is. His non-physical self is using his brain like a musician uses a piano.[202]

Here's a summary[203]:

1. One unified conscious entity notices details, makes logical inferences from them and creates a deduction.
2. Materialism knows no brain mechanism for that.
3. So materialism is insufficient to describe our consciousness.

6. Sherlock can do science

Sherlock was invented by a medical doctor, Arthur Conan Doyle, and uses forensic science in his detective work.[204] But if our brains evolved to survive on the Stone Age savannah, why can they do forensic science or astronomy or philosophy, or write complex detective novels or symphonies? You might say these extra features are nice to have, but they require a bigger brain, and that means a bigger head, and thus a more difficult birth, a longer infancy and more years vulnerable and dependent. Those things could be a survival disadvantage.

If you can track a gazelle, spear it, and feed your children, natural selection doesn't care what you believe, because evolution is "driven exclusively by physical causes".[205] Yet we seem to have more mental abilities than we needed to survive.

Atheist John Gray sees the problem. He argues with those who think science can find truth and make us free, saying, "[I]f Darwin's theory of natural selection is true this is impossible. The human mind serves evolutionary success, not truth. . . Darwinian theory tells us that an interest in truth is not needed for survival or reproduction. . . Truth has no systematic evolutionary advantage over error."[206]

And Charles Darwin, writing around the time Sherlock was invented, admitted, "With me the horrid doubt always arises, whether the convictions of man's mind, which has been developed from the mind of the lower animals, are of any value or at all trustworthy."[207]

Plenty of "lower animals" survive very well without rationality.

Cognitive scientist David Hoffman goes further in his book, *The Case Against Reality: how evolution hid the truth from our eyes*. He says we have no idea what reality is, or if it even exists, because evolution has "endowed us with senses that hide the truth and display the simple icons we need to survive long enough to raise offspring. . . You may want truth but you don't need truth. Truth would drive our species extinct. You need simple icons that show you how to act to stay alive. Perception is not an objective window on reality."[208]

Did you spot a problem with this? Hoffman doesn't say how he knows. And if he is right, no-one could know anything. But he raises an interesting question.

Let's think about this another way. Imagine you and I are two evolving cavemen. We see lightning, and you say, "Ugh, storm god angry!" and run into a cave. I say, "Why fire in sky?" and run into a cave. Which one survives? We both do, because we both ran into a cave, and survival depends on what we do, not what we think. Materialism says your thought is no more than an event in your nervous system, a group of braincells sending out messages to glands and muscles to make your body respond. Those braincells might also cause a belief in your consciousness, but that's only a by-product. The main event is what your cells *do*—because thoughts can't cause anything. And Christian philosopher Alvin Plantinga calculated that by the time two cavemen make 100 decisions to survive, the chances of their *beliefs* being correct even 75% of the time will be about one in a million, because evolution doesn't select for beliefs, it selects for actions. This means it's highly unlikely that we'd evolve into rational beings.[209]

This is called the Evolutionary Argument Against Naturalism. Atheist philosopher Thomas Nagel says it's the "deepest problem" of materialism, and no-one has "proposed a credible solution."[210] Nagel sees that materialism "provides an account of our capacities that undermines their reliability, and in doing so undermines itself."[211]

Survival depends on what we do, not our thoughts. So in a materialist worldview, we would not expect to evolve so many non-essential abilities, including rationality. The fact that we are rational is a major challenge to materialism.

And so. . .

Materialism would mean that your thoughts are a chance by-product of brain chemistry that evolved for survival. But Sherlock's abilities show that our consciousness is just as real as our body, but not only physical; and this suggests that Mind is fundamental in the universe.

Is your Mind just your Brain?

"I am a brain, Watson. The rest of me is a mere appendix."

So said Sherlock in *The Adventure of the Mazarin Stone*. But was he right? Materialism has to say your mind is nothing more than your physical brain—it can't accept anything non-physical.[212] Yet there is growing evidence that the mind is non-physical, and that our mental states are not just brain states. Such as:

1. Thoughts alter body chemistry

Laughing can seriously improve your health, says medical research from the respected Mayo Clinic. "Negative thoughts manifest into chemical reactions that can affect your body. . . decreasing your immunity. By contrast, positive thoughts can actually release neuropeptides that help fight. . . illnesses."

Mayo researchers say laughter "increases the endorphins that are released by your brain".[213] Your thoughts, feelings and attitudes can speed up healing.[214] Anxiety and depression affect your blood vessels and heart, but psychotherapy can improve them.[215] It's like King Solomon wrote 3000 years ago, "A merry heart does good like a medicine" (Proverbs 17:22).

That contradicts materialism, which says that minds can't influence the physical world any more than you can move a billiard ball just by thinking. It says your brain drives everything that happens in your mind—a theory called "upward causation". But clearly there's also "downward causation", as your thoughts affect your body, including your brain. Thoughts have physical effects that materialism cannot explain.

2. Grow a brain!

When Romanians toppled a brutal Socialist dictatorship in 1989, charity workers found over 100,000 children in State orphanages in appalling conditions. Most had been fed and kept clean but their paid carers had no time to give them hugs, baby-talk or play. Looking at their two-year-old brain scans breaks your heart—smaller brains, larger furrows, missing white matter under the cortex, which means less connection and slower thinking. Most had no diseases—it was neglect and lack of bonding or attachment that had been so devastating.

Harvard paediatrics professor Charles Nelson said that if you're lying in your cot "staring at a white ceiling, or no one is talking to you, or no one is soothing you when you get upset", then your brain areas for vision, language and emotion don't develop properly. Neglect "is awful for the brain" and, without affection and attention, "the wiring of the brain goes awry."[216]

Many Romanian orphans were adopted by kind people worldwide who enjoyed playing affectionately with them. This produced "neurotrophic substances that allow nerve cells to grow", and after six years their brain development had almost caught up developmentally. Tragically, children who remained in the orphanages never caught up.[217]

We wouldn't expect this phenomenon if the "mind = brain" story were true.

There is growing evidence that we are not determined by our brains: in many ways *we* determine our brains—they become who we choose to be.[218] It's like body-building. Learn a language or a new guitar chord and you are laying down new connections between braincells, causing physical changes in your brain. Forget to practise and those pathways fade like a bushland track no-one walks on. That's neuroplasticity.

Psychiatry professor Thomas Fuchs says our brain and mind have a "reciprocal relationship" and develop each other, and that this "strongly contradicts any reductionist notions of the brain as the creator of the mind."[219]

3. Your mental state is not your brain state.

Imagine a pink elephant.

Got it?

If doctors put you in a multi-million-dollar fMRI machine and scan your brain, they won't find a pink elephant. Even brain surgery won't. Your mind has a pink elephant in it and your brain doesn't, and that shows they're not the same thing.[220]

Let's put that another way:

1. If we can find one thing that is true of your consciousness that is not true of the brain, then they are not the same and materialism is false.
2. Consciousness can include an imagined pink elephant that is nowhere in the brain.
3. So materialism is false.[221]

Of course, recent advances in Brain-Computer Interface (BCI) neurotechnology are beginning to decode pre-speech brain activity into words, sounds and facial expressions.[222] This is impressive, but we are still a long way from being able to access the contents of a person's mind against their will.

You know your state of mind better than anyone, even though you know less about your brain state than a neuroscientist does. Minds are best known from the inside, but brains are known from the outside. Knowing lots about one doesn't mean knowing lots about the other—so they must be different things. Neuroscientist Benjamin Libet said our minds "cannot be observed or studied by an external observer with any type of physical device. In this sense, subjective experience (the conscious mind) appears to be a non-physical phenomenon."[223]

Wait a second—a brain scientist just said there's a non-physical phenomenon? That's a huge hole in materialism, which is built on the claim that third-person scientific research can (eventually) explain absolutely everything.

4. Your mind is first-person, science is third-person

Scientific materialism relies on objective third-person description ("The neurotransmitter crosses the synapse"), but consciousness is subjective and first-person ("I feel optimistic, not tired"), so science is unable to access our consciousness. If consciousness were merely physical, that should be easy.

Try this logic:

1. Physical objects (like your toaster) can't genuinely make "I" statements. (e.g. "I prefer rye sourdough.")
2. I can make "I" statements. (e.g., "I prefer rye sourdough.")
3. So I'm not only a physical object.[224]

This argument is a threat to scientism, the view that science will discover the cause of everything, since everything is physical. Consciousness keeps embarrassing that theory, decade after decade.

5. You can't explain mental experience in physical terms

Imagine I was born blind. Now try to tell me what it's like so see the colour red. You could say, "It's the colour of Mexican salsa." I've tasted that but haven't seen it. You could say, "Red looks hot." I've experienced how heat feels but can only imagine how it *looks*. You can tell me facts ("Red means stop" or "Red is light of 700 nm wavelength") but these are "propositional"[225], and they don't give me *what it's like* or the "raw feel" of experience, which philosophers call qualia or phenomenology. Words can't express an experience, because when I use the dictionary, it just gives me more words. Experience is something you must have yourself. It's like when someone asked Louis Armstrong what jazz is, and he said, "If you gotta ask, you ain't never gonna get to know."

Or imagine this. You're flying fast using only your body. You're seeing nothing, but feeling safe because the sounds and sonar you sense are telling you exactly where you are. You land on a cave roof and fall asleep upside down hanging on by your feet. Waking up hungry, you catch a moth in your mouth and crunch into it. You call to your wife and her masses of body hair bounce your voice back to you with a fuzzy, sexy sound like a distorted guitar. . . rowrrrrr, baby! Can you imagine enjoying that? I can't, thanks anyway. (Shudder!). Philosopher Thomas Nagel's famous essay "What Is

It Like To Be A Bat?"[226] argues that even if you knew every scientific fact about bats, that would not let you into their inner life—also called their subjectivity, qualia or phenomenology.

Conscious experience is beyond description by science.

So how do some materialists respond to the fact that materialism can't explain qualia? They deny that qualia exist! (We saw that in the previous chapter.) If they're right, "no one has ever really suffered"[227], and no-one has felt the bliss of love, the taste of eggplant parmesan, the muddy beauty of a jazz chord, or the rush of skiing through powder.

Nagel writes: "Conscious subjects and their mental lives are inescapable components of reality not describable by the physical sciences."[228] This points to even more realities that go far beyond physical things—more things in heaven and earth, Horatio, than are dreamt of in materialist philosophy.

6. Your brain has physical properties. Your mind doesn't.

Stand on your bathroom scales and think of a pie. Now think of two pies. Did your weight increase? No, because thoughts don't have weight. Fantastic, think of mango cheesecake as much as you like! Thoughts in your mind don't have height, temperature, location, hardness, length, area, mass, resistance, viscosity, angular momentum or any other physical properties. Thoughts and minds are non-physical. But your brain has physical properties.

A radiographer could measure the volume of your brain, but if someone asks, "What's the volume of your memories of your mother?", that may be poetic but it's not scientific.

Has your mind ever wandered to the person you love or to the ski slopes when you're at work? Then you know minds are non-spatial and don't have a location. And "spatially arranged matter" could hardly "conspire to produce nonspatial mental states".[229]

We could say:

1. Physical objects have physical properties like mass, height, temperature, location or volume.
2. Your thoughts don't have physical properties.
3. So your thoughts are not (only) physical objects.
4. So there are real, non-physical things in the universe.

7. Unity across time

Have you seen your kindergarten photos lately? You're still that same person, though every cell in your body has been replaced many times over, including your braincells. You're completely different physically, but it's still you. So there must be more to you than your physical self.

You can replace a computer's hardware and not lose the software and data, and the human equivalent might be variously called mind, spirit or soul, "a substance with an essence constituted by the potential for thought, belief, desire, sensation and volition".[230]

Conclusion:

There's no shortage of eminent scientists who think people are both physical and non-physical. Neurosurgery professor Michael Egnor finds that his 30 years of experience in operating rooms and laboratories contradict the materialist view that matter is all there is to a person: "Human beings straddle the material and immaterial realms."[231]

If minds are real but immaterial things in the universe, then belief in God would be reasonable. As philosopher Keith Ward puts it, "To believe in God is not to take a leap of blind faith beyond reason. It is to take a leap of faith in reason as the ultimate principle of reality."[232]

Summary: the argument from consciousness and reason to God

Here are some other ways to put this argument simply:

1. I'm conscious.
2. Physical things are not conscious.
3. So I'm not only physical.[233]
4. So materialism is false and dualism is true.
5. Dualism is consistent with the existence of God.

   Or:

1. We can do science and (at least partly) understand the universe.

2. This intelligible universe and our minds that grasp it are the products of either blind chance or intelligence.
3. Intelligence is much more likely.[234]

Further reading:

Joshua Rasmussen, "The Foundation of Mind", in *How Reason Can Lead to God: A Philosopher's Bridge to Faith* (Downers Grove: Downers Grove: IVP Academic, 2019)

Sharon Dirckx, *Am I Just My Brain?* (Epsom: The Good Book Company, 2019)

Alvin Plantinga, *Where the Conflict Really Lies: Science, Religion, and Naturalism* (Oxford University Press, 2011), ch.10

Victor Reppert, "The Argument from Reason", in William Lane Craig and J.P. Moreland (eds), *The Blackwell Companion to Natural Theology* (Malden: Wiley-Blackwell, 2012)

Victor Reppert, *C.S. Lewis's Dangerous Idea: In Defence of the Argument from Reason* (Downers Grove: IVP, 2003)

6

Choose Your Own Morality?

Evidence from Morality / Axiology

There are no objective values.
. . .if there are objective values, they make the existence of a god more probable than it would have been without them. Thus we have a defensible argument from morality to the existence of a god."

—ATHEIST PHILOSOPHER J.L. MACKIE[235]

What is the difference between right and wrong, good and bad?
There is no moral difference between them.

—ATHEIST PHILOSOPHER ALEX ROSENBERG[236]

Intrinsically valuable, thinking persons do not come from impersonal, non-conscious, unguided, valueless processes over time. A personal, self-aware, purposeful, good God provides the natural and necessary context for the existence of valuable, rights-bearing, morally responsible human persons.

—CHRISTIAN PHILOSOPHER PAUL COPAN[237]

*This chapter contains general descriptions of sexual assault.

A NEW YORK FASHION designer's party was in full swing when a woman screamed for help. She was being sexually assaulted in an upstairs bedroom.

Sir Alfred Ayer heard her and charged into the room. He saw an extremely muscular man forcing himself on a young model, and asked him to stop.

The man shouted, "Do you know who the f*** I am? I'm the heavyweight champion of the world!" He wasn't lying. He was Mike Tyson.

Ayer was 77 years old, and one punch from Iron Mike could have ended him, but he was a heavyweight of another kind—an Oxford professor of philosophy. He said, "I suggest that we talk about this like rational men."

As the prof argued with the boxer, the model ran out of the room. She was unknown in those days but went on to be a globally famous supermodel—Naomi Campbell.[238]

Would you say the professor was a hero or an idiot for risking his life like that? I'd call him an absolute hero for helping someone else at risk to himself. But here's the twist—he didn't believe in right and wrong. Professor Ayer spent his professional life arguing that ethics had no supporting facts or evidence, because the physical world was all we could really know. Maths and science could be verified as real, but morality was just opinion and any "God-talk" was plain foolish. He didn't believe in objective morals—he was a moral relativist or moral sceptic, not a moral realist or moral objectivist.

Which are you?

Moral relativists

I find some people feel they are moral relativists because they don't want to judge others and they value tolerance. They also don't like to feel guilty themselves. But if you think a bit more about relativism, some serious problems appear.

- Relativists don't believe in objective right or wrong, so any morals they accept could only be their subjective opinion. They can't say *anything* is wrong, any more than you could say I'm wrong for liking strawberry ice cream if you like choc chip. So that means they can't logically prove rape is wrong. They can only say they don't like it. If someone says they do, how can a relativist prove their opinion is not just as valid as yours? And that goes against a commonsense view that rape is always wrong.

- Relativists can't argue that racism or slavery or genocide are objectively wrong, because who says your moral opinion is better than some warlord or slave trader's?
- Relativists can't logically criticise bad behaviour or praise good behaviour because nothing is truly good or bad—that's just opinion.
- Relativists can't try to become a better or more moral person, because no one can say what is more moral or less.
- For relativists, laws are society's opinion at the time, not timeless principles.
- Relativists can't say that someone must be tolerant, because who says intolerance is wrong? People could get some advantages from excluding others.
- Relativists can't even tell someone "Don't force your morality onto me!"—because that person could reply, "Who says I can't? Who are you to tell me what to do?"

See the problem?[239]

I've often talked about this at universities, and I'll never forget one young woman who debated with me in question time. She said her upbringing in one particular religion had left her with a lot of guilt, and now as an adult she had rejected their rules as illogical and sexist and damaging. She felt her religious family didn't love her any more, but she had made good friends outside it and was damn well running her own life, and didn't need any god to tell her how. I really warmed to her. I said, "I'm sorry to hear that happened to you, and I bet it still hurts. You didn't deserve to be excluded and judged by dumb religious arrogance based on old-fashioned, man-made rules and I'm glad you're thinking for yourself now. I think the way you were treated was absolutely wrong—and that shows me that there is a right and wrong."

She nodded, so I continued, "I don't want to put you on the spot, but maybe I can make my point with one question: Is rape wrong? Always? Everywhere?"

The theatre went very quiet.

She replied, "If I say no, every woman in this room will tear my argument apart..."

A male voice chimed in, "So will every sane man." There was a roar of approval.

When that died down, she continued, "Anyone who says rape could ever be right doesn't need a moral philosopher. They need a psychiatrist. Hopefully in prison." Huge cheer.

She continued, "But if I say that rape could never be morally right, then you'll say that I've found at least one solid, objective moral truth, won't you? And there could be more."

I laughed and applauded. "Exactly. You read my play. And even one objective truth would be enough to make a moral realist of me."

"I need to think about that", she said.

"Great", I continued. "And with basic logic, moral relativism shoots itself in the foot. If someone says, 'There are no moral truths', that very statement is trying to tell you a moral truth and, if they're right about that, then they're wrong. It's like Roger Scruton said: 'A writer who says that there are no truths, or that all truth is merely relative, is asking you not to believe him. So don't.'"[240]

I often wonder how she's going now.

Moral realists

I find most people are moral realists underneath. They think right and wrong really exist, even though some individuals may not believe in them, or not feel like doing a duty or avoiding a wrong action.

Some people are scared off moral realism because they assume we are saying:

- I understand all moral issues.
- I always do what my morals say.
- I am capable of judging other people.

But those would be foolish and arrogant claims. Moral realism should make you pretty humble about how much you don't understand, about mistakes you have personally made and about your inability to read the motives of others. But I think there is a moral truth out there, and I try to get close to it. I'd much rather that than accept a philosophy that's too flimsy to say rape is wrong.

In stopping the rape, Prof Ayer was acting like a moral realist. His actions were better than his philosophy. But if a priest rapes a choirboy, he is probably the opposite: his religion teaches moral realism but his actions are much worse than his philosophy.

The moral argument for God

The moral argument is often misunderstood as saying "Only religious people can be moral"—which is obviously, laughably wrong, and would be smug and arrogant for a religious person to say. Even the Bible rebukes religious people for terrible behaviour at times. The moral argument actually goes like this:

1. Real and objectively binding moral obligations do exist. (e.g. Rape is always wrong.)
2. Real and objectively binding moral obligations cannot be based on anything other than the existence of a good and moral God.
3. Therefore, God exists.

Atheists have attacked both premises of that argument.

On premise 1, many atheists have been moral relativists because, like Professor Ayer, they cannot find a logical foundation solid enough to build morality. For example, Friedrich Nietzsche said there are "no moral facts whatever". (Again, does he want us to believe his statement is factual about morals? If so, it's self-contradictory.) He said people only think there are moral facts because they feel a debt to fit in with society and honour their forefathers.[241] Nietzsche scorned people in Western cultures who try to throw out Christianity and yet keep morality. He wrote, "When one gives up Christian belief, one thereby deprives oneself of the right to Christian morality. For the latter is absolutely *not* self-evident: one must make this point clear again and again."[242]

Similarly, J.L. Mackie's book, *Inventing Right and Wrong*, claims that we humans may think our moral thoughts and words are real and objective, but they are not. This is called "error theory". Mackie sees that morals would be very "queer" things in a materialistic world made only of particles, and would be beyond the ability of science to discover: "If there were objective values, then they would be entities or qualities or relations of a very strange sort, utterly different from anything else in the universe."[243] Some argue that we must be moral relativists because we cannot find any foundation for morals in a naturalistic, materialistic world.[244]

And yet some atheists have seen that moral relativism comes at a staggering cost—the inability to say *anything* is right or wrong. Atheist philosopher Kai Neilsen faults this view: he says wife-beating and child abuse are absolutely wrong, and so

> It is more reasonable to believe such elemental things to be evil than to believe any sceptical theory that tells us we cannot know or reasonably believe any of these things to be evil. . . I firmly believe that this is bedrock and right and that anyone who does not believe it cannot have probed deeply enough into the grounds of his moral beliefs.[245]

So more recently, atheists have accepted that objective morals are real (premise 1 in the moral argument), and looked for foundations other than God (trying to disprove premise 2). They have tried to build objective morals on science (evolutionary biology), society and/or individual choice.

Let's see what you think of their attempts. We'll use rape as the example of a moral absolute. Can their theories muscle up and condemn it?

Where might we get real, objective morals?

1. Biology?

It broadly makes sense that a group of animals that cooperates and treats each other well has a higher chance of survival than one that doesn't. No society that approves of theft or murder would survive for long, and evolutionary theory is all about survival. Some see this as the basic idea behind human morality.[246] But that view also has major problems.

Firstly, individual animals can get a survival advantage from rape or, as biologists call it, sexual coercion or forced copulation.[247] Male orangutans punch, kick and bite females to force 90% of sexual encounters. Male diving beetles hold females underwater, threatening to drown her unless she submits.[248] Similar tactics are common in dogs, dolphins, polar bears, and salmon. Males routinely injure the female, risk her life, cost her energy, and restrict her ability to choose a better partner, which means her offspring may be of lower quality than she deserves. So this may not help the *species* improve overall, but it certainly can get the *individual* male a higher quality partner than he deserves, and increase his "success in passing on his genes to the next generation".[249] So why wouldn't he?

And why wouldn't human animals? Rape can spread a man's genes, increasing his chances of survival. A genetic study found that a staggering 8% of the men in Asia today are descendants of the Mongol warlord Genghis Khan—which means 0.5% of the world's population are his descendants.[250] How did he become the all-time survival-of-the-fittest champion? By raping countless captive women. And encouraging his sons to do the same, spreading his genes even further.

Biology is about survival, not ethics. A female redback spider will usually eat the male she has just mated with.[251] If cannibalism gives her more energy to raise her babies, then why not? She's programmed for the survival of her genes, not some ethical principle like loving your neighbour.

This ugly reality was unthinkable to Susan Brownmiller, who wrote the pioneering book about rape, *Against Our Will*, back in 1975. She claimed "no zoologist, as far as I know, has ever observed that animals rape in their natural habitat, the wild." In fact zoologists had, but Brownmiller wanted to argue that rape was not biological or "natural"—it was socially conditioned by the patriarchy. She wrote, "It is nothing more or less than a conscious process of intimidation by which all men keep all women in a state of fear".[252] So rape was about power, not sexual desire. If rape was socially conditioned, not biological, then it could be stopped by education and culture change. In 2013, though, Brownmiller reluctantly admitted that a "vocal handful of neo-Darwinians theorize that rape is a cost-effective strategy for males. . . to spread their genes widely with a minimal amount of parental investment." She hated that idea: "What a fancy argument for rape, and for the failure to pay child support, as natural behaviour!"[253] Brownmiller seems to assume that if something is natural, then it must be right or moral or even inevitable for us humans. A more recent feminist, Louise Perry, challenges that. She faces the biological facts about rape so as to suggest more realistic ways to prevent it. Her argument is based on the idea that not everything natural is good or right or moral.[254]

Since rape clearly is biological and "natural", it would be disastrous to take our moral absolutes from nature.

Selfish genes

Secondly, how could we get morals from selfish genes?

As atheist biologist Richard Dawkins puts it, "we are survival machines—robot vehicles blindly programmed to preserve the selfish molecules known as genes."[255] And selfish genes need to "survive at the expense of their rivals".[256] Dawkins described it this way:

> So long as DNA is passed on, it does not matter who or what gets hurt in the process. . . Genes don't care about suffering, because they don't care about anything. . .
>
> if the universe were just electrons and selfish genes, meaningless tragedies. . . are exactly what we should expect, along with equally meaningless *good* fortune. Such a universe would be neither evil nor good in intention. It would manifest no intentions of any kind. In a universe of blind physical forces and genetic replication, some people are going to get hurt, other people are going to get lucky, and you won't find any rhyme or reason in it, nor any justice. The universe we observe has precisely the properties we should expect if there is, at bottom, no design, no purpose, no evil and no good, nothing but blind, pitiless indifference. . . DNA neither knows nor cares. DNA just is. And we dance to its music.[257]

How on earth do you build solid morality on that? Dawkins tries: "there are occasions when genes maximize their selfish welfare at their level, by programming unselfish cooperation, or even self-sacrifice, by the organism at its level."

In case that makes you feel warm inside, read the next sentence: "But group welfare is always a fortuitous consequence, not a primary drive. This is the meaning of 'the selfish gene.'" So it's not actually generous. It doesn't care for you unless you can help it. It's selfish to the core.

Dawkins argues that some morality is based on mistakes. He says some birds look after other birds' chicks because evolution programs rules of thumb like "look after small squawkers".

> The rule misfires if another baby bird somehow gets into the nest. . . Could it be that our Good Samaritan urges are misfiring, analogous to the misfiring of a reed warbler's parental instincts when it works itself to the bone for a young cuckoo? An even closer analogy is the human urge to adopt a child.

He says these are "precious mistakes" and "good" misfirings.[258] But realistically they waste effort and resources that your selfish gene wants you to spend on your children. They lower your survival chances, especially if things are tight, like in a famine, and can be fatal to you or your offspring. He's trying to sneak nice cuddly values into a "survival of the fittest" model which is actually based on ruthless competition, and they don't fit. These are external measures of morality that he is choosing, and not giving reasons for his choice.

And his view makes kindness a *mistake*, so morality would be a delusion, not something real. So bye-bye to moral realism.

Dawkins has also written that "at the same time as I support Darwinism as a scientist, I am a passionate anti-Darwinian when it comes to politics and how we should conduct our human affairs."[259] He said, "I feel that one of the reasons for learning about Darwinian evolution is as an object lesson in how not to set up our values and social lives."[260] He ends his book *The Selfish Gene* by saying we can overcome "the tyranny of the selfish replicators" because nature has given us consciousness.

What a giant leap of logic![261] I mean, have we now moved beyond evolution? Evolution is only interested in the "four Fs": fighting, feeding, fleeing and... reproduction. It cannot create moral values. And if you start with Dawkins' universe of valueless matter and energy, how do you get to human rights and morality? Where are the chances that objective morality would evolve randomly in an amoral, unthinking universe of matter?[262] How can science move from telling us what is to what ought to be? And if our consciousness was shaped by ruthless, bloody competition on the African savannah, why would it suddenly point us towards cuddly niceness to everyone?

In case that leap wasn't big enough for you, Dawkins has also said, "I call myself a cultural Christian... It seems to me to be a fundamentally decent religion."[263] If evolutionary biology could provide us with decent morality, why would he want to parachute in some Christian values?

Atheist Kai Neilsen writes

> We have not been able to show that reason requires the moral point of view, or that all really rational persons... need not be individual egoists or classical amoralists. Reason doesn't decide here. The picture I have painted for you is not a pleasant one... Pure practical reason, even with a good knowledge of the facts, will not take you to morality.[264]

But if God made and cares for all people (and animals), and summed up that care in a moral law, we would have a solid basis for objective, timeless morality, for human rights, and for our most cherished and deeply held values.

The atheist philosopher J.L. Mackie nails it:

Moral properties constitute so odd a cluster of properties and relations that they are most unlikely to have arisen in the ordinary course of events without an all-powerful god to create them.[265]

Darwinian ethics?

Thirdly, Darwinism doesn't produce ethics, as Charles Darwin himself saw in my home country. He visited Australia's island state of Tasmania, where Aboriginal men had fought to defend their land and women from settlers and convicts. Europeans had rounded them up at gunpoint and forced them onto a freezing island where almost all died out. (Read the tragic story of Truganini.). Darwin's comment? "This most cruel step seems to have been quite unavoidable" and now the colony "enjoys the great advantage of being free from a native population".[266]

He said Australian Aboriginal people were the second-lowest form of human life, a possible link between man and ape. And he made a sad prediction. "At some future period, not very distant as measured by centuries, the civilised races of man will almost certainly exterminate, and replace, the savage races throughout the world."[267] "Wherever the European has trod, death seems to pursue the aboriginal", he wrote. "The varieties of man seem to act on each other in the same way as different species of animals, the stronger always extirpating the weaker."[268] This was the evolutionary idea of survival of the fittest taken to its logical conclusion.

Yet Darwin may not have heard of Maria Lock. She was the daughter of a tribal chief named Yarramundi, and was invited into a school at Parramatta run by Christian missionaries. In 1819, at just fourteen years old, Maria came top of the state of New South Wales in the final examinations.[269] She married a freed convict in St John's Church, Parramatta, and they had ten children. Maria received a large land holding. Many people in the area today are proud to be her descendants.

But it didn't take long for Darwin's ideas to move from science books to government policy. Aboriginals were seen as a "dying race" and were not capable of learning. It was decided that they should be trained to be servants and farm workers. They were considered a "child race" who could not go beyond Year 3. Even in the 1960s, the Aboriginal Welfare Board said they lacked the necessary IQ.[270]

It's hard to imagine how much Aboriginal people have suffered and missed out because of this social Darwinism. Why are we not pushing Charles Darwin's statues over?

As one historian put it, "one of the few persistent barriers to social Darwinist theory in Australia was the Christian doctrine that all human beings were of 'one blood'".[271] A Bible text quoted in these debates said that "God has made from one blood all the nations of people on earth" (Acts 17:26).[272] This religious assumption would give all people equal value and rights, rather than ranking them on a theoretical scale of evolutionary development.

Accidental ethics?

Fourthly, and more broadly, why would we expect biology to have any ethics to it? If we are the accidental by-products of random evolution on a tiny planet in a mindless universe where particles move at random without any purpose, and we may be replaced by a higher species or die out, why would our ideas affect reality? What objective value could we have? If we found that a "love thy neighbour" morality helps us survive, that still wouldn't make it objectively true. Why would we expect that morality to be floating above us somehow or written into the reality of the universe somewhere? Our made-up morals would die out with us. Atheist philosophers see this problem. Atheist philosopher Thomas Nagel says "an evolutionary self-understanding would require us to give up moral realism—the natural conviction that our moral judgments are true or false independent of our beliefs."[273]

Michael Ruse supports this: "Considered as a rationally justifiable set of claims about an objective something, ethics is illusory. . . [and] without foundation. Morality is just an aid to survival and reproduction, and has no being beyond this. . . [And] any deeper meaning is illusory."[274]

That doesn't produce objective right and wrong. Atheist James Rachels says

> The traditional supports for the idea of human dignity are gone. They have not survived the colossal shift of perspective brought about by Darwin's theory. It might be thought that this result need not be devastating for the idea of human dignity, because even if the traditional supports are gone, the idea might still be defended on some *other* grounds. Once again, though, an evolutionary

perspective is bound to make one sceptical. The doctrine of human dignity says that humans merit a level of moral concern wholly different from that accorded to mere animals; for this to be true, there would have to be some big, morally significant difference between them... But that is precisely what evolutionary theory calls into question... [and] a Darwinian may conclude that a successful defence of human dignity is most unlikely.[275]

Legal philosopher Joel Feinberg said he believes human rights should be unconditional and unchangeable, and should belong to all humans rather than depending on merit. We can base value on merit or intelligence, but that will not make everyone equal, and a dolphin will outrank a handicapped child. In the end, Feinberg cannot find a logical basis beyond a feeling or attitude.[276]

The Moral Landscape?

The best attempt to show how evolutionary biology could motivate moral behaviour is a book called *The Moral Landscape* by the atheist philosopher Sam Harris. He calls moral relativism "nonsensical" and says, "I think there is an absolute right and wrong."[277] That's a great start, and he then tries to build solid morals on Darwinism, with its ideas of competitive survival and the selfish gene, and he suggests four evolutionary reasons why we might behave unselfishly:

a. Kin selection. We might suffer or even die for our children—because they carry a copy of our genes.

b. Reciprocation. I might help you and your children if you help me and my children.

c. Reputation. I might be unselfish if it gets me and my children a good reputation. If my community thinks I'm a good guy, they're more likely to help me and this could improve our chances of surviving and thriving.

d. Sexual advertising. Being generous shows you're a fantastic person and makes people more likely to reproduce with you. Charles Darwin also wrote about this.

Let's think whether these reasons work in the real world. Can they motivate people to care for others? Imagine you can go online and quietly donate to a boarding school that takes very young girls out of child sex brothels in Bangkok, and gives them a free education in a caring environment, increasing their chances of a good job and a future. (You can. A friend of mine runs one of many schools like that.) What might motivate you to give?

a. Kin selection won't help, because these girls are not your relatives. You'd be more likely to give your money to your own children or your nephews and nieces.

b. Reciprocation won't help, because there's almost zero chance that these children could ever pay you back—so that's a bad investment.

c. Reputation might motivate you to give a public gift and tell everyone about it. But that's not actually caring about the children—it's caring about how you look. One of the worst child sexual predators, the billionaire Jeffrey Epstein, gave large donations to charities. These boosted his image and made him powerful friends—even presidents and royalty—and allowed him to keep abusing young girls.

And if appearance is all that matters, it would be cheaper simply to lie about your giving.

d. Sexual advertising? Some research found that generally "prosocial men were rated as more physically and sexually attractive, socially desirable, and desirable as dates".[278] People who are "altruistic" (meaning they help others at cost to themselves) were seen as desirable long-term partners, and women preferred altruistic men for one-off dates—yet men did not have a preference for altruistic women.[279] Men tended to donate more when they were with a potential partner[280], and give four or five times more when the fundraiser was an attractive woman. Men also did "competitive helping" and gave more when another man had given a large donation—but women did not.[281] These gender differences may be explained by the fact that women bear a heavy cost in childbearing, and desire a competent, generous man to support them in that, while men look for other factors.

So sexual advertising would not encourage women to give, and men could find less expensive ways to attract a mate.

Yet people do donate their money and time to the orphanage, and feel great about it. Harris's theory doesn't really explain why. I'd say his attempt to build objective morals and values on a neo-Darwinian view of nature was not successful.

2. Society?

Many people think our morals come from the societies we live in. Again, there is some logic to this. Individuals constantly fighting would lead to a life that is "solitary, poor, nasty, brutish and short"[282], while and working together in a society can give us safer, richer, more social, longer lives. And so we make a "social contract", agreeing not to lie, steal, cheat or do violence so that we can get on with our neighbour—as long as they do the same.

But while societies do influence us in good ways, are they a reliable source for all our morals? What if you live in a society with a rape culture, for instance? In parts of South Africa, one in four men have raped and one in five have gang-raped, saying it is "fun" and "what boys do", or a good way to punish an annoying woman or keep her in her place under male dominance. They feel "peer pressure" to rape. Some even believe that sex with a virgin will heal them of AIDS.[283]

Parts of India have a culture where police don't bother to enforce rape laws, especially against rich or high caste men. Society blames women for being raped, and fear of shame stops many of them from reporting the crime. Rape is even used as revenge on the victim's father or husband.[284]

In Pakistan, a woman called Mukhtaran Bibi was "honour-raped" by a local council as punishment for a crime her brother supposedly committed. She was expected to suicide in shame, but somehow she had the courage to stand, and international media took up her case and brought power to bear. She eventually won and is now a human rights educator.[285]

Societies get things wrong. Many societies in history have gotten slavery wrong for centuries. We applaud people like William Wilberforce and Bibi who stand up to whole societies and are brave enough to call out evil, even when almost everyone else disagrees with them. And that would mean that some things remain true even if no-one in a society sees them or believes them. Human sacrifice is wrong even if not one Aztec knew it. Morals transcend societies. So trying to get solid morals from a society alone involves serious relativism. It's hard to have a social contract if so many people disagree about what the contract is.

If you're a moral relativist, you cannot condemn rape in other societies. That's just their way of doing things and you can't judge. That view is ridiculous, and shoots moral relativism in the brain.

Another problem is that the social contract is based on self-interest. So if my neighbour is helpful, I would help him. If he becomes very needy or drains my resources, I may not be motivated to help him. It is religion that goes one better with the command to "Love thy neighbour".

Further, who should I include in my social contract? Everyone in the world? Even enemies who are trying to take what I have? Even poor people in countries who will never help me? Or only people who are rich enough to help me? And what is my duty to them anyway? To give to them at heavy cost to me, or just not to harm them? Many people disagree about these questions, so the social contract is far from clear.

The social contract also has a problem with motivation. Think how much we spend on locks and alarms and computer security each year globally. If we could trust the social contract, we could spend that money on much better things, but individuals make a calculation: if I can get an advantage by cheating, or stealing, or free-loading off the work of others with very little risk of being caught, why wouldn't I? Surely the most self-interested outcome would be enjoying the fruits of cheating while enjoying a positive social reputation. This sound sociopathic, but the social contract cannot really motivate moral choices, and needs to spend a lot on deterring people from breaking the contract.[286]

Perhaps the greatest challenge to social contract theory is Social Darwinism, which applies evolutionary theory to the most advanced animals of all—humans.

Let's imagine a counter-factual scenario. Imagine Hitler won World War II, with help from King Edward VIII in England, who didn't abdicate, and Joseph P. Kennedy, who became President of the USA. (Both men admired the Nazis.) Your Science professor explains that the world used to be infested by dangerous pests called Jews and lower races like Blacks and Asians, but our beloved Führer gave us the final solution to that problem. He had the strength and moral clarity to rid the world of them, which seemed sad and even perhaps immoral at the time but actually cleared the best of our species—the tall, blonde Master Race—to find its rightful place on top. We are the fittest and so we should survive at their expense, and we are constantly getting better, evolving towards the Superman or Übermensch. Your History professor quotes Hitler's view on human rights, that there was "only one most sacred human right . . . namely to ensure the preservation of the best of humanity in order to make possible a nobler development of this nature."[287] So it was right of the Führer to rid us of dangerous ideas like democracy and a free market. There are no books or academics who say differently. (They were quietly removed from universities before you were born.) And you can't get to know any non-Whites or hear their stories, because they are extinct. No-one in the world says this race-based mass murder was wrong.

Question: Does that make it morally right?

I say no. Never.

If you agree, then you are a moral realist or objectivist.

On religion, Hitler and many leading Nazis were members of the Church for political purposes, but Hitler said of Germany

> You see, it's been our misfortune to have the wrong religion. Why didn't we have the religion of the Japanese, who regard sacrifice for the fatherland as the highest good? The Mohameddan religion too would have been much more compatible to us than Christianity. Why did it have to be Christianity with its meekness and flabbiness?[288]

Reichsführer Heinrich Himmler added:

> The German people . . . have learned once again to value people racially—they have turned away once again from the Christian theory . . . which ruled Germany for more than a thousand years and caused the racial decay of the German Volk [people], and almost caused its racial death.[289]

What Christian theory? The idea that all people have equal value and the weak and poor need special care.[290] This idea clashes with the Darwinist view that the weak should die and make way for the strong, so that the next generation will have strong parents and the race will be improved. And Social Darwinism became the Nazi's justification for murdering some 6 million Jews, 5.7 million Soviet citizens, 1.8 million Poles, 250,000 disabled people, 250,000 Roma gypsies and more.

So we can't really get objective right and wrong from society. Cross that option off the list.

3. The individual?

We humans clearly do make moral decisions ourselves, and that is an important part of our freedom and individuality. But are our own thoughts and feelings enough to decide what is moral? Can we be totally morally autonomous?

What if a man enjoys rape? Would that make it morally right?

Surveys have suggested that around 30% of men *might possibly* consider forcing a partner into sex if they could be sure they would not be caught[291], and an estimated 10% of men in Western countries have forced sex or would be likely to.[292] These can't easily be identified, but they tend to be low in empathy, make decisions impulsively, enjoy risk-taking, be promiscuous, act hyper-masculine, and seem hostile and disagreeable.[293] Can we expect someone like that to have a moral conscience, or even care about anyone or anything much, other than consequences to themselves? Can we trust them to decide what is moral? Hardly.

Men who are more likely to rape might sincerely believe rape myths[294], like these: She said no but I know she meant yes. She wore a skimpy dress so she was asking for it. She's that kind of girl—I hear she's had plenty of other guys from work. I paid for dinner so she owed me. She complained but that was just trying to look like a "good girl". She came to my house, so she wanted it. She got drunk with me, knowing what would happen. I'm very passionate, and when she flirted with me, I couldn't stop. I love her so it's OK. We're married, so that's always consent.

Or women who rape might believe rape myths, such as: A male can't be sexually assaulted, except by a gay man—they all secretly want sex any time. I'm the hottest female teacher in this school, so he was lucky to have me even though he was underage. He was very mature for his age. He got aroused eventually so he must have wanted it.

Rape myths like these deny or minimise the trauma, excuse the perpetrator, blame the victim, and even make the victim blame themselves. Believing them can make perpetrators more likely to offend, make victims less likely to report, and make police, juries and even judges less likely to deal with crimes properly.

Rape myths show that people can be ignorant—sometimes purposely—and biased and selfish, and can believe myths and tell themselves convenient lies. It's easy to see that weakness in others, but harder to see in ourselves that we may need to change our own thinking or educate our consciences. Even Aristotle, the father of logic and rationality, saw women and slaves as "naturally inferior beings", lacking fundamental human rights.[295] That might make us a little less confident that we know best. Wise people look for objective ways to check their beliefs, recognising that the individual alone doesn't always see objective morality.

4. God?

Let me be crystal clear that this argument *doesn't* say that believers are better than non-believers. Even the Bible often criticises religious people for being immoral, sometimes worse than non-religious people.[296]

This argument says that if there are real moral truths—and clearly there are—then their origin can't be explained other than by God's existence.

Atheist writers Peter Singer and Helga Kuhse admit that the best way to justify belief in human rights and human value would be the Judaeo-Christian idea of humans bearing the image of God.[297] That gives humans a value that mere matter cannot give.

As we've seen, philosopher J.L. Mackie didn't believe in God or objective morals, but he said that if objective moral values did exist, then they would "make the existence of a god more probable. . . Thus we have a defensible argument from morality to the existence of God."[298] I think he's right about that. I do believe in objective morals, so they give me one more reason to think God exists.

The Bible claims God writes a moral law in every person's heart—even for people who don't believe in God, so they can "instinctively do what the law requires" and have a conscience that either condemns or excuses them. (Romans 2:14-15). You'd expect a God who cares about everyone to give commands that are objective, not biased on grounds of gender, race, social class or religion (Galatians 3:28). You'd expect a Creator to make moral commands that suit who we are and match reality, and that promote human happiness and wellbeing.

If God holds everyone morally accountable, rewarding good choices and punishing evil, then this is a powerful motive to do the right thing. We might even put others before ourselves or even self-sacrifice—a soldier taking a bullet for a friend—because God would reward that after death.

This argument has a weakness—it won't tell you *which* God. But common sense suggests it will be a good and totally ethical God, not one who rewards men who kill thousands by flying aeroplanes into buildings and gives them 72 women to rape in the afterlife.

I find it interesting that the moral teaching of Jesus Christ seems to have considered most of Harris' categories and explicitly asked people to do even better.

   a. It goes beyond kin selection: "If you are kind only to your family and friends, what have you done more than anyone else? Don't even the pagans do that?" (Matthew 5:47)

   b. It goes beyond reciprocation:
   "When you put on a dinner, don't just invite your friends... and rich neighbours, because they will repay you by inviting you back. Rather invite the poor, the crippled, the lame, and the blind. Then at the resurrection of God's people, God will pay you back for inviting those who could not repay you." (Luke 14:12–14)

   It also says, "Do unto others as you would have them do unto you", the famous Golden Rule. That's very different from what reciprocation theory would say: "Do unto others only if they will do unto you."

   c. And Jesus' ethic goes beyond advertising or reputation theory: "Be careful not to do your 'acts of righteousness' in front of people, to be seen by them. If you do, you will have no reward from your Father in heaven. (Jesus, Mt 6:1)

   d. Jesus doesn't mention sexual advertising, since he advocates loving monogamy.

Going further, Jesus promotes unselfish altruism. For example, one of his most famous teachings is the story of the good Samaritan, who cares for an injured man from an enemy nation, risking his own safety and spending his own money on him. So Jesus even advocates self-sacrificial altruism: "No-one has greater love than this: laying down his life for his friends." (John 15:12–13)

And even:

> You have heard that it was said, 'Love your neighbour and hate your enemy.' But I tell you: Love your enemies and pray for those who persecute you, so that you may be sons of your Father in heaven. He causes his sun to rise on the evil and the good... (Matthew 5:43–45)

These morals are based on the assumptions that every person is a child of God, made in God's image and loved by God, and thus hugely valuable, and also that God rewards and punishes people's moral choices.

This seems the only solid foundation for objective morals and ethics. No other explanation really works in a convincing way.

Summary: The Moral Argument for God's Existence (aka The Axiological Argument):

Human reason and conscience often motivate people to act morally, even when it is not in their own selfish interests. Both reveal a moral law, but we cannot find a source for it in the natural world. This points to a supernatural Lawgiver.[299]

We could sum it up like this:

1. Real and objectively binding moral obligations do exist.

2. If God did not exist, then real and objectively binding moral obligations would not exist. (Because evolutionary biology, societies and individuals are not a solid enough foundation.)

3. Therefore God exists.

The moral argument does *not* say that religious people are necessarily more moral than non-religious people.

And the moral argument alone doesn't say which God or gods exist, but it does suggest kindness and fairness, and the moral teaching of Jesus Christ is impressive.

The moral argument can be added to other arguments in this book to build a cumulative case.

See also:

David Baggett & Jerry L. Walls, *Good God: Theistic Foundations of Morality* (Oxford University Press, 2011)
Paul Copan and Mark D. Linville, *The Moral Argument* (Continuum, 2015).
William Lane Craig, "Moral Argument", in *A Reasonable Faith*, 172–83.
Gregory R. Peterson, 'Out-Group Altruism and the New Atheism', in Amarnath Amarasingam (ed), *Religion and the New Atheism: A Critical Appraisal* (Leiden/Boston: Brill, 2012)

7

Does Suffering Disprove God?

Suffering as Evidence Against God; and a Free Will Defence

Epicurus's old questions are yet unanswered.
Is he [God] willing to prevent evil, but not able? then is he impotent.
Is he able, but not willing? then is he malevolent.
Is he both able and willing? whence then is evil?

—DAVID HUME[300]

Earth has no sorrow that heaven cannot heal.

—THOMAS MOORE

THE ACTOR STEPHEN FRY was asked what he as an atheist would say if he met God at the Pearly Gates of heaven. He let fly a passionate speech that has been viewed over 10 million times:

> I'd say, bone cancer in children? What's that about? How dare you? How dare you create a world in which there is such misery that is not our fault. It's utterly, utterly evil. Why should I respect a capricious, mean-minded, stupid God who creates a world which is so full of injustice and pain. That's what I'd say.[301]

He went on:

> Yes, the world is very splendid but it also has in it insects whose whole life cycle is to burrow into the eyes of children and make

Does Suffering Disprove God?

> them blind. They eat outwards from the eyes. Why? Why did you do that to us? You could easily have made a creation in which that didn't exist...
>
> It's perfectly apparent that he's monstrous, utterly monstrous, and deserves no respect whatsoever. The moment you banish him, your life becomes simpler, purer, cleaner and more worth living.

Fry is qualified to comment, having suffered bi-polar disorder and other struggles, as his moving and beautifully-written autobiographies describe, and having attempted suicide a number of times.

We'll look at the logic in a minute, but first let's go with Fry's powerful emotion and imagine God has been banished. Adios, Dios! Are we happy now? Hmmm, we still have bone cancer. And the West African *Loa loa* worm. But now we're on our own, without even the slimmest hope that there could be a kind Someone somewhere who might care for us after all the suffering. Afterlife is a hope that most people alive today find attractive in some form or other.[302] If that just went in the bin, is life looking "more worth living"? Not to most people, I'd say.

I'd say the problem of evil doesn't skip over atheists, and atheism doesn't help.

I'll never forget making a documentary in Rwanda just after the genocide where 800,000 Tutsi people were murdered in 100 days, mostly in face-to-face attacks by Hutu neighbours with *panga* knives. I interviewed Samuel, whose family had been attacked in their home. Enemies had burst in their door swinging machetes and dismembered his wife and two of their children before he could even blink. Samuel somehow snatched up their three other young children and ran out the back door. He fled all night with his children on his back and in his arms, then hid all day in a drain under a highway. He travelled every night for a week, scrounging food and water and coaxing the children to sleep by day, until they reached safety. When I met him, he was working for an aid agency managing road reconstruction, and raising his children. I asked him if he had given up on God after his terrible loss. He said

> I have already lost so much. Why would I also lose my dearest friend, who understands my tears and will one day give my loved ones back to me in a new, joyful world?
>
> This hope strengthens me to keep going. I tell my troubles to a kind Father who listens sympathetically and suffers with me, having watched his own son die at the hands of enemies. I trust there is a plan, even though I do not see it yet. One day God will

rid the world of suffering and evil. And so I keep on, and I find this life worth living. And I encourage my children.

Who wouldn't want that kind of comfort in suffering and sorrow? Yet I find people who are attracted to it emotionally, but can't rationally believe it. So let's see if the evidence and logic give us any reason to hope.

The Logical Problem of Evil

This well-known argument—at least as old as Epicurus in 300BC or the Buddha in 500BC[303]—aims to use evil and suffering to prove the non-existence of God. Here's a summary:

1. An all-knowing (omniscient) God would know about suffering.
2. An all-loving (omnibenevolent) God would want to stop suffering.
3. An all-powerful (omniscient) God would have been able to stop suffering.
4. But we suffer.
5. So there is no all-knowing, all-loving, all-powerful God.

"Oh dear", says God, "I hadn't thought of that." And He vanishes in a puff of logic.[304]

Or does He?

The philosopher J.L. Mackie[305] was definite that suffering "disproved" belief in God. That's a big claim, but Mackie used the cricket bat of logic to hit any counter-arguments over the fence.

When people argued that "good cannot exist without evil", Mackie replied (in summary):

a. Who says it can't? Why couldn't you have only good? If God created all the laws in the universe, then *God* must have made evil necessary. By that logic, God would be the cause of evil.
b. If God could have created without any evil or suffering, why didn't He? And if He couldn't, then He isn't omnipotent.
c. This argument suggests good and evil work together, and "denies that evil is opposed to good". That would mean evil is actually almost good—a claim that makes no sense, and weakens the idea of evil to a vague relative term.

Does Suffering Disprove God?

    d. It also suggests the world should contain "just enough evil to serve as the counterpart of good." Yet there seems to be far too much evil in the world to believe this.

I'd have to admit Mackie won that one.

Some argued that suffering and pain make people develop sympathy, kindness, heroism and other virtues of character. That is of course partly true—think of Stephen Fry doing charity work for mental health agencies. But Mackie slogged this argument:

    a. In a perfect world, people wouldn't need virtues like sympathy (because no one else would suffer) or heroism (because they wouldn't need to fight anything). And isn't it obvious that we would all be happier if there wasn't any suffering at all?

    b. Suffering may produce some heroes, but it makes many, many people broken, demoralised, cowardly, defensive, callous and cruel. Why would a kind God cause that?

    c. This argument tries to justify first-order evil (pain) by second-order good (good character traits). But first-order evil (pain) could also cause second-order evil (bad character traits). You might try to argue that second-order evil then causes some kind of third-order good, but what if it also produces third-order evils? How long will we be stuck in this regress? And why wouldn't God just stop first-order evil right from the start?

I find it hard to fault his logic here.

Mackie also considered the argument that evil is "due to human freewill" and that "it is better on the whole" that people "should act freely, and sometimes err" than be mere robots pre-programmed to do good. He attacked that argument too, saying that God should have created people "such that they always freely choose the good", "beings who would act freely but always go right". God could have done this because "there are no limits to what an omnipotent being can do".[306] But God didn't do this, so God is either not good or he's not omnipotent.

And that's where I think Mackie's argument falls over. Did you see the problem?

The Free Will Defence

In summary, Mackie had said:

1. Evil exists.

2. It would not exist if a good, all-powerful God existed, because

    a. God would create people who always freely choose to do good, because there are no limits to what an omnipotent God can do

    b. a good God would destroy evil

3. So a good, all-powerful God does not exist.

Maybe you've already found the glitch that Christian philosopher Alvin Plantinga found: it's logically impossible to create people with genuine freedom and zero chance of ever doing anything wrong. *Genuinely* free people would always have the real possibility of making at least one mistake. Plantinga said God "cannot *cause* or *determine* them to do only what is right. For if He does so, then they aren't significantly free after all; they do not do what is right *freely*."[307]

Mackie had claimed there was "no possible world" in which suffering could exist with a good, all-powerful God, but Plantinga showed it was very possible that God may have a good reason to allow some suffering, because making people free could be worth the price.

Imagine two worlds:

- In World A, you can't hurt anyone else and no-one can hurt you. Everyone is pre-programmed to do good all the time.

- In World B, you might get hurt by other people's choices or even your own, but you have free will.

Which world would you want to live in?

I've asked thousands of people, mainly on campuses, and I've never seen one person choose World A. People want world B because they can choose to love whoever they want, can be loved, and can have individuality, artistic expression, creativity and the liberty to define their own lives. In World A, you can't love or be loved, you can't choose what matters to you, and you are controlled from the inside—worse than any dictatorship. In World B, you might choose to hurt other people, and others may choose to hurt you—and ironically, people might even choose things like slavery

Does Suffering Disprove God?

and rape[308] that take away the freedom of other people—but you can also do acts of kindness and goodness because you want to. And you have *love*.

People often tell me they might like to have *part* of World A. They'd like God to stop child abusers. Maybe dictators. But then they start to disagree on how much God should control. Should He stop people from selling drugs? Using drugs? Smoking near children? Smoking at all? Should God stop overweight people eating ice-cream? When would people start complaining that God was a dictator, a control freak? Conversely, some say God should control us more, and has allowed us too much freedom.[309] But no-one ever wants the full World A, and you can't really have *part* of World A. You're either significantly free or you're not.

And if love is God's highest value, then He would never create World A, because without freedom, love is impossible. And the Bible's God defines himself as love: "God is love."[310]

But wait. If God *couldn't* have made free people and guaranteed their good behaviour, does that mean He's not omnipotent? No, because omnipotence doesn't mean God has to be able to make a square circle, or a married bachelor, or a bowling ball that is both heavier and lighter than an egg. Even the Bible admits that it's "impossible" for God to do some things—e.g. to lie, to deny his own nature or be tempted by evil.[311] So omnipotence includes the ability to do things that would be impossible for us (e.g. to create the universe), but not to do logically impossible things—that's just silly talk.

In Plantinga's words, a world

> containing creatures who are sometimes significantly free (and freely perform more good than evil actions) is more valuable... than a world containing no free creatures...
>
> To create creatures capable of moral good... [God] must create creatures capable of moral evil; and he can't give these creatures this freedom to perform evil and at the same time prevent them from doing so. God did in fact create significantly free creatures but some of them went wrong in the exercise of their freedom: this is the source of moral evil.[312]

Plantinga called this the "free will defence"[313] against the logical problem of evil.

Mackie tried to defeat the Free Will Defence with another interesting argument: he claimed that if God really lets people be free, then He can't be omnipotent because he is not controlling everything. This is called the Paradox of Omnipotence. Can an omnipotent God make something which he cannot later control? If he can't, then He is not omnipotent now. If he can, then He is not omnipotent later. I think this problem disappears if you say that God has the power to control every person—every atom in the universe!—but can choose not to when and where He wishes.

Today, most philosophers, including many atheists, agree that Plantinga's Free Will Defence has defeated Mackie's Logical Problem of Evil.[314] Atheist William Rowe, for instance, finds the free will defence is "a fairly compelling argument for the view that the existence of evil is logically consistent with the existence of... God."[315]

I certainly don't claim Plantinga has written a full explanation of suffering and evil—how it began, what it is, where it resides, how it will end—let alone given us emotionally satisfying answers to all our questions about your personal suffering or mine. Rather, he used a "small target" argument for the skinniest possible rebuttal: Mackie said it's impossible to believe in a good, all-powerful God because suffering exists, and Plantinga shows the two could be compatible if there is free will.

And that's not just a nerdy argument—it can be a major comfort and hope. I've seen too many friends suffer a tragedy which not only hurts them but also convinces them that God doesn't exist—and so they lose what used to be their major source of support and hope just when it's most needed. Plantinga's logic helps at a time like that. Put simply, suffering is still a problem (oh really, Captain Obvious?) but it doesn't disprove the existence of God.

Since Plantinga, most atheist philosophers have abandoned Mackie's Logical Problem of Evil, and moved to a softer, small target version which they call "the probabilistic argument from evil". Let's take a look at that.

The Probabilistic Argument from Evil

This softer version of the argument doesn't try to claim that suffering *logically disproves* God, but says that the existence of so much extreme, pointless suffering makes it *improbable* that a good God exists. (It's also called the "evidential argument from evil", because it claims that suffering is *evidence* against God.)

Philosopher William Rowe[316] gives two examples that are heart-ripping and powerful:

- a young deer is horribly burned in a forest fire that was started by a lightning strike, suffers for days, then dies
- a five-year-old girl is raped, severely beaten and strangled to death by her mother's drunk boyfriend (in a news report)

The deer suffers what is called "natural evil", the suffering caused by nature without human involvement, e.g. tsunamis, diseases, predation by animals. The child suffers "moral evil", for which human choice is responsible. Rowe uses both in his argument:

1. There are examples of terrible suffering which an omnipotent, omniscient, totally good Being could probably have prevented without losing anything good or permitting some equal or worse evil.
2. An omniscient, omnipotent Being would prevent these examples of suffering if that Being was wholly good.
3. Therefore, that Being does not exist.

Rowe later zoomed in on point 1, admitting that there could possibly be reasons that it was wrong, if allowing these cases of suffering achieved some actual good. But after long and careful thought, he could not think of any goods that made sense. He added that there must have been a huge number of cases of suffering since humans and deer existed, and this makes it likely that at least *some* could have been prevented.

Paul Draper[317] makes a softer case, arguing that these "gratuitous" evils are not explained very well by theists, so he suggests the "hypothesis of indifference", which says that if any supernatural being exists at all, it doesn't seem to care about horrendous evils.

The weakness of this probabilistic / evidential argument is that it's based on debatable probability. Even if it fully succeeds, it doesn't *disprove* God, it merely provides *some evidence against* God's existence. I'll also show in a minute that it provides *some evidence for* God. And I'd suggest that any evidence *against* God is outweighed by the many other *lines of evidence for God*, some of which I've outlined in this book. So this version of the argument from evil is "not *as much* of a problem as it is often alleged to be".[318]

Rowe is right that both moral evil and natural evil need to be explained by any credible view of the world. Atheist materialism would see them both as random bad luck requiring no explanation—they just are. Yet, crucially, that offers no possible solution. Theism can explain moral evil as humans misusing their God-given free choice, and can also fit natural evil into a balanced view of nature—giving us countless things we need to survive and to enjoy life and also involving suffering. In Stephen Fry words, nature is "very splendid" but also contains cruelty. In a biblical view, the genius comes from God and the suffering comes from nature being "fallen" below God's original intentions as a result of the choices of the first humans. Thus it even suggests that natural evil may be caused by moral evil. While the Bible is short on detail here, we are beginning to see how our lifestyle choices affect not only our bodies and psyches but, through recent discoveries in epigenetics, how our smoking, drinking or even our attitudes may affect our grandchildren. And our current science offers some understanding of how environmental systems connect, so that cutting down forests in one country can cause devastating floods in the country downstream. This requires more explanation than we have space for, but the crucial point is that theism says God is working on a plan to restore nature and human nature.

As well as moral evil and natural evil, Christianity also considers "metaphysical evil", the idea that there are angels or spirits, basically non-physical intelligences, who are influential on humans and on nature. If there is a supernatural arena, this would not be surprising.

Evil as evidence *for* God?

A boy named Jack lost his mother when he was nine, felt very unhappy at school and, at nineteen, entered hell in the trenches of World War I, serving in the Somme and being wounded by a shell that killed two of his friends. He said all this made him a pessimist and an atheist[319], and he was "very angry with God for not existing" and "equally angry with him for creating a world."[320]

I could be wrong, but I think I hear a similar anger in Stephen Fry using words like "monstrous" and "stupid" for a God he thinks doesn't even exist. In Samuel Becket's absurdist play *Endgame,* where a character prays for rescue, then angrily shouts, "The bastard! He doesn't exist!" Are they angry at Santa Claus and the Easter Bunny for not existing? Yet they rage against the non-existence of a real source of goodness and hope. I agree—it would be awful if a good God didn't exist! I think they have stumbled on a big truth by intuition.

But Jack re-thought the problem of evil, as he explains:

> My argument against God was that the universe seemed so cruel and unjust. But how had I got this idea of *just* and *unjust*? A man

Does Suffering Disprove God?

> does not call a line crooked unless he has some idea of a straight line. What was I comparing this universe with when I called it unjust? If the whole show was bad and senseless from A to Z, so to speak, why did I, who was supposed to be part of the show, find myself in such violent reaction against it? . . .
>
> Of course I could have given up my idea of justice by saying it was nothing but a private idea of my own. But if I did that, then my argument against God collapsed too—for the argument depended on saying that the world was really unjust, not simply that it did not happen to please my fancies. Thus in the very act of trying to prove that God did not exist—in other words, that the whole of reality was senseless—I found I was forced to assume that one part of reality—namely my idea of justice—was full of sense. Consequently, atheism turns out to be too simple. If the whole universe has no meaning, we should never have found out that it has no meaning: just as, if there were no light in the universe and therefore no creatures with eyes, we should never know it was dark. *Dark* would be a word without meaning.[321]

Later in life, Jack would find faith, reluctantly at first, and would express the case for God so well that I often quote him in this book—not by his nickname, Jack, but by his real name, Professor C.S. Lewis.

I applaud Stephen Fry's passionate desire for kindness and justice in the world—it could be a hint of the God-shaped gap that Pascal said is in everyone. I admire atheists who help others overcome suffering. I've often seen them in refugee camps and children's wards, in schools and youth centres and courts, showing admirable skill and what I would call God-like love—and all without any supporting belief that there is a Source of these things in the universe. I believe God's Spirit is influencing them towards love and virtue even if they think religion is bunk, and I always think that these great people deserve a better view of the world—one that offers an outside source of comfort and hope.

Further, the fact that we can identify and define evil is evidence of that there are objective moral values. And remember from last chapter that good old J.L. Mackie wrote

> If. . . there are. . . objective values, they make the existence of a god more probable than it would have been without them. Thus we have. . . a defensible argument from morality to the existence of a god.[322]

So evil can actually be evidence *for* God. The logic goes like this:

1. Evil exists.
2. We can't define evil without objective moral values.
3. So objective moral values exist.
4. Objective moral values would not exist if God did not exist. (See chapter 6 for why.)
5. So God exists.

A suffering God?

The English priest John Stott expressed one answer to the problem of pain and suffering that centred on the cross of Jesus Christ:

> I could never myself believe in God, if it were not for the cross. The only God I believe in is the One Nietzsche ridiculed as 'God on the cross'. In the real world of pain, how could one worship a God who was immune to it? I have entered many Buddhist temples in different Asian countries and stood respectfully before the statue of the Buddha, his legs crossed, arms folded, eyes closed, the ghost of a smile playing round his mouth, a remote look on his face, detached from the agonies of the world. But each time after a while I have had to turn away. And in imagination I have turned instead to that lonely, twisted, tortured figure on the cross, nails through hands and feet, back lacerated, limbs wrenched, brow bleeding from thorn-pricks, mouth dry and intolerably thirsty, plunged in God-forsaken darkness. That is the God for me! He laid aside his immunity to pain. He entered our world of flesh and blood, tears and death. He suffered for us. Our sufferings become more manageable in the light of his. There is still a question mark against human suffering, but over it we boldly stamp another mark, the cross which symbolizes divine suffering. 'The cross of Christ . . . is God's only self-justification in such a world' as ours.[323]

Suffering: a (partial) Christian explanation

It would take a whole library to summarise the many answers people have suggested to this problem, and at least a large book to outline a full Christian response. But here's a sketch of one:

1. God wanted a universe where people could love each other and Him.
2. Pre-programmed love is no love at all—it's robotics. So God made humans responsible moral agents, free and intelligent.
3. Freedom always brings the risk that humans could ignore God's brilliant advice *and their own best interests*. And this has real consequences.
4. Evil in the world results from human choices.
5. Meanwhile, the presence of evil does not stop loving relationships. And free, intelligent beings can still choose the good.
6. Christianity says God is working on a plan to deal with evil:
   a. God lived a good human life in the person of Jesus of Nazareth, including suffering in many of the ways we do. This would show God understands human life by experience.
   b. Jesus' death by crucifixion absorbed the consequences of human mistakes and paid the moral debt they created.
   c. God offers forgiveness for those honest enough to admit that evil is not just 'out there' but in every human heart.
   d. God's Spirit works to influence every person towards choosing the good.
   e. One day God will re-create a good world in which there is "no more death, nor sorrow nor crying" (Revelation 21:4). We'll still be free—but our experience with evil will increase our understanding and trust for God, and mean we'll never want to experiment with evil again. Ever. So God will finally get what God always wanted—intelligent beings who love each other and God and completely love life.
   f. The joy and pleasure in the afterlife—an infinite amount—will make even the most horrendous past suffering seem little in comparison, and God will wipe away all tears from people's eyes.

So I'd say good old J.L. Mackie was more right than he may have known when he wrote, "An all-powerful God would be able to stop suffering". I believe God can and will. It may just be taking some time because God leaves humans free and takes time to persuade us.

Imagine a world without suffering. No bone cancer. A different diet for the *Loa loa* worm. I'd love to see how Stephen Fry would feel in his first minute there.

Summary: suffering

1. Suffering and evil make people seriously question whether an all-powerful, all-loving, all-knowing God exists.

2. But God may have a good reason for permitting some suffering for a time—e.g. because you can't create people free and guarantee they will not misuse it.

3. The existence of evil can be a logical argument *for* the existence of God, since evil cannot be defined without objective morals, and objective morals have no foundation without God.

4. Faith in God can be a profound comfort and source of hope during suffering, and Christianity teaches that God is working on an ultimate solution to all human suffering—which is a far more satisfying belief than atheism offers.

5. This belief seems even more credible when combined with other evidences for God as outlined in this book.

See further:

Amy Orr-Ewing, *Where is God in all the Suffering?* (Epsom: The Good Book Company, 2020)

Dan Paterson & Rian Roux, "How could a good God allow suffering?", in *Questioning Christianity: is there more to the story?* (Chicago: Moody Publishers, 2021)

Rebecca McLaughlin, "How could a loving God allow so much suffering?', in *Confronting Christianity* (Wheaton: Crossway Books, 2019)

John C. Peckham, *Theodicy of Love: Cosmic Conflict and the Problem of Evil* (Grand Rapids: Baker Academic, 2018)

William Lane Craig, The Problem of Evil www.reasonablefaith.org/writings/popular-writings/existence-nature-of-god/the-problem-of-evil

John Dickson, *If I were God, I'd end all the pain: struggling with evil, suffering and faith* (Sydney: Matthias Media, 2002)

William A. Dembski, *The End of Christianity: Finding a Good God in an Evil World* (Nashville: B&H Publishing, 2009)

Tim Keller, *Walking with God through Pain and Suffering* (Penguin, 2015)

8

Hitler's moustache

Evidence from Religious Experience

*This chapter contains descriptions of war crimes and violence.

TODAY HE WOULD KILL thousands of Americans without warning.

He said he was fighting "a sacred war to liberate Asian nations that had been suffering... under the rule of the whites for 200 long years"[324]—yet he had previously bombed Chinese and Korean people, confident that his supposedly superior race was destined to rule Asia. He admired Nazi racial theory—though it actually excluded him—and he even copied Hitler's moustache. His name was Commander Mitsuo Fuchida.

He led 353 Japanese aircraft off carriers towards Hawaii. Arriving over the US naval base at Pearl Harbour, his torpedo planes hit the *USS Oklahoma*, which then capsized, killing 429 sailors, most just 17 or 18 years old. A bomb hit the *Arizona*'s ammunition room and a fireball shot 1000 feet into the air as 1,177 American boys were burned, drowned or gutted by shrapnel. Some sailors swam for safety but died screaming as floating fuel oil caught fire.

Fuchida took photos and felt "a warm feeling" as he counted four battleships sunk and three severely damaged.[325] Later, landing on the aircraft carrier with his fuel tanks near empty and control wires shredded, he was hailed as a hero.

In Pearl Harbour, makeshift hospitals were treating thousands of burns patients. A witness described "men running around crying like babies, in a state of shock, screaming, 'Let me at those yellow bastards!' or

"They killed my best buddy!'" There would be memorial services for weeks, with 669 graves marked as unknown.

Japan's Emperor Hirohito, self-declared offspring of the Sun goddess, declared war on the USA and the British Empire after the attacks. Japan had also bombed British ships and seized Hong Kong. Taking Singapore, they left British soldiers hanging from trees with their severed genitals shoved into their mouths.

Fuchida bombed the Australian city of Darwin and sank British ships near Ceylon.

Japan seemed unstoppable. They promised they would liberate "a hundred million Asians tyrannized by... whites." But they attacked China, saying, "Take All, Burn All, Kill All". They torched 100,000 people in Sungchiang, slaughtered 350,000 in Szuchou and killed 350,000 in the infamous Rape of Nanking. A Nazi businessman, John Rabe, was so disgusted by the brutality in Nanking that he wrote a complaint letter to Adolph Hitler, and sheltered Chinese people in his back yard. A Japanese soldier described gang rapes and bayonetted babies: "I beheaded people, starved them. . ., burned them, and buried them alive, over two hundred in all. It is terrible that I could turn into an animal and do these things. There are really no words to explain".

Some 300,000 women from China, Korea, and the Philippines were tricked into slavery as "comfort women", and each was forced to service 50 Japanese soldiers a day. Three-quarters of these women died of infection. At the war's end, survivors were shot and bulldozed into mass graves.

Within months, Japan ruled the Asia-Pacific. Over 320,000 Allied soldiers had been killed, wounded or captured.

America's president wanted a counterattack to confuse Japan and build American morale, so the celebrity pilot Jimmy Doolittle led a dangerous secret mission—to bomb Tokyo. He needed an aircraft carrier to put them within 450 miles of Japan so his bombers would have enough fuel to fly on to friendly China, but a fishing boat detected them 688 miles out. If they launched, they would have to ditch 200 miles offshore. There was a wild gale blowing, and it was breakfast time, so they could not fly at night as they had planned. They launched anyway.

In the last bomber, *Bat Out of Hell,* sat a farm boy named Jake De Shazer. He watched Doolittle's heavily loaded bomber, engines screaming, start its take-off run while the flight deck was pointing down at the ocean, timing it so the next giant wave would push the ship's bow up and kick Doolittle into the air. But his bomber dropped out of sight and de Shazer thought it had crashed into a wave. A huge cheer went up as the carrier crew saw the bomber climbing out through the sea spray.[326]

De Shazer's plane nearly blew off the back of the ship. A crewman worked desperately to save it, and lost his arm in a propellor. He shouted from his stretcher, "Give 'em hell for me!"[327]

They did. De Shazer fire-bombed an oil refinery and an aircraft factory, then *Bat Out of Hell* raced towards China. They would have crashed in the sea but for a strong tailwind that pushed them onwards to land. With fuel gauges on empty, De Shazer jumped into the stormy night, not knowing if he would land in Japanese occupied territory.

Japan was shocked by the first foreign raid on its soil in 700 years. Fighter squadrons and troops were moved back to defend the homeland.

The Chinese people helped Doolittle's airmen. As payback, Japanese troops would kill up to 250,000 Chinese civilians and test biological weapons in the area.

De Shazer landed in a cemetery, and was taken in by a Chinese man. Japanese troops caught the man, wrapped him in a blanket and doused him with petrol as his wife watched. A Japanese officer threatened to strangle her child if she did not throw the match. As he burned, the soldiers laughed, then burned the whole village anyway.

De Shazer was captured, blindfolded, hand-cuffed and interrogated under threat of death. Sharpened pencils were pushed between his fingers, or a lighted cigarette was pushed up his nose.

Three of Doolittle's fliers were tied to wooden crosses and shot. Emperor Hirohito ordered leniency for the others.

De Shazer's group was taken to a prison run by the Kempeitai military police. They were hit in the ear with rifle butts, water-boarded, stretched on a rack or hung up by handcuffs. If they blacked out, they were revived so they would suffer more pain.

They were barely fed. They became paranoid, suspecting spying and betrayal. In a stinking prison beside buddies dying of contagious diseases, some considered suicide but had no way to kill themselves. Some developed *beriberi* and drowned in the liquid filling their lungs. Some died of dysentery, dried out by diarrhoea. All were vitamin-deficient, with declining mental health.

Pilot Bob Meder led them in memory games to stay sharp and optimistic, but he slowly died because he simply was not fed enough. He was 26. De Shazer said, "My hatred for the Japanese people nearly drove me crazy."

For Meder's funeral, the Americans demanded a Bible. De Shazer had barely even opened one before, but in that hell-hole he read about heaven. He thought, "I can enjoy the pleasures of eternal life. . . no pain, no suffering, no loneliness in heaven. Everything will be perfect with joy forever."

He read about God as a kind father, and felt God became a friend: "Hunger, starvation, and a freezing cold prison cell no longer had horrors for me. . . Even death could hold no threat when I knew that God had saved me. . ." He read in the Bible, "If you confess. . . that Jesus is Lord and believe in your heart that God has raised him from the dead, you will be saved" (Romans 10:9). "My heart was filled with joy. I wouldn't have traded places with anyone".[328]

Soon after, a guard purposely slammed a metal door on his foot. De Shazer nearly hit back, but remembered Jesus' words: "Love your enemies. . .do good to them that hate you". So he spoke kindly to the guard. He got a weird look, but he persisted. Eventually they began talking, and there was no more beating. The guard even gave De Shazer a sweet potato—a great gift for a starving man. De Shazer was surprised that he could "make a friend out of an enemy because I had just tried."[329]

Wartime hatred was extreme. Fuchida said, "Our core aim was to kill kill kill as many Americans as possible. . . and put them through hell until the very end." The US fleet commander said, "Kill Japs, kill Japs, kill more Japs", promising the Japanese language would soon be spoken only in hell. *Life* magazine showed a nice American girl smiling at a souvenir from her soldier boyfriend—a Japanese skull.

Furious about Doolittle's raid, Japan attacked Midway Island, but America was ready, thanks to a crazy-brilliant code-cracker who worked in his pyjamas. Fuchida wasn't flying that day because of an appendix operation. He was on the lead carrier *Akagi* when American helldivers lobbed a bomb down its elevator shaft to the lower deck, where bombs and avgas were stored. He saw a chain of explosions: "Reluctant tears streamed down my cheeks as I watched the fires spread." Jumping into a lifeboat, he broke both his legs.

Returning home, Fuchida was hailed as a national hero, but privately he felt very sad that so many friends had died in battle or ritual suicide after defeat. Japan had lost 700 experienced airmen, 322 planes and four of the six carriers that had attacked Pearl Harbour.

Japan refused peace talks, telling every adult and child to fight to the death. Newspapers announced *Ichioku gyokusai!* One hundred million die for the country! America decided nuclear bombing would be kinder than that.

Fuchida was working in the city of Hiroshima, but was ordered to fly back to Tokyo the night before the city was destroyed by an atomic bomb. He was sent back next day to inspect the damage. (All other inspectors would later die of cancer after radiation.) He saw dead bodies everywhere, naked and burned. The few survivors suffered terrible thirst. Fuchida watched a boy getting water for his little sister, whose fingers were too swollen to hold the bowl. "Shortly before she died, she whispered, 'Brother, get revenge.'"[330] And in that moment Fuchida saw exactly what his country's problem was.

He watched Japan's leaders sign the peace treaty on an American warship in Tokyo Bay. What would America do now? Enslave or kill its enemies as Japan had done? General MacArthur said he hoped "a better world shall emerge out of the blood and carnage of the past—a world founded on faith and understanding. . . the dignity of man. . . freedom, tolerance and justice." Fuchida was impressed, thinking Japan wouldn't have done that if they had won.

He decided to write a book called *No More Pearl Harbors*, but struggled to find a foundation for peace.

Japan's surrender changed De Shazer's guards. "They never hit me nor hollered at me. . . A medical man came to my cell, and. . . shot some medicine into my arm. . . I was surprised to receive. . . milk, boiled eggs, . . .bread, and some nice, nourishing soup."

American paratroopers arrived and, after three years and four months, he was free.

De Shazer thought of his enemies. "I could not help wondering what would happen to Japan now. . . It would be an awful blow to suffer defeat. . . At this time the voice of the Holy Spirit spoke to me clearly: 'You are called to go and teach the Japanese people.'"[331]

De Shazer was uneducated and shy. He could barely even tell a joke. How could he teach Japan?

Meanwhile in Tokyo, Fuchida met lots of returning Japanese POWs who talked about an American girl called Peggy Covell. They said eighteen-year-old Peggy had

> started to care for the injured Japanese prisoners of war with all her energy. She told us, 'Everyone, if you should have any inconvenience or if you are in need of anything, please let me know.'
>
> Japanese prisoners thought there might be some hidden intention . . . They could not understand why a Yankee girl would suddenly appear and offer to help them. However, there was nothing feigned about what she did. She. . . provided nursing care to the injured prisoners who were missing an arm or a leg, to the extent that even most family members would not . . .
>
> As this continued. . ., the prisoners were moved by her. . . 'Lady, why do you treat us so kindly?' The woman hesitated at first, but they kept pressing her for an answer. She finally said, 'Because my parents were killed by the Japanese Army.'[332]

Peggy's parents, Jim and Charma Covell, had been Baptist missionaries in Japan. Seeing war looming, they left for the Philippines and sent their children home to America for their education. When Japan invaded Manila, they escaped to the mountains, serving local people and building a church. Then Japanese soldiers appeared, saying Christians were spies and would be executed. They took them up the mountain one by one, beheading the adults and bayonetting the children.

When Peggy heard, she imagined her parents at the mercy of people with no mercy, and she hated the Japanese with all her heart. She knew she was meant to love her enemies, but her hatred was stronger than anything.

She heard from people who had witnessed her parents' death. They said they were tied and blindfolded, but kept praying for their enemies. It hit her that her parents had prayed God's blessing on the people killing them! Then how could she do any less? Being fluent in Japanese, she looked for a POW camp where she could help prisoners. The more she did for them, the more she felt forgiveness.

The soldiers asked, "Why do you do this?"

Peggy replied, "Because the Japanese Army killed my parents, but the Holy Spirit has washed away my hatred and has replaced it with love."

The POWs found this confusing. By their Samurai code, it was honourable to avenge your parents, even if it took a lifetime or more. Their code said Peggy was weak and lacked family pride. It was dishonourable to forgive your family's killers.[333] But Peggy was so kind that they began to wonder if Peggy was right and the Samurai code was wrong.

Peggy avoided publicity, but returning POWs spread her story across Japan. Fuchida was "immensely moved" by it. The old warrior was hoping to "put an end to the bitterness of hatred." He wondered if hate and war and endless human revenge could be stopped by spiritual love and forgiveness.

He was farming—not earning much but finding time to think. "I was ashamed of my arrogance, my former self . . . While all the friends I had in the world abandoned me, I felt deeply that God alone, as the creator, accompanied me with his never-changing grace, and I was alive because of his blessing."

In a Tokyo station, someone handed Fuchida a booklet titled *I Was A Prisoner of Japan*, about an American airman who spent forty months in prison, mostly in solitary confinement. The American had written that, at first

> the bitterness of my heart against my captors seemed more than I could bear.
> I had heard about Christianity changing hatred between human beings into real brotherly love, and I was gripped with a strange longing to examine the Christian's Bible to see if I could find the secret . . .

The writer said he found new spiritual life. Seeing the "guards who had starved and beaten me and my companions so cruelly, I found my bitter hatred for them changed to loving pity." He read about Jesus being beaten by soldiers, spat on and nailed to a cross, but

> He tenderly prayed in His moment of excruciating suffering, 'Father, forgive them for they know not what they do.'
> I too prayed for God to forgive my torturers, and I determined. . . to do my best to acquaint the Japanese people with the message of salvation. . .
> My love for the Japanese people was deep and sincere. . . I know that it came from God."[334]

The booklet was written by—you guessed it—Jake De Shazer.

Fuchida found this "exactly what I was seeking. Since the American had found it in the Bible, I decided to purchase one myself, despite my traditionally Buddhist heritage."

He found some parts confusing. Then he read about the Son of God being tortured by soldiers and saying, "Father, forgive them, for they know not what they do." Fuchida said,

> It was like having the sun come up. I was certainly one of those for whom He had prayed. The many men I had killed. . . in the name of patriotism. . . I did not understand the love which Christ wishes to implant within every heart.
> I seemed to meet Jesus for the first time. I understood the meaning of His death as a substitute for my wickedness, and so in prayer, I requested Him to forgive my sins and change me.

Fuchida contacted a pastor, who taught him more about the Bible. He felt shy to speak about his new faith, but one day stood up in public and said, "I am Mitsuo Fuchida, . . .who commanded the air attacking forces against Pearl Harbour. . . But now I'm a Christian, and I want to let you know how I became one. All Japanese want peace . . . I know the brutality and the cruelties of war better than most people. Now I want to work for peace. But how can mankind achieve a lasting peace?"

A crowd gathered, the first of many that would hear Fuchida speak. Newspaper headlines boomed, *Pearl Harbor Hero Converts to Christianity*. Fuchida's war buddies tried to get him to forget this "crazy idea", but instead he wrote a book, *From Pearl Harbour to Calvary*.

De Shazer had studied at a Christian college in America. He married Florence ("the most attractive young lady I had ever met") and they came as missionaries to Japan. Arriving at the docks, Jake was shocked to see

40 reporters eager to interview him. He had no idea that Christians had handed out a million copies of his story. Crowds came to see the man who could forgive his enemies, and he spoke four or five times a day for the next six years. Thousands of Japanese became Christians, including two of his prison guards.

He was invited to meet the son of the emperor who had stopped his execution. He thanked him, and explained the teaching of Jesus to him.

At one public meeting, he noticed a young woman staring. She came to a Bible class in his home and eventually admitted her fiancé had died in the war and she had intended to kill De Shazer as revenge—but his message had changed her thinking. She became a Christian.

The De Shazers worked in Japan for 30 years and started 23 churches, including in Nagoya, the city Jake had bombed from his plane *Bat Out Of Hell*.

Fuchida and De Shazer became friends and did public talks together in Osaka. Newspapers reported that 500 people became Christians.

Fuchida spoke all over Japan and America, making friends of old enemies and showing the love and grace of Jesus.

And he shaved off his Hitler moustache.

Can religious experiences like these be evidence for God?[335]

If you have a religious experience yourself, it can be strong evidence—as long as you are rational, not emotionally manipulated, drugged, hypnotised or seriously mentally ill. It can be profoundly life-changing.

Some say other people's religious experiences are not much help[336], but it seems fair to treat them like a witness in court, showing "critical trust" unless there are reasons to doubt them.[337] We could ask logical questions. Is this witness competent to observe and remember? Rational? Trustworthy and honest? Lacking bias or a motive to lie? And has the claimed religious experience had a positive effect on their lives? (Not that we should expect a perfect saint.)

I think Fuchida and De Shazer pass these tests, so I believe their claims about experiencing God. Sceptics say religious experiences tend merely to copy a person's existing beliefs, but that's not true of Fuchida, whose experience gave him Christian beliefs not found in his Buddhist upbringing. He ran what some would call a religious "experiment"[338] by calling out to a

God he hadn't believed in, asking if that God existed. And while De Shazer had Christian parents, he had zero interest in religion himself until he suffered the unthinkable, and then he spent his life teaching forgiveness to old enemies. Something has to explain that.

I'm not claiming this as knock-down proof that God exists, but it's more evidence to add to a fairly large pile. And it could make you want to try the religious experiment yourself. The logical evidence in this book can be a launch ramp to allow you to look for a personal connection with God.

Summary:

1. Religious experiences can be evidence for God, as long as the person is a reliable witness: not manipulated, drugged or seriously mentally ill.
2. Many reliable people report religious experiences.
3. This suggests there is a God.
4. Anyone can try a "devotional experiment" by searching for God.

9

So far, so God

Is Evidence Enough?

GOD WALKS INTO A bar and sees a man having a quiet drink.

"Hello, Ivan", says God. "I'm God."

"Nyet", says Ivan. "I don't believe in you. I am Communist. Marx said religion is mind-numbing drug."

"Well, have you heard of the miracle of turning water into wine? Watch this."

There's a flash, Ivan looks down at his glass and sure enough, what used to be clear liquid is now deep red. He tastes it—and it's sparkling grape juice! (Because even in this joke, God wouldn't offend Alcoholics Anonymous, Muslims, or the Salvation Army).

Ivan frowns.

"Now do you believe in me?", asks God.

"Nyet."

So God leaves.

The next night God walks in again. "Hello, Ivan. Do you believe in me now?"

"Nyet."

"Do you need more evidence?"

There's another flash, and grape juice appears in Ivan's glass again. He groans and rolls his eyes.

"Now do you believe in me?"

"Nyet!"

So God leaves.

He comes back the third night. "Hello, Ivan. Do you. . .?"

Ivan puts his hand over his glass and says, "OK, OK, if I say I believe in you, will you leave my vodka alone?"

As a nineteen-year-old, with the evidence for God beginning to pile up in my mind, I can remember the moment in Manning Bar at Sydney University when I realised I needed to decide whether to stay open to evidence or to ignore it and hang onto the vodka of hedonism and escapism. It was clear that God was going to be inconvenient to some parts of my lifestyle. Looking back, I think God probably spirited himself into that bar and persuaded me of the infinite benefits he offered—love, joy, peace, etc.

So I could really relate to a young bloke who spoke to me years later after I gave a lunchtime talk at the University of New South Wales. He said, "I didn't want to say this in question time, but I think your case for God and Jesus is probably true. The problem is that if I believed them, I'd have to stop taking a different girl back to my dorm every night, and I don't want to."

I immediately liked the guy. I said, "What if loving one great woman for life and developing intimacy with her could make you both happier than just physical pleasure without love and commitment? Plenty of studies link hookup culture to anxiety and depression. And what if sleeping around now shrinks your ability to experience intimacy long-term, and makes your future marriage more likely to break up? Decades of research suggests this. What if Jesus' moral teaching results in more happiness and satisfaction over your lifetime?"

He said he couldn't imagine that, so he didn't want to believe in God. I felt sad when he walked away. I can only hope he reconsidered later. If there is a God brilliant enough to make us and kind enough to want us, then I can't imagine a better source of advice.

But we are not just minds needing evidence. We are people with feelings and desires and relationships, and our choices are complex.

That young bloke would have related to Aldous Huxley, who grew up in a proudly atheist family—his grandfather was "Darwin's Bulldog", who famously debated clergy who opposed evolution. Huxley wrote:

> The pure love of truth is always mingled to some extent with the need, consciously or unconsciously. . . to justify a given form of personal or social behaviour. . .

> The philosopher who finds meaning in the world is concerned... to prove that it is most clearly expressed in some established religion...
>
> The philosopher who finds no meaning in the world is... concerned to prove that there is no valid reason why he personally should not do as he wants to do...
>
> For myself as, no doubt, for most of my friends, the philosophy of meaninglessness was essentially an instrument of liberation from a certain system of morality... We objected to the morality because it interfered with our sexual freedom... The supporters of these systems claimed that... it embodied the meaning (the Christian meaning, they insisted) of the world. There was one admirably simple method of confuting these people and justifying ourselves in our erotic revolt: we would deny that the world had any meaning whatever.[339]

Buying hedonism at the expense of meaning in life seemed like a bad deal to me, especially when an intelligent morality could make life's pleasures last longer.

I'm fascinated by Thomas Nagel. He's an avowed atheist, yet I've often quoted him in this book because he supports some of the most solid arguments for God. As we've seen, he says the Neo-Darwinian story of evolution can't explain the origin and diversity of life, because it's too unlikely—probability theory destroys it.[340] He thinks evolution would not produce logical minds.[341] He thinks materialism can't explain consciousness, and says that if we got our minds that way, then they couldn't be rational. He thinks objective morals cannot be explained by naturalism.[342] So why is he an atheist? I don't pretend to know, but he writes:

> I want atheism to be true and am made uneasy by the fact that some of the most intelligent and well-informed people I know are religious believers. It isn't just that I don't believe in God and, naturally, hope I'm right in my belief. It's that I hope there is no God! I don't want the universe to be like that. My guess is that this cosmic authority problem is not a rare condition and that it is responsible for much of the scientism and reductionism of our time.[343]

Even intellectuals are not just intellectuals—they have other motives. I appreciate Nagel being honest about it.

So far, we've looked at some of the evidence for and against the existence of God. There are plenty more lines of argument for and against that I wish I could fit into this book.

But for now, here's a Q&A that summarises how the two views, atheism and theism, deal with some of life's biggest questions.[344] You might find it interesting to use it as a tool to see which way you're leaning.

Questions about us:

	Atheism/ Materialism	Christian theism:
Where did we get consciousness and reason?	We don't really have them! Or else they arose somehow from non-conscious physical processes.	They were given from the Mind behind the universe, and mind is just as real and foundational as matter.
Where did we get personhood?	We don't actually have it! Or it somehow arose from impersonal physical processes.	From a personal God.
Where did we get free will?	We don't really have it! Or it arose from deterministic physical processes beyond our control.	God has given us minds that can think freely.
Where does our desire for purpose and meaning come from?	From purposeless, meaningless physical processes.	From God's loving intentions for us.
Where did we get our Intrinsic value, human rights and worth?	We can't prove them on any factual basis, just opinion. Or they somehow arose from valueless physical processes.	From being made in God's image, wanted and loved like God's children.
Where did talent & giftedness come from?	A lucky spin of the genetic roulette wheel.	A gift to use to make life good for others and ourselves.
Why do we suffer?	Bad luck. The universe doesn't care. Then you die.	Because of misuse of human free will, which in turn has damaged nature. God cares and knows how it feels and will one day repair everything. "Earth has no sorrow that heaven can't heal."

	Atheism/ Materialism	Christian theism:
What is our future?	Unpredictable randomness, then death. And that's it. Eventually the solar system ends with a bang or a whimper. No-one cares—there's no-one out there.	Unpredictable stuff and death in the short-term but eternal bliss in the long term. Doing interesting things with great people and tourism in an infinite universe. Knowing a kind and endlessly fascinating God.
What can we wish each other?	Good luck!	God's blessings.

Questions about the universe:

	Atheism/ materialism	Christian theism
What caused the fine-tuning that made the universe *just right* for human life in so many ways?	Blind chance.	Kind design.
Why is there any order?	Unexpected luck.	Intention of a precise Mind.
Why is there so much beauty?	Accidental/ incidental.	An aesthetic Creator.
Why do we have senses?	For survival.	For survival and, importantly, enjoying life.
How did the universe begin?	From nothing by nothing.	Created from nothing but God's energy ($e=mc^2$).
How did life begin?	From non-living matter.	From a living God.

Questions about ideas:

	Atheism/ materialism	Christian theism
Truth is…	…constructed by humans in their circumstances (so it's contingent and conditional on "my" view).	…observed from realities in the universe God created (so it's consistent and transcends "me").

	Atheism/ materialism	**Christian theism**
Morality is...	...constructed by us, and therefore relative, as it can't arise from non-moral physical processes.	...defined by God, and therefore reliable. It's focussed on love and wellbeing, consistent with God's moral character.

For me, the right column seems more rational, more intuitive and more likely to make life happy and fulfilling. What do you think? We could rank ourselves on a seven-point scale:

1. Strong Atheist (There is definitely no God.)
2. Moderate Atheist (I don't think there is a God.)
3. Strong Agnostic (No one can know if there is a God.)
4. Agnostic (I don't know if there's a God or not and don't really care.)
5. Open Agnostic (I'd be interested to see evidence on God.)
6. Moderate Theist (I'm pretty sure there is a God.)
7. Strong Theist (There definitely is a God.)

You might what to ask yourself where you're sitting now. (I'm about a 6.75.). What arguments move you either way? Where do you feel you'd like to be? Why?

Wherever you are on the scale, you might want to try talking to God in your own words. If there is no God, you will have wasted a few minutes. If there is a God, you may get a response—though it may not be how you expect. I tried this "devotional experiment" myself, and I loved the results.

So far in this book we've looked at some logical evidence for *a* God. Now let's look at evidence for the Christian view of God, and see if that moves you up the scale.

10

Jesus and the Non-Christian Historians

Historical Evidence of Jesus

"It is even possible to mount a serious, though not widely supported, historical case that Jesus never lived at all, as has been done by, among others, Professor G.A. Wells of the University of London in a number of books, including *Did Jesus Exist?*"

—ATHEIST BIOLOGIST RICHARD DAWKINS[345]

As a child, I received instruction both in the Bible and in the Talmud. I am a Jew but I am enthralled by the luminous figure of the Nazarene [a name for Jesus]. . .
No one can read the Gospels without feeling the actual presence of Jesus. His personality pulsates in every word. No myth is filled with such life. . .
No man can deny the fact that Jesus existed. Nor that his sayings are beautiful."

—THEORETICAL PHYSICIST ALBERT EINSTEIN[346]

"He certainly lived, and in my view he too was a kind of religious genius. . . and his teachings have impacted the world ever since."

—ATHEIST PROFESSOR OF NEW TESTAMENT BART EHRMAN[347]

Do historians think Jesus existed?

Let's not ask Christians who want to believe or atheists who don't. Let's check a range of academic historians in public universities, who analyse historical sources and test their ideas in peer-reviewed journals.

Let's start by consulting a trusted reference source like *The Oxford Classical Dictionary*. This 1,700-page tome describes Jesus' life and his death by crucifixion.[348] The fourteen-volume *Cambridge Ancient History* does too. *The Cambridge History of Judaism* has chapters on Jesus' life, death by crucifixion, teaching, and reputation as a healer. It doesn't say he was resurrected, but it says his disciples "were absolutely convinced that Jesus had been raised and was Lord" and many "were certain that he had appeared to them".[349]

Why do these critical reference works record Jesus in history? Because Greek, Roman and Jewish historians of the time mention him. It's very surprising that they bothered. After all, "Jesus was a marginal Jew leading a marginal movement in a marginal province of a vast Roman Empire", so it would be remarkable if "any learned Jew or pagan would have known or referred to him at all in the 1st or early 2nd Century."[350]

Yet they did.

But let's not get starry-eyed. Most of these historians thought Jesus was shameful and stupid[351] because he was executed by crucifixion. Graffiti on a wall in Rome from around AD200 shows a donkey-headed man hanging on a cross and a young man praying to him. The caption is "Alexamenos worships his god." There are two massive insults here—obviously the donkey-headed god but also the crucifixion itself, because the Romans saved crucifixion for serious criminals, and associated it with guilt and shame, like an electric chair or hangman's noose.[352] We are used to seeing crosses on churches or hospitals (originally started by Christians) or in flags of countries with Christian histories, and sometimes forget that it would be at home in a museum of torture. Cicero said crucifixion "cannot by any possibility be adequately expressed by any name bad enough for it."[353] The historian Seneca wrote:

> Is there such a thing as a person who would actually prefer wasting away in pain on a cross—dying limb by limb one drop of blood at a time—rather than dying quickly? Would any human being willingly choose to be fastened to that cursed tree, especially after the beating that left him deathly weak, deformed, swelling with vicious welts on shoulders and chest, and struggling to draw every last agonizing breath? Anyone facing such a death would plead to die rather than mount the cross. (*Epistulae morales* 101.14)

Jesus and the Non-Christian Historians

In the Graeco-Roman world, worshipping a crucified God would be unheard of, and just plain weird and shameful.

Yet these hostile witnesses are very valuable. People who despised Christ and Christians would never dream of making anything up in order to support a religion they rejected and called weird. And writers who record embarrassing details also show an objectivity that makes us trust them more. When historians look for sources, they want as many as possible (for cross-checking), they want them early (writing near the events they describe, while they can check the facts with living witnesses), and they want them independent (not just copying each other).

What did Greek, Roman and Jewish historians say about Jesus?

1. Tacitus, AD115

Have you heard the story of Emperor Nero fiddling while Rome burned? We're not sure he played the fiddle, but we know a six-day fire destroyed 70% of the city. An eight-year-old boy was there, who grew up to be Rome's finest historian[354], as well as a lawyer and governor. For such a brilliant orator, he had a strange name—Tacitus ("silent"). He wrote an 18-volume history, *Annals of Imperial Rome*, using his access to the Senate archives.

Then 51 years after the Great Fire of AD64, Tacitus (AD 56—120) sat down to write about it. He recorded a rumour that Nero himself had secretly ordered the fire to be lit, hoping to rebuild Rome better. This was damaging to Nero's public image.

> Therefore, to stop the rumour, Nero substituted as culprits, and punished in the utmost refinements of cruelty, a class of men, loathed for their vices, whom the crowd styled Christians. Christus, the founder of the same, had undergone the death penalty in the reign of Tiberius, by sentence of the Procurator Pontius Pilatus... (Tacitus, *Annals*, 15.44)[355]

Tacitus calls him Christus, a title given to Jesus. (Christus is from a Greek word meaning "Anointed One", which is the meaning of the Hebrew title "Messiah"). A Roman audience would understand the connection between Christians and the name Christus more easily than the name Jesus. Tacitus says Jesus was executed by order of the Roman governor Pilate (who governed AD 26-36) during the reign of Tiberius (AD 14-37), just as the Gospels say.[356] And like the biblical book of Acts, Tacitus records how Christianity spread after Jesus' death:

the pernicious superstition was checked for a moment, only to break out once more, not merely in Judea, the home of the disease, but in the capital itself, where all things horrible or shameful in the world collect and find a vogue.

He describes the torture of Christians by Emperor Nero after Rome burned:

> First, then, the confessed members of the sect were arrested; next, on their disclosures, vast numbers were convicted, not so much on the count of arson as for hatred of the human race.
>
> Mockery of every sort was added to their deaths: they were covered with wild beast skins and torn to death by dogs; or they were fastened on crosses, and, when daylight failed were burned to serve as lamps by night. Nero had offered his Gardens for the spectacle, and gave an exhibition at the Circus...
>
> So... there arose a sentiment of pity, due to the impression that they were being sacrificed not for the good of the public but for the ferocity of a single man."
> (*Annals*, 15.44)

Tacitus hates Christianity—calling it "shameful", a "superstition" and a "disease". He was definitely a hostile witness, so when he records Jesus' execution, we know it is historical fact.

He says the spread of Christianity slowed for a while after its leader was executed, but then it became well-known as far away as Rome within 30 years. Eyewitnesses of Jesus's crucifixion would still have been alive at this time, and Tacitus saw Christians who were willing to be killed—even with torture—rather than deny their experience of Jesus.

2. Pliny the Younger, AD112

Mt Vesuvius blew up in AD79, drowning the city of Pompeii in lava. Pliny's uncle (also called Pliny) hurried there to report on the volcano. He invited his nephew to sail right up close with him in a small boat, but the younger man wanted to watch from a safe distance. His uncle was overcome with fumes and died on the beach, but Pliny the Younger (AD 61–113) lived to write a description for his friend Tacitus.

Pliny the Younger—that's Gaius Plinius Caecilius Secundus to you—went on to be a lawyer and senator who governed the Roman province of Turkey. He found Christianity was spreading fast, and wondered what to do, so he wrote to Emperor Trajan over in Rome in AD112. He didn't need

Jesus and the Non-Christian Historians

to mention that Christ had been executed in Judaea under Pilate, since "his friend Tacitus (governor of neighbouring Asia) made this clear" and we can "assume it was common knowledge among Roman bureaucrats".[357] Like Tacitus, Pliny elsewhere calls Christianity a "foreign cult" (*superstitio*), "degenerate" and "contagious". Pliny had killed some Christians and interrogated others who gave up their faith when threatened with death. He writes:

> They assured me that the sum total of their error consisted in the fact that they regularly assembled on a certain day before daybreak. They sang a hymn antiphonally to Christus as to a god. They also took an oath not to commit any crime, but to keep from theft, robbery and adultery, and not to break any promise or embezzle property entrusted to them. After this it was their custom to... come together again to partake of a meal...
> (*Letters*, 10.96)

Pliny provides important evidence of Christians worshipping Christ(us) as God very early, which seriously undermines the claim that Jesus was a mere man who came to be considered a god in myths that developed over time.

3. Suetonius, AD120

Suetonius was a great friend of Pliny, who called him "quiet and studious, a man dedicated to writing", and indeed he wrote a history of Julius Caesar and other emperors. Pliny got Suetonius a job managing historical archives for the emperors Trajan and Hadrian. Hadrian's wife, the empress Vibia Sabina, was famous for her beauty. Hadrian proudly put her gorgeous face on coins and had her image carved in stone, but privately he had a teenage male lover and Sabina had no children. Hadrian was quite harsh and mean to her, and she had an affair with guess who—the quiet and studious Suetonius. When the emperor found out, the historian was nearly history. He barely escaped with his head, and sadly Sabina suicided.

Suetonius may not have been a great relationship advisor, but he was a great historian. Like Tacitus, he records how Nero had treated Christians:

> Punishment was inflicted on the Christians, a class of men given to a new and mischievous superstition.
> (*Nero* 16)

He also records that the emperor Claudius

> expelled the Jews from Rome, since they were always making disturbances because of the instigator Chrestus.
> (*Lives Of The Caesars*, vol V)

Many historians think these disturbances are the protests that often broke out around Jewish communities when Christians taught publicly[358] that Jesus was the Messiah or Christus. Suetonius wrote "Chrestus", probably using an alternate spelling.[359] Some historians claim Chrestus (meaning "useful") was a common name for slaves, so this Chrestus could have been anybody. Yet Chrestus was a pagan name, not used by Christians or Jews, so it wouldn't fit a Jewish agitator.

The emperor blamed the Jews for these riots, since most of the first Christians were Jewish. The New Testament records similar disturbances in other cities, and Claudius expelling Jews from Rome.[360] Claudius ruled from AD 41–54, just a decade or two after Jesus' death. So Suetonius records controversy around public presentations of the story of Christ(us) in Rome very early.

4. Josephus, AD93

Flavius Josephus was a Jewish aristocrat and general. He fought against Roman armies for nearly five years until he was captured. He knew Israel was losing to Rome, the superpower of the day, so he encouraged his fellow Jews to surrender rather than have their capital, Jerusalem, and its Great Temple destroyed. They ignored him, even throwing darts over the wall at him as he begged them to stop fighting a losing battle. He was there as they faced the horrors of siege warfare and the tragic destruction of Jerusalem, and he recorded that history. It is brutal and tragic reading.

Josephus guessed that the Roman general Vespasian would become emperor, and he really backed the right horse. Vespasian set him free and paid him for fifteen years to write history. He even let him live in an apartment in his palace in Rome. Josephus produced *Jewish War* and *Jewish Antiquities*, brilliant histories describing prominent public figures like Herod, Pontius Pilate and Caiaphas, who are also mentioned in the Gospels.

One of the prettiest buildings I've seen is the Ambrosian Library in the Italian city of Milan, also the home of fashion and Ferraris. And an ornate manuscript there is one of the oldest copies of Josephus' work. They make you wear white gloves to read it. Remarkably, Josephus describes the preacher John the Baptist being executed by King Herod Antipas, who feared his influence (*Antiquities* 19:116–10), just as the Gospels say.[361]

Josephus also records the execution of James the brother of Jesus. It was led by a High Priest named Ananus, who was "bold. . . in his temper, and very insolent".

> So he convened the judges of the Sanhedrin and brought before them a man named James, the brother of Jesus who is called the Christ, and certain others. He accused them of having transgressed the law and delivered them up to be stoned. (*Antiquities* 20:200–201, 203)

Ananus was the son of the high priest who, in the Gospels, accused Jesus before the Roman governor Pontius Pilate.[362] By killing James, the leader of the early church[363], Ananus was knocking off his religious competition.

This quote leaves no doubt that Jesus lived. It records, fairly and neutrally, that some people called him the Christ or Messiah: some translate it as calling Jesus "the so-called Christ".[364] It confirms that James was Jesus' brother and a leader in the early church, as the Bible says.[365] Scholars take the quote as "certain"[366], and it tells us Jesus' name, commonly used title, and the name and fate of one of his brothers.

Josephus also gives us a more controversial quote. Some scholars see it as totally fake, while some accept it all, but most see it as a genuine text with some sections added later by Christians.[367] I will use italics for the sections that experts believe were added.

> About this time there lived Jesus, a wise man *[if indeed one ought to call him a man]*. For he was one who wrought surprising feats and was a teacher of such people who accept the truth gladly. He won over many Jews and many of the Greeks. *[He was the Messiah.]* When Pilate, upon hearing him accused by men of the highest standing among us, had condemned him to be crucified, those who had in the first place come to love him did not give up their affection for him. *[On the third day he appeared to them restored to life, for the prophets of God had prophesied these and countless other things about him.]* And the tribe of Christians, so called after him, has still to this day not disappeared." (*Antiquities* 18:63–65)[368]

Perhaps the extra lines were added in the margin as personal comments and later merged into the body text.[369] But even after you remove the obviously

Christian parts, you are still left with Jesus being called a "wise man", a doer of "surprising feats", condemned by leaders, as well as the statement that Christianity has not died out *yet*.

There is another version of Josephus in an Arabic book, which is much more neutral. It says Jesus "was perhaps the Messiah" and that after his disciples "reported that he had appeared to them". This is fair, reporting what Christians said without agreeing with them, and it agrees with Josephus saying Jesus "was called the Christ", not that he was the Christ.

Josephus' second quote about Jesus is somewhat debatable, though with a solid core of fact, while his first undeniably shows Jesus as a fact of history.

5. Mara bar Serapion, AD73+

Mara bar Serapion was taken prisoner by the Romans after his home city in Samosata (modern-day Samsat, in Turkey) was captured. He wrote encouraging his son to be wise, even though good people can be mistreated by the powerful. He gives three examples: Socrates in Athens, Pythagoras in Samos and the wise king of the Jews in Jerusalem. He wrote:

> What advantage did the Athenians gain from murdering Socrates? Famine and plague came upon them as a punishment for their crime. What advantage did the men of Samos gain from burning Pythagoras? In a moment their land was covered with sand. What advantage did the Jews gain from executing their wise king? It was just after that their kingdom was abolished.
>
> God justly avenged these three wise men: the Athenians died of hunger; the Samians were overwhelmed by the sea and the Jews, desolate and driven from their own kingdom, live in complete dispersion.
>
> But Socrates is not dead, because of Plato; neither is Pythagoras, because of the statue of Juno; nor is the wise king, because of the "new law" he laid down.[370]

Mara is writing just three years after Roman armies destroyed Jerusalem (in AD70), with terrible loss of life.

His other writings make him sound like a Stoic, not a Christian, and he says Jesus lives on through his new law, not through resurrection. (Jesus gave his followers a "new commandment" in John 13:34.). Mara doesn't use the name Jesus, but he takes it as common knowledge that the Jews had one man who claimed to be a king, who had wise sayings, and was killed within a generation of the destruction of Jerusalem. So Mara is a very early non-Christian source for Jesus' existence and His execution.

6. Lucian of Samosata, AD 165

Lucian (AD 125—180) wrote satire and had a wild sense of humour. He thought any belief in the supernatural was ridiculous, and mocked all religion as a scam to make money from superstitious people.

He wrote a fictional story about a Cynic called Peregrinus, an insane adulterer and paedophile who murdered his own father. Christians took pity on Peregrinus, and he took advantage of their generosity, getting free food and accommodation. In Lucian's story, the gullible Christians started worshipping him as a god. He misbehaved, hoping to die as a martyr, but the governor couldn't be bothered executing yet another nutter. So Peregrinus suicided in a fire to get attention.

Lucian's whole story mocked Christian martyrdom and the death of Jesus. Christians can laugh at it because it's so unlikely, especially the part about worshipping a man, considering many were actually martyred for refusing to worship a man who thought he was a god—the emperor. Lucian mentions that Christianity was started by "the one whom they still worship today, that man who was crucified in Palestine for introducing the new cult to the world"

He mocks Christians:

> The poor fools have persuaded themselves above all that they are immortal and will live forever, from which it follows that they despise death and many of them willingly undergo imprisonment. Moreover, their first lawgiver taught them that they are all brothers of one another the moment they transgress and deny the Greek gods and begin worshipping that crucified sophist and living by his laws. So they despise all things equally and regard them as common property, accepting such teaching without any sort of clear proof. Accordingly, if any quack or trickster... comes among them he can acquire great wealth in a very short time by imposing on simple-minded people.
> (*The Death of Peregrinus* 11–13)[371]

Bahahaha, those silly Christians!

But Lucian has left us a record of the crucifixion of Christ in the Roman province of Judaea (now part of Israel) as a well-known and unremarkable historical fact.[372] He describes Christians worshipping Jesus as God quite early on. He shows their willingness to suffer and die for their belief that they would live forever. I wonder how Lucian would feel about leaving us such useful historical evidence for Jesus. I expect he'd be horrified—but he might belly-laugh at the irony. This joke's on you, bud.

7. Celsus (AD175)

A philosopher named Celsus was one of the first writers to slam Christianity. He read the Gospels, but poo-hooed the idea of virgin birth, claiming Mary gave birth to Jesus after an affair with a Roman soldier called Panthera. He said Jesus was short, ugly and stupid, and that uneducated sailors and tax collectors followed him because he dazzled them with sorcery that he learned as a boy in Egypt:

> having tried his hand at certain magical powers, Jesus returned from there, and on account of these powers gave himself the title of God.[373]

He says Jesus taught his followers to beg and steal for a living and that, when Jesus died, hysterical women made up the story of the resurrection. His famous quote was, "No wise man believes the gospel."

Celsus' book is more a satire than an independent historical source, and yet two things fascinate me: one, he associates Jesus with supernatural events; and two, he never questions whether Jesus really existed in history.

8. Thallus (c.AD55)

A Greek historian named Thallus wrote about a darkness at the time Jesus of Nazareth was crucified. This darkness is also described in the Gospels[374], but Thallus argues that it was caused by an eclipse of the sun. A Christian writer named Sextus Julius Africanus (AD 160—240) argues with Thallus, arguing the darkness was supernatural. It's lucky he did, or we wouldn't know what Thallus said—his three volumes called *Histories* are lost to us. Africanus' book *World History* was written around AD200—but that's lost too. Fortunately, Africanus is quoted by Georgius Syncellus (d. AD 810) in his *Chronicle*, written in the 800s.

This third-hand source is not the strongest but it's not nothing. We see Thallus rejecting a supernatural explanation of the darkness, which we'd expect a non-Christian writer to do. But he never questions whether Jesus existed or died by crucifixion. In fact, he records the crucifixion of Jesus in his history book within about 30 years of its occurrence—a very short gap in historical terms.

9. The Talmud (AD200s[375])

Second to the Hebrew Bible, the Talmud is the most important book of Jewish belief and daily living. It's more like a library—one English edition has 73 volumes—and it was collected from traditional sayings for centuries. When Pope Gregory (AD 540—604) and the Church of the Middle Ages felt insulted by its comments about Jesus and his mother Mary, some Talmud manuscripts were changed, either by Christian censors or Jews afraid of persecution. Since then, scholars have added back the missing lines. One passage reads:

> On the Sabbath of the Passover festival, Yeshu the Nazarene was hanged.
> For forty days before execution took place, a herald went forth and cried: 'Here is Yeshu the Nazarene, who is going forth to be stoned because he practiced sorcery and enticed Israel to apostasy. Anyone who can say anything in his favour, let him come forth and plead on his behalf.' But since nothing was brought forth in his favour, he was hanged on the eve of Passover."
> (*The Talmud*, baraitha Sanhedrin 43a)

This is an independent historical source giving us Jesus' name (Yeshua or Yeshu in Hebrew), his home town (Nazareth), the date he died (around Passover), the method of his death (the word hanging was sometimes used for crucifixion), and the charges against him: sorcery (suggesting his miracles were real or at least taken seriously), and enticing Israel to apostasy (that's taking people to a new religion). These details match the Gospels exactly. The last two accusations are backed up by Justin Martyr, who wrote in AD140 that Jewish authorities had called Jesus "a magician and a deceiver of the people."[376]

This source is brief and written well after the events, but it is striking that these "contemporaries in the first and second century saw no reason to doubt Jesus' existence."[377]

Conclusion

We've seen a number of non-Christian historians reporting on Jesus:

- his name and title in various languages: Yeshu, Chrestus, Christus, and the wise king;
- his brother's name, James;
- his teaching;
- reports of supernatural events;
- his death, linked to both Roman and Jewish histories; and
- the Christian community that spread his story even under intense persecution.

These writers are hostile to Christianity, and yet they offer independent backup to key details from the Gospel stories, which gives me a reason to read the gospels as credible history.

In fact, it's really hard to find an expert who says Jesus didn't exist.

But wait! Professor George Wells says, "Jesus probably never existed at all". That was in the documentary *Jesus: The Evidence* and Richard Dawkins' bestseller *The God Delusion*. Dawkins calls Wells a professor at the University of London, but doesn't tell us his subject area—maybe because it's German language. Das ist gut! But it gives him no special expertise about aerodynamics or orthodontics—or first-century history. So we need to evaluate his arguments on their merits, not any supposed authority. Wells wrote a book on Jesus back in 1975, but he never tested his ideas in the argy-bargy of scholarly debate. He wrote straight to the public, who may or may not know better. Scholars have largely ignored him. John P. Meier, a leading scholar on the historicity of Jesus, says in a brief footnote that Wells quotes out-dated sources, uses "simple affirmation, supported not by argumentation" and wrote just another "popular Jesus book that I do not bother to consider in detail."[378]

Atheist journalist Christopher Hitchens wrote in *God is Not Great* that Jesus' existence was "highly questionable".[379] But guess how many scholars he quoted in support. Yes, zero.

Christian historian John Dickson, a visiting scholar at Oxford University, has said, "if anyone can find a full professor of Classics, Ancient History or New Testament in any accredited university in the world who thinks Jesus never lived, I will eat a page of my Bible." That hasn't happened so far.

Summary: Jesus in history

1. Almost all ancient history academics today, Christian and non-Christian, believe Jesus of Nazareth was a figure of history who was crucified by the Roman governor Pontius Pilate, and whose followers claimed he had physically appeared to them after his death.

2. Leading historians Tacitus, Pliny, Suetonius and Josephus mention him, as do writers like Mara bar Serapion, Lucion of Samosata and Celsius, and he appears in the Jewish Talmud.

See also:

John Dickson, *The Christ Files: How Historians Know What They Know About Jesus* (Sydney South: Blue Bottle Books, 2006)
———. *Investigating Jesus: An Historian's Quest* (Oxford: Lion, 2010)
Paul Barnett, *Finding the Historical Christ* (Cambridge: Eerdmans, 2009)
Rhodes Eddy & Gregory A. Boyd, *The Jesus Legend: A Case for the Historical Reliability of the Synoptic Jesus Tradition* (Grand Rapids: Baker, 2007)

11

Jesus & predictions: can you find a hole in this?

Evidence from Fulfilled Prophecies

"It's difficult to make predictions—especially about the future."
—DANISH PROVERB

"You dummies! So slow to believe all that the prophets have predicted! Didn't Messiah have to suffer these things and then enter his glory?"
—JESUS TO TWO DISCIPLES (LUKE 24:25–26)

"Do you want hard evidence for the existence of God?", my uncle Winston asked me as we waited for a chairlift at the ski resort of Thredbo.

"No" would have been my honest answer. But he was one of my favourite people, with an intellect like a surgical scalpel, so I listened politely. He said, "If you can find a hole in this logic, I'll eat my hat." I looked at his woollen ski beanie and we laughed.

By the time our chair reached the top of Mt Crackenback, he had summarised the Seventy Weeks prophecy found in the Bible's book of Daniel. He claimed it predicted the date of Jesus Christ's arrival and his death 500 years before it happened, as well as two events in the history of Jerusalem—and all with super-human accuracy.

"Are you going to read my palm as well?" I asked him as we prepared to get off.

JESUS & PREDICTIONS: CAN YOU FIND A HOLE IN THIS?

He snorted, but seriously challenged me to take a close, critical look and find the loophole.

I thought about it during our run down the mountain. "Let me see if I get this", I said in the next chairlift line. "This prophet Daniel in 550 BC predicts, firstly, that his ruined city of Jerusalem will be rebuilt, and secondly, 483 years after the order to rebuild, Israel's king or Messiah will appear. Daniel says, thirdly, that 3½ years after that, Messiah will be killed. Then fourthly, Jerusalem will be destroyed again."

He nodded.

"And you say history matches these predictions accurately—Jerusalem's rebuild starts in 457BC, Jesus appears 483 years later in AD27 and dies 3½ years after that in AD31, then Jerusalem is destroyed in AD70. And you say such detailed knowledge of the future is far beyond human ability, so it must have come from a superhuman mind, i.e. God."

"Right."

"Come on, that's easy", I said. "Someone wrote history after it happened and pretended this guy Daniel had predicted it beforehand."

"Good try", he grinned at me. "But in Jerusalem, there are manuscripts of Daniel's book dated centuries before..."

"Oh..."

That was awkward. I really didn't want there to be a God. That would spoil my fun. So when I got back home, I hit the university library, aiming to make my uncle eat his beanie.

I found that the great scientist Sir Isaac Newton had written about the Seventy Weeks prophecy. His logic was simple: if a prediction comes true beyond human ability, then there must be a God. God gave prophecies because "the event of things predicted many ages before, will then be a convincing argument that the world is governed by providence."[380]

I found this claim in the Bible too. Jesus made a prediction and added, "I am telling you about this before it happens so that when it does happen, you will believe that I am who I am."[381] And the prophet Isaiah has God claiming he is worth trusting because he can "make known the end from the beginning" and "foretell what is to come."[382]

It's also clear that accurate predictions are well beyond human ability. If you can reliably predict future events, come and spend one day with me at the stock exchange. If you know someone who's genuinely psychic, let's go and see them—and let's not make an appointment, because they'll already know we're coming. But I remember reading a newspaper article about a psychic convention that had been cancelled due to unforeseen circumstances. Oops!

The future is too hard to predict. Think of the Decca Records executive who rejected an unknown musical group and said, "We don't like their sound, and guitar music is on the way out anyway." He didn't sign The Beatles. Or the great economist John Maynard Keynes saying, "We will not have any more crashes in our time" in 1927—two years before the stock market crash and Great Depression that shredded the global economy for a decade. Or the twelve publishers who turned down an unknown writer's story about Harry Potter that went on to make J.K. Rowling a billionaire. We humans can only guess. Accurately telling the future in detail would be at least some evidence of the supernatural.

So I took a critical look at the Seventy Weeks. I'll summarise what I found. But first a warning: Isaac Newton called this prediction "the foundation stone of the Christian religion". Foundations are heavy and require serious digging—and same with this prophecy. So don't just take my word for it. Dig for yourself.

Daniel's prediction

In 606/605 BC, the armies of Babylon smashed through the walls of Israel's capital city, Jerusalem. A teenage Jewish nobleman named Daniel was taken as a slave to the city of Babylon in modern-day Iraq. His genius was soon noticed and he began serving in the king's palace. Despite huge pressure to conform to his colonial masters, he managed to keep his religious identity.

Daniel constantly thought about his home city of Jerusalem and its enslaved people, and claimed God gave him a vision about it:

> Know therefore and understand
> That from the going forth of the command
> To restore and build Jerusalem
> Until Messiah the Prince,
> there shall be seven weeks and sixty-two weeks.
> The street shall be built again, and the wall,
> Even in troublesome times.
> And after the sixty-two weeks
> Messiah shall be cut off, but not for himself.
> And the people of the prince who is to come
> Shall destroy the city and the sanctuary..."
> (Daniel 9:25–26, NKJV).

If you read it carefully—maybe a few times—you can see it predicts four main events:

1. Jerusalem would be restored and rebuilt

This was not easy to guess, since many ancient cities never recovered from wartime destruction. When the empire of Babylon conquered a country, they weakened it with a divide-and-rule policy, mixing different ethnic groups together so they would not unite and rebel. And Babylon attacked Jerusalem a second time in 586 BC, levelling it after 2½ years of brutal siege warfare and deporting its remaining people as slaves. Jerusalem was in ruins for well over a century. Its temple, a marble and gold masterpiece built in the prosperous age of King Solomon around 960BC, was a sad ruin.

In 539BC the Persian Empire defeated Babylon and dominated the region. King Cyrus the Great allowed enslaved peoples to go home, and showed respect to their cultures and religions. This was written on a clay tablet called the Cyrus Cylinder:

> I returned the images of the gods... to their places...
> I gathered all their inhabitants and returned to them their dwellings.
> (Line 30–33)

Cyrus' cylinder is now seen as one of the first declarations of human rights—a copy is in the United Nations building in New York City.[383] Some historians say Cyrus was less interested in human rights than in building unified countries with strong economies so that he could tax them—but either way, the Edict of Cyrus in 539BC freed the Jews.

Then a later Persian king told the Jews to rebuild Jerusalem and even gave them resources to remake their temple. His name was Artaxerxes I, nicknamed Longimanus (long-handed) because his right hand was longer than his left—you can see it in the picture on his spectacular tomb, carved into rock at Naqsh e Rostam in Iran (the most beautiful and friendly country I have visited). Artaxerxes wrote this decree for a Jewish leader called Ezra[384], and the Jews went to work rebuilding Jerusalem and its wall, facing nasty opposition from enemies but overcoming the predicted "troublesome times" and getting the job done under a leader called Nehemiah.

King Artaxerxes gave this decree in 457 BC—and Daniel said Messiah would appear 483 years after that.

2. Messiah would appear

Ever since Israel's King David defeated the aggressive Philistines around 980 BC, the Jews had been looking for a "son of David" to save them from their enemies. Many prophets had predicted details about this king or Messiah (in Hebrew *Mashiach*, "Anointed One"), and Daniel now foresaw that he would come 483 years after the order to rebuild Jerusalem.

Daniel's exact words were "seven sevens" plus "sixty-two sevens". Jews thought in seven-year periods just as we think in decades. The Ten Commandments gave them a Sabbath day of worship and relaxed family time every seven days, and other laws allowed a sabbatical year of recreation and no work every seven years.[385] (Talk about work-life balance!) So the "7 and 62 weeks are understood as 69 seven-year periods."[386] Within the first seven "weeks" (49 years), the temple was rebuilt.[387] The Jewish Talmud says, "A week in Daniel means a week of years." (*Yoma* 54a).

So it's (7 + 62) weeks of years = 69 x 7 = 483 years.

If the time period starts in 457 BC and runs 483 years, then it ends in AD 27—remembering that there was no year 0. (I felt safe copying Sir Isaac Newton's figures—he wasn't a bad mathematician.)

And AD 27 is an accepted date for the public ministry of Jesus,[388] who was called Messiah[389] or Christ (Greek, "Anointed One"). Jesus' first public speech was:

> "The time is fulfilled and the kingdom of God is near.
> Repent and believe the good news."
> Mark 1:15.

What time was fulfilled? The time predicted by Daniel. Jesus said Daniel was a prophet that readers should understand.[390]

But then...

3. Messiah would die after 3½ years

This was truly shocking. Israel was a small nation kicked around by big empires—Egypt, Assyria, Babylon, Greece, Rome. Their last king had gone by 586 BC, when the Babylonians killed his sons in front of him and poked his eyes out, then chained him and fed him like a dog at the king's table. After that, who wouldn't want some military pride back! Israel expected Messiah to raise an army and defeat their conquerors, making them number one.

But Daniel was clear that Messiah would die. No wonder his prediction was not very well-known.

When Jesus became popular, crowds hoped he might be Messiah. He could feed an army with loaves and fishes! He could heal any wounded soldiers so they could fight on! They tried to make him king, but he slipped away.[391] Jesus was clear that was not his mission. He told his disciples he had to die—and they hated the idea and promptly ignored it.[392] They wanted a military hero, not a dead guy.

Historians agree that Jesus of Nazareth, called the Christ, was killed on a cross by Roman soldiers after trials in Jewish and Roman courts.

Daniel had said Messiah would be "cut off but not for himself" (Daniel 9:26). The Hebrew *karat* means to be killed, like lambs sacrificed in the Jewish temple and Jesus was called "the lamb of God who takes away the sin of the world".[393] Christians see Jesus' death as the ultimate "sacrifice" to pay for human guilt and sin, God accepting the cost of forgiveness and absorbing the consequences of our mistakes. Daniel had predicted his death would be "not for himself"—but for others.

But the word *karat* also means to make a covenant or legal deal: this was often done by killing an animal (see Genesis 15:10, 18; Jeremiah 34:13, 18.) "The prophecy thus identifies the Messiah with the sacrifice of the covenant. Like the lamb, His death made possible a covenant and assured divine forgiveness. All this was a language that the Israelites, living in a context where sacrifices were a part of daily life, could easily understand."[394]

I noticed one more stunning detail—Daniel says exactly when Messiah would die: "In the middle of the week" (Daniel 9:27) The middle of a seven-year week is 3½ years—and the gospels record that Jesus died after 3½ years of ministry, likely in AD31.

So Daniel's third prediction came true as Roman soldiers nailed Jesus to the cross. The Romans would also fulfil the fourth.

4. Jerusalem and the temple would be destroyed again

Notice the sad words of the prophecy: "And the people of the prince who is to come shall destroy the city and the sanctuary" (Daniel 9:26b)

Jesus had been surprisingly kind to the Roman soldiers who had invaded his country. By law, they could force citizens to carry their pack for a mile, but Jesus told his followers to go a second mile, not in weakness but in dignified kindness. He healed a Roman centurion's servant. One of his disciples, Simon, had been one of the Zealots who plotted violent resistance against Rome, but Jesus taught love of enemies and turning of cheeks. After all, who could defeat Rome, whose roads stretched from India to Britain to North Africa to Turkey, and whose legions enforced *pax Romana* with predictable violence for rebels? If Jerusalem had taken Jesus' advice, Rome would never have attacked.

But a generation later, Jerusalem's leaders raised a fist to Rome, refusing to pay tax. The Romans rolled their eyes yet again about the rebellious province of Judaea, and sent them warnings. The army under Titus and Vespasian widened the roads and brought in military hardware—huge siege engines that could catapult rocks over city walls or smash through them. Jerusalem was surrounded by armies. Their last chance came from Flavius Josephus, who had fought as a Jewish general but was now captured by the Romans. He stood at the city wall and begged Jerusalem's leaders to submit to Rome, pay tax and let people live. Their reply was a volley of darts that just missed him.

And Josephus records what follows—the terror of siege warfare, the starvation and cannibalism, the slaughter, demolition and enslavement. I can't read it without tears.

The Roman general Titus gave orders that Jerusalem's temple must not be harmed because it was one of the wonders of the world—built of the finest marble floated in from Italy, and topped with beaten gold that shimmered in the sun—but a Roman soldier noticed Jewish soldiers were using the Temple as a hideout and, in a moment of fury, threw a torch into its roof timbers. It burned for days. In the resulting pandemonium, the Roman army flooded into the city just as Daniel had foreseen.[395] They tore the city apart stone by stone and took hideous vengeance on its people. Many Jews had died in the siege and in the fighting, but now the Romans slaughtered more, taking others as slaves to dig in salt mines or row ships across the Empire. From this date—AD 70—they and their children would become wanderers, living anywhere but home for nineteen centuries. It really was one of the great tragedies of history, though the Romans celebrated and boasted of it, carving it into stone in the Victory Arch of Titus. You can see it today in Rome, including the *menorah* or sacred candlestick snatched from the Jerusalem's Great Temple to boast that Roman gods were better than anyone else's.

Jesus & predictions: can you find a hole in this?

With tears in his eyes, Jesus had warned Jerusalem of what was coming, quoting Daniel's predictions.[396] He told people to escape from Jerusalem when they saw it surrounded by armies.[397] That seemed ridiculous. How on earth could civilians escape from a besieged city? Yet Josephus records that the Romans arrived and surrounded Jerusalem, then left to punish another city. Everyone who took Jesus' advice was able to escape, and many ran to the town of Pella, across the Jordan River. Then the Romans returned, and the rest is bloody and tragic history.

Daniel's prediction was looking tragic but impressive... but hang on a minute... Was I getting too emotionally involved in this story?

Not so fast! The loopholes

Stay critical, I told myself. Don't get sucked in by this emotive religious stuff. And you, gentle reader, have probably already thought of obvious ways this prediction could be faked:

1. What if the prediction was written after the events?

The most likely explanation seemed to be that someone had faked this prophecy. They may have had good motives—trying to bring people comfort and hope, or make sense of meaningless tragedy by suggesting a made-up god had a plan—so they wrote a fictional prophecy predicting events that had already happened, and pretended it had been written earlier by Daniel.

I soon found my uncle Winston was right, and my post-eventum theory didn't stand up.

   a. The Dead Sea Scrolls are a collection of manuscripts from around 300BC to 100AD, discovered in Qumran in 1946. They include 8 manuscript fragments from the book of Daniel, and the earliest is dated to around 150BC. We know that from the palaeography, the scientific study of writing techniques. I've checked this in an interview with Professor Shalom Paul, the leading expert at Hebrew University in Jerusalem, whose team used high-tech dating methods.
   b. Daniel is mentioned in the historical books of Maccabees, written 134–34 BC. (1 Maccabees 2:59, 60).

That would be enough. If Daniel's prediction is written by about 150 BC and accurately predicts events around 180 years later, I would see that as super-human. But I found evidence that the book of Daniel was written even earlier than that.

c. It appears in the Septuagint (LXX), the Greek translation of the Hebrew Bible that began in around 250BC and continued for a century or so.

d. And Alexander the Great read from the book of Daniel in about 330 BC. According to Josephus, Alexander had just defeated the cities of Tyre and Gaza and marched toward Jerusalem, where some of his advisers wanted him to be brutal. Alexander was surprised when a procession of Jewish priests came out to meet him, so he left his army and went to meet them. They carried a scroll of Daniel's writings, including his prediction in chapter 8 that the Greek goat would smash the Persian ram. Alexander was flattered to be mentioned in someone's holy book—though they somehow didn't read him the prediction that he would die when he was strong. (He died at 33.) So rather than destroying Jerusalem, Alexander gave them a tax discount! Every seventh year they could keep their Sabbath year and pay no tax. Josephus wrote:

> And when he [Alexander] went up into the temple, he offered sacrifice to God, according to the high priest's direction, and magnificently treated both the high priest and the priests. And when the Book of Daniel was showed him wherein Daniel declared that one of the Greeks should destroy the empire of the Persians, he supposed that himself was the person intended. And as he was then glad, he dismissed the multitude for the present; but the next day he called them to him, and bid them ask what favours they pleased of him; whereupon the high priest desired that they might enjoy the laws of their forefathers, and might pay no tribute on the seventh year. He granted all they desired.
> (Flavius Josephus, *Antiquities*, Book XI, Ch viii, 5)

e. The prediction itself claims to be written in "the first year of Darius", which is 538/537 BC.

Jesus & Predictions: Can You Find a Hole in This?

So this is not post-eventum prophecy. Independent sources date it at least three and a half centuries before, and the text itself claims it was written five centuries before.

2. What if Jesus wasn't the Jewish Messiah?

It hit me that most Jews say Jesus was not the Messiah! I double-checked by reading a number of Jewish writers, and they said Jesus was not Messiah! Ha! Eat your beanie, Uncle Winston!

But then I carefully read their reasons. Rabbi Eckstein wrote:

> Not only were the biblical prophecies foretelling the dawn of world peace and political harmony unfulfilled, quite the opposite occurred—Jews lost sovereignty over the land of Israel, the temple was destroyed, and exile and suffering became the mark of their collective condition...
>
> If he were truly the Messiah he should not have died in the first place![398]

Yet Daniel's Seventy Weeks prophecy predicts exactly these things! Dying doesn't show Jesus was a failed Messiah, it shows he was the biblical Messiah.

Rabbi Eckstein is of course correct that many biblical predictions do speak of Messiah as a conquering king who brings peace to the whole world: read Psalm 2 or 72, or Daniel 2, 7, 8, 10, 11 or 12. Yet many others speak of Messiah suffering and dying, e.g. Psalm 22 and Isaiah 53. Which of those two sets of predictions do you think were more popular with an oppressed people? Even Jesus' disciples expected him to be a military Messiah. When he said he would die, they pushed back hard. He had to explain to them how the two kinds of predictions fit together: "You dummies! So slow to believe all that the prophets have spoken! Didn't Messiah have to suffer these things and then enter his glory?"[399] He made clear that he had come the first time to die for the sins of the world, but promised to come a second time to rule.

I worked on a documentary interviewing Jewish visitors at the Western Wall in Jerusalem, and I discovered three main views of Messiah. One was that he was still to come. Another was that the idea of Messiah was just a metaphor to encourage people to be like Messiah themselves, and "save the world" in small ways. A third group said that, since the Holocaust, they couldn't even believe in the reality of God, let alone God's king on earth. Rabbi Professor Dan Cohn-Sherbok says many Jewish people find that "totally implausible", so they "rely on themselves to shape their own destiny." "Instead of looking to a heavenly form of redemption, the Jewish community must now rely on itself for its own survival and the redemption of the world." He doubts many foundations of Jewish faith, arguing that Jews should "free themselves from the absolutes of the past" because "these ancient doctrines can be superseded by a new vision of Jewish life which is human-centred in orientation." He finds it is no longer "plausible to assert that any religious outlook is categorically true" and Jews should "recognise that their Scriptures are simply one record among many others" not "possessing truth for all humankind."[400] So he has given up on the idea of a Messiah coming at all, and dropped almost any claim to truth from God.

Yet Daniel 9 has been crucial for many Jewish people finding Jesus as God's Messiah for both Israel and the wider, non-Jewish ("Gentile") world. Many were shocked to find Messiah has already visited, and that learning from him brings them closer to God, not further away. My friend in a group called Jews for Jesus wears a T-shirt that says: "Jesus Made Me Kosher".

Christianity is often seen as destructive to Judaism, and I have to admit that some churches have been horribly anti-Semitic. During the Nazi era, some churches displayed a sign saying *Juden sint hier unerwünscht* (Jews are unwelcome here) while the crucifix up the front had the initials INRI— Iesus Nazarenus, Rex Iudaeorum, or Jesus of Nazareth, King of the Jews. Did no one see the irony? Jesus was crucified naked but most crucifixes had a loincloth covering the fact that he was a circumcised Jewish man.[401] Jesus the Jew worked in Jerusalem, did everything he could for its people and wept at the thought of its future destruction. His followers should love Jews no less.

So was Jesus the Jewish messiah? Yes—even if he was unrecognised by many. And even this was predicted by the prophet Isaiah:

> Who believed what we tried to tell them?
> Who noticed God's hand at work?
> ...He had no image or majesty to draw our attention,
> No special appearance that made us want him.
> He was despised and rejected by people,
> A man who knew sorrow, well acquainted with grief.
> People turned their faces away from him.
> He was despised, and we thought he was nobody.

> Yet it was our grief he was carrying, our sorrow that he shouldered...
> He was wounded for our arrogant foolishness,
> And punished for our sins.
> He endured a flogging to make us well,
> And because of his wounds, we are healed."
> (Isaiah 53, my translation)

3. What if Daniel scored one lucky prediction among a lot of failed guesses?

In short, no. Reading his whole book takes less than two hours and reading a good commentary on it will show lots of predictions that have come true, and some predictions that point to events that are still future.

4. What if it's all in how you read it?

I've heard some vague, fluffy predictions that could mean almost anything, but this one clearly states a city (Jerusalem), a start date ("the command to... rebuild"), an event ("Messiah the Prince"), a clear time period (7 sevens + 62 sevens = 69 sevens = 483 years) and another event ("Messiah shall be cut off, but not for himself") and a time period ("in the middle of the week = 3½ years).

These things need careful explanation 2500 years later in a very different culture, but it's clear language and you can read it yourself.

And so...

Having read and thought about this for months, I jotted down some conclusions:

- Daniel strikingly accurate:
  - Jerusalem rebuilt
  - Messiah arrives 483 years later
  - Messiah dies 3½ years after that
  - Jerusalem destroyed

- No loopholes I can see.
- Easy to imagine a homesick Jew dreaming of his city being rebuilt, and Messiah coming. Wish fulfilment doesn't make it really happen.
- Hard to imagine a homesick Jew dreaming of Messiah being killed (contrary to expectations) and Jerusalem being destroyed again (too sad to imagine).
- Odds of a human predicting dates at this level of detail five centuries out? Near zero.
- Daniel said God revealed it. If that's true, then:
  - There must be a God
  - God knows the future.
  - God cares about humans
  - Jewish history is important
  - Jesus' life and death important
  - Forgiveness for mistakes

But wait, there's more. . . and more. . .

But then everything got much more complicated. Reading the Gospels, I noticed they mentioned dozens of other predictions about Messiah that came true in Jesus of Nazareth. Here's one.

Every school Christmas play has the Wise Men, who come from the East on camels and give gifts to baby Jesus. Cute—except it's political dynamite. These foreign leaders visit King Herod in Jerusalem and ask him where the new king of the Jews has been born. Herod feels threatened, even paranoid, about any rival. He has killed family members to keep power, but he plays along and calls in the priests and religious academics to ask where Messiah will be born. They quote a prediction from Micah, a prophet who lived seven centuries earlier, saying that Messiah would be born in Bethlehem.[402] So the wise men go there and give their gifts to Jesus. Herod sends soldiers there to kill all boys under two just to be sure—but the gospel of Matthew says this terrible tragedy was predicted in a quotation by Jeremiah the prophet around 600 years earlier.[403] Luckily Jesus is not killed because Joseph and Mary have sold the gold and perfumes from the wise men and escaped to Egypt, which is also predicted by the prophet Hosea[404] 750 years

JESUS & PREDICTIONS: CAN YOU FIND A HOLE IN THIS?

earlier. After taking refuge in Egypt, the family hears Herod is dead and returns, but they move North to avoid Herod's son and settle in the town of Nazareth. Matthew says this is because the prophets predicted Messiah would be a Nazarene.[405] Matthew later shows Jesus moving to Capernaum, and says this fulfils a prophecy by Isaiah.[406]

One simple story, and five predictions? Seriously? I saw it would not be easy to understand these predictions beforehand. One prophet says Messiah will be born in Bethlehem, another says he'll come from Egypt, and another from Nazareth, another from the Capernaum area. . . That seems contradictory—until they all happen to Jesus.

The gospel writers keep saying that dozens of details of Jesus' life were predicted by Hebrew prophets centuries before—the town of his birth, the tribe he was born into, the date his public life started, the date of his death, the fact he'd be killed by piercing his hands and feet (predicted by David[407] around 960 BC), and many more.

I won't pretend all these predictions are easy to interpret. Some still baffle scholars. Some use complicated symbolism and typology and obscure cultural references. But they are impressive. And even the most liberal scholars say the prophets wrote at least 150 years before Jesus, since we have them in the Dead Sea Scrolls.

What do you think are your odds of picking the town of birth for your country's leader in 100 years? Or how he or she will die? What are the odds of dozens of predictions like this being correct by chance if there is no God?

A mathematician and an astrophysicist walked into a bar and. . . actually no, they soberly considered eight Messianic prophecies, and tried to estimate the probability of Jesus Christ fulfilling them by chance. You could question some estimates as educated guesses, but Peter Stoner and Dr Robert Newman[408] tried to be very conservative and still found the odds were approximately one in one hundred million million million. That's one chance in 100,000,000,000,000,000,000.

Then they considered 48 prophecies, and estimated the odds at one chance in 10^{157} or 10,000,000,000,000,000,000,000,000,000,000,000,000,000,000,000,000,000,000,000,000,000,000,000,000,000,000,000,000,000,000,000,000,000,000,000,000,000,000,000,000,000,000,000,000,000,000,000,000,000,000,000,000.

Yet some scholars estimate that Jesus fulfilled 332 prophecies. Using our smallest type font, that number would fill a whole chapter of zeroes.

Predictions this accurate seem well beyond human ability, suggesting they have supernatural origins.

I told my uncle Winston what I was discovering and how it was developing my thinking faith, and he said with typical understatement, "Good. I like my ski beanie."

Summary: prophecy

1. The Seventy Weeks prediction was fulfilled in striking detail centuries later. And many other detailed predictions came true in the life of Jesus.
2. Accurate predictions of exact details in the distant future are beyond natural human ability.
3. This suggests a supernatural source for this information, namely God.
4. These predictions also draw attention to the importance of Jesus' life and death.

Further reading:

Jacques B. Doukhan, *On The Way To Emmaus: Five Major Messianic Prophecies Explained* (Clarksville, Lederer Books, 2017)
Jacques B. Doukhan, *Secrets of Daniel: Wisdom and Dreams of a Jewish Prince in Exile* (Hagerstown: R&H Publishing, 2000).
Rich Robinson, "The Top 40 Messianic Prophecies"
https://jewsforjesus.org/learn/top-40-most-helpful-messianic-prophecies

12

Jesus and Afterlife: four agreed facts

Evidence for the Historical Resurrection of Jesus, Part I

There are no gods, no purposes, no goal-directed forces of any kind. There is no life after death. When I die, I am absolutely certain I am going to be dead. That's the end for me.

—PROFESSOR WILLIAM B. PROVINE, BIOLOGIST[409]

If Christ has not been resurrected, your faith is worthless, you're still under condemnation for your sins, everyone who has died believing in Christ is gone forever, and Christians are the most pitiful of people. . .
If the dead are not resurrected, let us eat, drink and be merry for tomorrow we die. . .
But Christ has indeed been raised from the dead. . .

—ST PAUL, FIRST LETTER TO CORINTHIAN CHRISTIANS 15:17–18, 32, 20

AUSTRALIA'S RICHEST MAN WAS playing polo when he slumped forward on the neck of his pony. He had suffered a heart attack, and lay dead on the turf for eight minutes until an ambulance arrived and resuscitated him. Later he told a reporter, "Son, I've been to the other side and let me tell you, there's f***ing nothing there. . . There's no one waiting for you, there's no one to judge you, so you can do what you bloody well like."[410]

But Kerry Packer had only experienced heart death, not brain death, where cells decompose due to enzyme release and dropping pH, and a process called autolysis causes widespread cellular destruction. The body changes colour (livor mortis), stiffens (rigor mortis) and cools (algor mortis), and pathologists use these tests to determine time of death.

So if Jesus Christ was pronounced dead at around 3pm Friday, then by Sunday morning 40 hours later, he would be well beyond mere resuscitation. Coming back to life would require all his body cells to be replaced and start functioning at the same time, which is of course totally unknown in medicine or biology. It would be about as difficult as making a human in the first place.

If there's no God, forget it. It's a fairytale.

But if there is a God—as the evidence in previous chapters suggests—then it would be possible.

How could we know 2,000 years later? We can't use the scientific method, because historical events can't be repeated in a lab. Historical claims like this stand or fall on the kind of evidence that historians and lawyers use—the testimony of witnesses.

Christianity has always claimed to be based on facts of history. It doesn't make vague, fluffy claims that are impossible to prove or disprove. ("The Flying Spaghetti Monster appeared only to me, but I can tell you what he says and you will feel fire in your bosom. . .") In the quote at the top of this chapter, the Christian apostle Paul is confident enough to hang all his credibility on one historical question –the resurrection of Jesus of Nazareth.

Is there any evidence for this claim? Surprisingly, there are four crucial facts accepted not just by Christians but by almost all ancient historians who study the accounts of Jesus, because they come from primary sources written by eyewitnesses.[411]

Of course, many historians reach different conclusions about these facts—we'll discuss those in the next chapter—but almost all accept these basic facts as a starting point:

1. Jesus was a real person of history, and died by crucifixion

Crucifixion was common in the Roman Empire as punishment for slaves and rebels. How do you motivate a slave whose life was already a hopeless grind? Threaten him (or sometimes her) with a slow death—days of agony and public shame. It hurt much more than being burned or fed to wild animals in a public show, let alone having your head quickly cut off by a sword. Tacitus called it "the extreme penalty", Josephus "the most wretched of deaths", and Cicero "cruel and disgusting".[412] It was also humiliating and shameful.

Slaves made up a third of the population of Rome, so the Romans lived on constant fear of an uprising. In 73 BC, a slave gladiator named Spartacus led 70 other gladiators in a rebellion, raising an army of 70,000 escaped slaves. It took a huge effort to defeat them, after which 6,000 of the slaves were crucified along the Appian Way. People who saw their bodies displayed mile after mile beside this major road would get a clear message: Don't rebel or you will die after days of absolute agony.

When Jerusalem rebelled and a Roman army destroyed it in AD 70, Josephus reports clusters of crosses so thick you could barely walk between them. He says Roman soldiers "out of anger and hatred amused themselves by nailing them in different positions."[413] Other historians record people being crucified upside down, or nailed through the genitals or with a sharp stake up the backside.[414]

We saw in the last chapter that Tacitus recorded Jesus' crucifixion, as did Josephus, Lucian, Mara and the Talmud. The sceptical scholar John Dominic Crossan sums it up: "That he was crucified is as sure as anything historical can ever be."[415]

But did he die? After more than 40 medical and scientific studies on his crucifixion, the answer is clear.[416] (This section is rather gory.)

The damage started the night before. Jesus knew he faced an agonising death the next day, and the biographer Luke, a medical doctor, described him sweating "great drops of blood".[417] Dr Frederick Zugibe explains this as a medical condition in which a patient haemorrhages into the sweat glands. It has been seen in people condemned to execution or dreading enemy bombing.[418]

Then Jesus was arrested and faced six interrogations or trials in the five hours from around 1 am until dawn with no sleep. Guards punched him in the face while his hands were tied and he was blindfolded.[419] The Roman governor Pontius Pilate had him flogged.[420] A Roman scourging was deadly serious. The whip or *flagrum* had pieces of stone or bone on the end of its strings, and a soldier called a *lictor* would pull it in a way that cut deep into the muscle tissue of the back, buttocks and thighs. This caused blood loss serious enough to send a victim into haemorrhagic shock.[421] It was known that 39 lashes was the limit for most people to stay alive.[422] Dr Thomas Miller says many patients would die after that unless they received intensive care with intravenous fluids, blood transfusions, oxygen and wound care to stop blood loss.[423]

Then the soldiers made a crown of thorns and pressed it into Jesus' scalp.[424] Dr Zugibe describes nerve damage and severe shooting pains across the face, increasing the chances of traumatic shock.[425]

The crowd still wasn't satisfied, so Pilate ordered that Jesus be crucified. Soldiers stripped off his robe, ripping away drying blood and causing more bleeding. Then he had to pick up a wooden crossbeam weighing around 50kg and carry it 800 metres. By now, the 33-year-old carpenter was so weakened that he collapsed under that load, so soldiers grabbed someone out of the crowd, an African man from Libya named Simon of Cyrene.[426]

The crossbar was laid on the ground and Jesus was nailed on. Archaeologists have found crucifixion spikes six inches long, hammered through the heel-bone or calcaneum, the strongest bone in the foot.[427] Nails also went through the wrist between the two forearm bones, the radius and ulna.[428] The nails were bent over at the top to stop the prisoner escaping.[429] Nails would likely crush nerves and produce the most severe shooting pains, called causalgia.[430]

Then the cross was lifted up vertically and dropped into a hole. Mayo Clinic researchers say that the weight of Jesus's body pulling down on his outstretched arms would have "fixed his intercostal [rib] muscles in an inhalation state", making it difficult to breathe out. He would have had to lift his body weight up on the nails and rub his lacerated back on the rough wood every time he exhaled. Shallow breathing would hurt less, but it would cause a buildup of carbon dioxide in his blood (hypercarbia), which in turn could cause muscle cramps, confusion and even coma.[431]

Victims could stay like that for days. Birds might peck out their eyes, animals could eat them alive—suffering was the whole idea. Our word for the worst pain—excruciating—comes from *ex crucis* ("out of crucifixion"). Jesus was offered a drink of wine mixed with gall, which would have dulled his pain, but he refused it,[432] perhaps wanting mental clarity to the end.

It was then a race as to what would kill the victim first—asphyxia if he became too exhausted to lift himself up[433], or heart failure[434] or cardiovascular collapse[435], dehydration[436], hypovolemic shock (the drop in blood pressure due to blood loss or severe dehydration)[437], a blood clot in the lungs[438], or infection spreading from wounds.[439]

If Roman soldiers wanted to be kind, they might asphyxiate the victim quickly by lighting a smoky fire near his cross or smashing his lower legs with a mallet (*crurifragrum*) so he couldn't lift himself up to breathe out. This was seen as *kindness.* As Jesus died, Jerusalem's leadership asked the Romans to break the legs of the crucified men so that no one would be on the cross on the Sabbath. Soldiers came to do that but saw that Jesus was already dead.[440] Just to be sure, a soldier thrust a spear up under his ribs and John witnessed blood and water coming out.[441] Doctors believe the flogging would have caused a fluid build-up around the heart and lungs—known as pericardial and pleural effusion—and the spear pierced his heart and the pericardial sac around it.[442]

Jesus was dead.

2. His tomb was found to be empty on Sunday morning.

There's a major problem with this story.

Joseph of Arimathea, a wealthy and respected member of the Jewish council or Sanhedrin, asked Pilate for permission to bury Jesus. Pilate agreed, and Joseph placed the body in his own family's new tomb[443], an upmarket crypt cut into a rockface. Then a large stone weighing around 2 tonnes was rolled across the entrance. Mary Magdalene and other women watched the burial.[444] That's not the problem.

Another wealthy Sanhedrin council member, Nicodemus, had talked with Jesus privately some years before.[445] He now brought 35kg of myrrh and aloes, the expensive ingredients for a traditional Jewish burial.[446] The women would usually wrap the spices in among the graveclothes, but it was nearly dark and the Sabbath day of mandatory rest was beginning, so they hurried home, planning to come back and finish the job on Sunday morning. That's not the problem either.

The chief priests went to Pilate and reminded him that Jesus "the deceiver" had said he would come back to life on the third day. They worried that his disciples might steal the body and pretend Jesus really had risen, so they asked for a guard for a few days. Pilate gave orders and they put a seal over the stone opening and set a guard at the tomb.[447] Anyone breaking that seal would be contravening Roman imperial authority. Still not the problem.

At dawn on Sunday morning, Mary Magdalene, Mary the mother of James, Johanna, and Salome came to the tomb carrying spices and hoping to complete the burial ritual. They were stunned to find the tomb empty, and reported this to the other disciples.[448]

And there lies a major problem—the first witnesses were women. Of course that would not be a problem under modern Western law, but under Roman law, women, along with slaves, children and criminals, were "ineligible as witnesses in court."[449] Jewish law said that women, thieves, gamblers and slaves were usually "unfit to give testimony".[450] Josephus records the historical attitude behind this law: "But let not the testimony of a woman be admitted, on account of the levity and boldness of their sex."[451]

With this sexist attitude widespread in society, Christianity would be slammed for having female witnesses. The Greek philosopher Celsus (3.44) wrote in AD170 that Christians couldn't convince sensible people of the truth of Christ's resurrection. He said they "are able to convince only the foolish, dishonourable, and stupid, only slaves, women, and little children". Why?

> The chief witness is a hysterical female... half-crazy from fear and grief, and possibly one other of the same band of charlatans who dreamed it all up or saw what they wanted to see—or more likely simply wanted to astonish their friends in the tavern with a good tale.[452]

Even more embarrassing than that is the fact that even Jesus' disciples did not believe the women at first. Mary Magdalene, Joanna, Mary the mother of James and other women came to tell the men that they had seen Jesus' tomb empty—as Jesus had asked them to—and *the men did not believe them*. "Their words seemed to them like idle tales"[453]—even though these women were their close friends. How embarrassing! Men who would travel the world telling the story of Jesus' resurrection did not believe it the first time they heard it—partly due to sexism.

"But to us as historians this... is gold dust", says Professor N.T. Wright, because if anyone made these stories up for people of those days to believe them, they would never have women as lead witnesses. That would wreck their credibility. "The early Christians would never, never have made this up."[454]

One mark of authentic testimony is if it's awkward for the person who tells it. This is called the "criterion of embarrassment". So having female witnesses in the story suggests it's authentic. (And could God have been trying to send a message about equality?)

Mary was so insistent that the male disciples decided to go and see for themselves, and Peter and John saw the tomb was empty. They would now become key eyewitnesses.

But it wasn't just individual disciples who discovered the empty tomb. It became a major problem for the authorities, both Jewish and Roman. On Sunday morning, some of the guards woke up, walked into the city and told the Chief Priests what had happened. The priests must have been furious, but they quickly came up with a cover story. They gave the guards a bribe and told them to say, "His disciples came at night and stole him away while we slept."[455] Can you spot the reasons why that's a lie? For one, how could you know what happened while you slept? For another, how could people roll a massive stone without waking you? And third, under Roman law the penalty for sleeping on guard duty was death, so if they were telling that story, how were they still alive? In fact, the priests had promised to speak to Pilate so the guards wouldn't be executed. Their cover story has serious holes, but it admits a major truth: Jesus' body was missing. All the authorities needed to do was to produce Jesus' body and they could have proved the resurrection story was a hoax. But they couldn't.[456]

This is accidental enemy attestation, which is even stronger evidence than claims by a supporter.

The empty tomb is only circumstantial evidence—it is consistent with a resurrection, but does not prove it—but we are about to see direct witness evidence.

3. Many people reported seeing him after his death, including some who previously doubted.

Most historians accept this. Gerd Lüdemann, an atheist professor of New Testament, writes, "It may be taken as historically certain that Peter and the disciples had experiences after Jesus' death in which Jesus appeared to them as the risen Christ."[457] Another atheist, Bart Ehrman, agrees: "It is a historical fact that some of Jesus' followers came to believe that he had been raised from the dead soon after his execution. We know some of these believers by name; one of them, the apostle Paul, claims quite plainly to have seen Jesus alive after his death."[458] Both of these scholars conclude that these were visions, not real sightings, but they accept that the disciples thought they saw Jesus.

A number of different people in Jerusalem at the time claimed they interacted with Jesus soon after his death:

- Four women—Mary Magdalene, Mary the mother of James, Johanna, and Salome—saw him and touched him near his tomb on Sunday morning (John 20:11–18; Matthew 28:1–10).
- Peter saw him sometime on Sunday (Luke 24:34; 1 Cor 15:5)
- Two disciples spoke with him on Emmaus Rd and ate with him (Luke 24:13–32)
- Ten disciples saw him, touched him and ate with him in an upper room on Sunday night (Luke 24:36–49; John 20:19–23). (Of Jesus' original twelve disciples, Judas had suicided after selling him out, and Thomas had given up his belief.)
- A week later, eleven disciples (this time including Thomas) ate with him and touched him. (John 20:24–31)
- His disciples saw him, talked with him and ate with him by the Sea of Galilee (John 21:1–25)
- Eleven disciples saw him in Galilee (Matthew 28:16–20; Mark 16:14–18)
- A crowd of 500 people saw him (1 Corinthians 15:6)
- His brother James saw him and talked with him (1 Corinthians 15:7)
- Eleven disciples saw him in Jerusalem over a 40-day period (Acts 1:3–8)
- The Christian-hating Paul saw and heard him in vision on Damascus Rd (Acts 9:1–19; 1 Corinthians 15:8).

Some of these people are even more interesting because they used to be sceptical about the idea that Jesus was Messiah or had been brought back to life after his death:

Jesus and Afterlife: four agreed facts

1. Jesus' half-brother James

You might think Jesus' biggest supporters would be his family.[459] But no, they didn't believe in him. At one point they thought he was "out of his mind" and wanted to force him into care.[460] None of his siblings were mentioned as present at his crucifixion or resurrection, though their mother Mary was there and would have reported every detail to them.

Then Jesus' brother James said Jesus appeared to him personally.[461] After that, James joined the early Christian church, calling himself a "servant" of his brother.[462] James was trusted as an eyewitness, and the new convert Paul came to him to check his facts.[463] James also led the Jerusalem church for 30 years[464] until, as Josephus records, he was stoned to death by Ananus, an aggressive high priest.[465] Under threat of execution, James could have said his brother wasn't resurrected. Why die for a story if you know it's not true? Yet James never wavered in telling what he knew to be true.

2. "Doubting" Thomas

When Jesus was crucified, his disciple Thomas left the others, depressed that his Messiah was a dud and worried that he might be the next one nailed. The disciples found him and told him that Jesus had come to their dinner on the Sunday night. They claimed, "We have seen the Lord!" but Thomas brushed them off, saying he wouldn't believe it unless he saw Jesus and touched his wounds. I admire his determination not to believe *blindly* in a second-hand story, but then again, the people who were telling him they had seen Jesus resurrected were friends he had known and trusted for years, and their new confidence was evidence in itself. Why not accept the testimony of trusted eyewitnesses? Maybe Thomas's pride was hurt that Jesus had appeared to others but not to him. But what did he expect if he hadn't shown up?

Either way, a grumpy, curious Thomas was with the disciples the next Sunday night and Jesus walked in through a locked door. He told Thomas to poke his finger in the wounds and to quit doubting and believe. Now Thomas had all the evidence he could want, and he knelt down and said, "My Lord and my God".[466]

Thomas spent the rest of his life telling people what he had seen, travelling through Turkey, Iraq, Iran, China and India. He taught in the seven synagogues in the Indian region of Kerala, where Jewish spice traders had lived for 900 years.[467] And arguably the world's oldest Christian church building is not in Jerusalem or Rome but in India—in Arappally, also called Thiruvithamcode. (Try saying that with a mouthful of aloo gobi.) Thomas the carpenter-turned-preacher built it in AD63. He was martyred in Mylapore near Chennai on 3 July AD72, and so India has an apostle's grave, just like Peter in Rome, Andrew in Greece, Bartholomew in Italy, James in Spain, Matthew in Germany, and Philip in Turkey.[468] Marco Polo said he visited Thomas's tomb.[469] And today, twenty million Indians are Thomist Christians.

I interviewed a young girl in a church in India who quoted Jesus' words to Thomas: "You have seen and believed. Blessed are those who have not seen and yet believed." She added, "That's me. And I have Thomas to thank for it."

What changed Thomas' mind? He was an eyewitness, convinced by evidence.

3. Saul the Christian-killer

Saul despised Christians as fools and heretics. As an ambitious young Jewish rabbi working to have them arrested, he watched the first Christian martyr, Stephen, being stoned to death.[470] You could call him a religious extremist.

Imagine Saul's shock when he had a vision of Jesus. He found this to be strong evidence that Jesus was in fact alive after death, but a supernatural vision was not his only evidence. Saul (later called Paul) did careful research with eyewitnesses. He spent fifteen days interviewing Peter and also James to check his facts a few years after Jesus' death.[471]

Saul / Paul travelled further than any other Christian apostle, writing over half the books in the New Testament along the way. He worked hard, was imprisoned, and five times suffered a flogging of 39 lashes, being "exposed to death again and again". "Three times I was beaten with rods, once I was stoned... in danger in the city, in danger in the country." He not only endured this, but did so happily! Why would he "delight in weaknesses, in insults, in hardships, in persecutions, in difficulties"? He gives the reason—"for Christ's sake".[472]

Clearly, he thought the story of Jesus promised him an infinite amount of bliss in the afterlife, and that it was worth any trouble in this life to offer that hope to other people. He said the sufferings of this life are not worth comparing to the glory that is coming.

4. The disciples

It may seem funny to put them on the list of sceptics, but they didn't really believe Jesus when he told them he would die and be resurrected. He predicted it often[473], yet they didn't get it or didn't take him seriously.[474] To be fair, it was hard to imagine and sad for them to think about. When they saw his empty tomb, their first thought was that someone had stolen the body![475] Then they didn't believe the women who reported having seen both the empty tomb and Jesus himself.[476]

Then just days later they had the bulletproof confidence to stand up in public and tell the story of resurrection even under threat—then take it around the world. What changed them? Evidence. Experience of the risen Jesus.

4. After initially being fearful, multiple eyewitnesses spoke publicly and wrote about his resurrection, even when they faced prison, torture and execution for it.

It's surprising to learn how many of the people who spoke and wrote about Jesus' resurrection were flogged, imprisoned and/or killed for it. The Roman Empire demanded certain duties from its citizens, including taking part in ritual sacrifices to Emperors who viewed themselves as gods. In that context, Christians who said "Jesus is Lord" would look disloyal and even could even seem threatening. The official Roman story was that after Caesar Augustus died, he was raised up to heaven by the gods, including his adoptive father Julius Caesar, who had also become a god. So the story of Jesus resurrecting to his Father in heaven could look like a cheap counterfeit copied from the Caesars, and blaspheming Roman gods. Yet that didn't stop the Christians telling what they knew to be true. They suffered threats, violent abuse by mobs and false accusations ("Christians burned Rome!" "Christians eat human flesh and drink blood!") Yet they kept on like the bravest soldiers. They saw their friends fall one by one and they kept on, giving people hope of a gracious and forgiving God and life after death.

There can be no doubt that they sincerely believed Jesus had risen—otherwise Christianity would never have taken off. Remember the *Cambridge History of Judaism* doesn't say he was resurrected, but it does say his disciples "were absolutely convinced that Jesus had been raised and was Lord" and many "were certain that he had appeared to them".[477]

If they had the slightest doubt that they really saw Jesus alive after his death, then a public flogging would put those doubts top of mind. Iron cuffs cutting off blood supply to your hands and feet would make you want to change your story. If you faced a slow, excruciating death for saying things you knew were not really true, you could very quickly say, "Sorry, I made that up to give people hope and make some money... I take it back"—and you could walk away free. Painless. *Alive.*

What sane person would throw away their life for a story of afterlife if they knew they had made it up?

If they did believe in God, would they think that deceiving people and selling false hopes would please God? Would he welcome religious conmen into heaven if they lied about the most important question of all? Then why throw away a chance at a real afterlife for a made-up story of afterlife? Surely as they faced death, at least one of them would develop some conscience and apologise if they had been lying.

But not one of them did. Not one.

Some might say, "Well, suicide bombers believe they'll have afterlife. That doesn't prove they're right." Yet suicide bombers believe what someone has told them. Jesus' disciples had seen and heard him for themselves and were in a position to know for a fact what had really happened. They believed what they had observed for themselves, and their absolute certainty did not crumble, even under torture.

Summary: key facts about Jesus

1. Jesus was a real person of history, who died by crucifixion.
2. His tomb was found to be empty on Sunday morning. (This is circumstantial evidence.)
3. Many people reported seeing him after his death, including some who previously doubted. (This is direct evidence.)

4. After initial doubt and fearfulness, many eyewitnesses wrote and spoke publicly about seeing him alive after he had died, even when they faced prison, torture and execution for it.

Where does that leave us? In the next chapter, we'll look at some possible conclusions.

Further reading (and search these authors on YouTube):

Josh McDowell and Sean McDowell, *More Than A Carpenter* (Carol Stream: Tyndale House Publishers, 2009)

Gary R. Habermas & Michael R. Licona, *The Case for the Resurrection of Jesus* (Grand Rapids: Kregel, 2004)

Paul Copan and Ronald K. Tacelli, *Jesus' Resurrection: Fact or Figment? A debate between William Lane Craig & Gerd Lüdemann* (Downers Grove: IVP, 2000)

Craig A. Evans and N.T. Wright, *Jesus, the Final Days: What Really Happened* (Westminster John Knox Press, 2012).

N.T. Wright, *The Resurrection of the Son of God* (London: SPCK, 2003)

13

Jesus and Afterlife: conclusions

Evidence for the Historical Resurrection of Jesus, Part II

Presumably what happened to Jesus was what happens to all of us when we die. We decompose. Accounts of Jesus' resurrection and ascension are about as well-documented as Jack and the Beanstalk.

—ATHEIST BIOLOGIST, PROFESSOR RICHARD DAWKINS[478]

A number of different theories, each of which might conceivably be applicable to part of the evidence but which do not themselves cohere into an intelligible pattern, can provide no alternative to the one interpretation which fits the whole.

—CHRISTIAN LAWYER, PROFESSOR J.N.D. ANDERSON[479]

WHAT CONCLUSIONS FIT THE facts about Jesus that we established in the last chapter?

You'll remember these facts were accepted not just by Christians but by most ancient historians and researchers into the story of Jesus:

1. Jesus was a real person of history, who died by crucifixion.
2. His tomb was found to be empty on Sunday morning. (Circumstantial evidence.)
3. Many people reported seeing him just days after his death, including some who previously doubted. (Direct evidence.)

Jesus and Afterlife: conclusions

4. After initial fear, many eyewitnesses wrote and spoke publicly about seeing him alive after he had died, even when they faced prison, torture and execution for it.

Since that first Sunday, people have come up with other theories to reinterpret or deny those facts. Let's look at the main ones that people use (sometimes in combination) to explain away any resurrection:

1. His disciples stole the body while the guards slept, then made up a resurrection story

The Jerusalem leaders came up with this conspiracy theory immediately[480], but it has many problems.

First, the soldiers reported that this happened while they were asleep, but how could they know what happened while they slept?

Second, if the soldiers truly admitted they had fallen asleep on duty, knowing that this was an offence the Romans would punish with death, why would they still be alive? Polybius[481] records that a soldier would be court-martialled and, if found guilty of sleeping, would receive the *fustuarium*, which meant his commander would lightly touch him with a cudgel or club, then all the soldiers would "fall upon him with clubs and stones, and usually kill him". If larger groups deserted their posts, the officers would make them march past and would choose every tenth man to be beaten to death by the other nine, a penalty called *decimation*. So how were the guards of Jesus' tomb telling this story and yet still alive and well?

Third, Matthew records that the guards were bribed.[482]

Fourth, how would Christ's disciples move a two-tonne stone without waking at least one guard? For that matter, would they have the courage to risk facing conflict with professional soldiers? When Jesus was first arrested, the disciples ran away like cowards. "They all forsook him and fled." The Sunday after he was executed, they were cowering behind locked doors "for fear" of the religious leaders.[483]

Fifth, most of Jesus' followers did not understand him when he said he'd resurrect, and doubted it even when trusted friends told them they had seen him. When he visited the disciples for dinner on the first Sunday night, they were afraid and "they still could not believe it because of their joy and amazement". Even after seeing him a number of times, the disciples met him and "worshipped him, but some doubted." And when he was about to leave, some asked him if he was going to be the political Messiah they hoped for, ejecting the Romans and giving Israel political power[484], so clearly they had trouble understanding Jesus' mission even after he had explained it to them so often.

Sixth, why would they tell this lie? How dumb would they have to be to bet their afterlife on a story they knew was fiction because they made it up? Would lying impress the God they believed had written the Ten Commandments, one of which condemns false witness? This story of resurrection completely went against the religion they were raised in, so it would hardly earn them fame or fortune or friends. And even if it did, they'd soon quit when the Roman Empire persecuted them. If this was a lie, surely one of the apostles would have broken under torture and admitted the lie. But none did.

This last point was made powerfully by Chuck Colson, the hard man and "evil genius" working for US President Richard Nixon. When Nixon's staff were found guilty of organising a break-in to bug their political opponents' office in Washington's Watergate building, the scandal brought down Nixon's presidency, and Colson served nine months in prison. As he was waiting to be arrested, a friend gave him a copy of *Mere Christianity* by C.S. Lewis (which you've seen quoted in this book), and he became a Christian. Critics said he was faking it to get a shorter sentence, but he stayed with his faith for the rest of his life. He said that one reason he believed in Jesus's resurrection is that if Christ's apostles were lying, there is no way that all of them could have kept a lie secret for 40 years under torture and prison. The crusty old political hard man wrote, "Watergate embroiled 12 of the most powerful men in the world—and they couldn't keep a lie for three weeks. You're telling me 12 apostles could keep a lie for 40 years? Absolutely impossible."[485]

Seventh, John describes a key piece of evidence. He writes that he entered the tomb on Sunday morning and noticed Jesus' graveclothes were there, neatly folded, and he immediately "believed".[486] He knew for sure that the body hadn't been stolen. Why?

Let's imagine you're one of Jesus' disciples and you've decided to steal his body and tell everyone he resurrected. You've snuck to the tomb in the dark, broken a Roman seal (an illegal action punishable by death) and rolled back a huge stone, which made a lot of noise but didn't wake even one of the armed guards (I know, I know, that's already quite unlikely). You're nervous about all the soldiers outside who could wake up at any minute and fight you. (Again, it's highly unlikely for a dozen discouraged civilians even to attempt that.). You and a few friends quickly grab the body to carry it away. Then imagine another disciple says, "Hey, guys, let's take his graveclothes off!"

What do you say?

"Great idea, Thaddeus, let's take ten minutes to unwrap all that cloth with the 35 kilograms of myrrh gum that stick it to different parts of the body, because carrying a body-shaped lump through the streets at dawn is not suspicious enough—let's carry a naked dead guy! And please take some more time to fold the graveclothes neatly because we don't want to leave a messy crime scene for our friends the Romans."

No. That's ridiculous and John knew it. The folded graveclothes were the cherry on the cake of all the other evidence he had seen for Jesus.

And 2000 years later, my mother told me, "If Jesus folded his graveclothes on the most exciting day of his life, then you're not too busy to make your bed." And now that she's sleeping the big sleep, those folded fabrics that John saw are part of the reason I think I'll see her again.

This theory of a stolen body doesn't explain fact 3, the 500+ people who reported seeing Jesus after his death—touching him, eating with him, talking with him at length. It doesn't explain fact 4, why the eyewitnesses risked persecution and death to spread the story of Jesus. Why would they do that if they knew it was false? It accepts fact 1 (that Jesus died) and tries to explain facts 2 (his tomb was empty), but it fails.

2. People hallucinated visions of him

Gerd Lüdemann, an atheist professor of New Testament, writes, "It may be taken as historically certain that Peter and the disciples had experiences after Jesus' death in which Jesus appeared to them as the risen Christ."[487] However, he claims these were not real-life, historical appearances, but illusions caused by a "shared hallucinatory fantasy".

The major problem with this theory is that, while individuals may hallucinate, and a crowd of people may use drugs and hallucinate on their own trips, there is no documented example of a crowd hallucinating the same thing at the same time, let alone at various times and places, and there is no known psychological explanation for such a phenomenon.[488] And these witnesses saw, heard and touched Jesus—more than 500 of them, both individuals and groups, on the road or in a house, day and night at different times over 40 days, not in one hyped-up group session. The diversity argues very strongly against them all experiencing the same vision.

Crucially, many of those who saw Jesus had been discouraged and depressed, not expecting him to come back. And they had no reason to expect a resurrection in their lifetimes, since Judaism only taught about a general resurrection at the end of time. Further, some of the people who saw him did not believe he was anything special—in fact they had thought he was mad. So why would they all hallucinate something they were not expecting?

One exception is Saul, also called Paul. He did have a vision of Jesus that started his belief in Jesus.[489] However, Paul claims this was a supernatural vision given to him by God, not a psychological hallucination from his own subconscious. A number of people in the Bible claim visions from God, so this is a fairly standard experience for prophets. And Paul later reported other visions where God spoke to him.[490] But crucially, Paul confirmed his vision of Jesus by carefully checking the historical facts with eyewitnesses, especially Peter and James.[491]

This hallucination theory tries to explain fact 3 (people reported sightings) but it doesn't really succeed, and it doesn't even touch facts 2 (his tomb was empty).

3. Myths about Jesus grew over time

Bart Ehrman and others have argued that Jesus was a popular teacher whose enthusiastic supporters added legends to his story over time: e.g. "Ooh, he walked on water!" "Ah, and he healed diseases!" These were not deliberate lies, but well-intentioned exaggerations, embellishments and hyperbole. The story just grew as time passed.[492]

One major problem with this theory is time. Imagine someone tries to tell you that Princess Diana died by assassination in New York. Millions of people remember a tragic car accident in Paris, and the new story wouldn't be accepted at least until that generation had died—if ever.

Myths would take time to over-write history, and yet Peter could stand up in Jerusalem just weeks after Jesus was crucified and tell a crowd of thousands about Jesus' miracles and not be contradicted. He even added "as you yourselves know" (Acts 2:22). Eyewitnesses could have challenged any fictional additions and stated very clearly "what had and what had not happened".[493] If Peter had made up this story, it would be risky in the extreme to tell it in a city where, just weeks before, Jesus was known to have been publicly executed and buried in a known tomb. He would very likely have been contradicted and shamed him for lying if the authorities simply produced Jesus' body for public inspection. They certainly had a motive to do that. But they never did.

And the first Christian was killed right there in Jerusalem for his resurrection faith within a few years, c. AD34. Stephen was falsely accused and, as stones were being hurled at him, he saw Jesus with God in heaven.[494]

The story of resurrection was repeated as the disciples travelled, and was then written down within around twenty years. Paul wrote his first letter to the church in Corinth in around AD53. He reminds them of a creed (or summary of belief) that he has already taught them:

> For what I received I passed on to you as of first importance: that Christ died for our sins according to the scriptures, that he was buried, that he was raised on the third day according to the scriptures, and that he appeared to Peter, and then to the Twelve. After that, he appeared to more than five hundred of the brothers and sisters at the same time, most of whom are still living, though some have fallen asleep. Then he appeared to James, then to all the apostles, and last of all he appeared to me also...[495]

Paul says he has already told them this on a previous visit to their city. He says he received this information from others, and elsewhere describes interviewing eyewitnesses of Jesus, including Peter and James, soon after his own conversion.[496]

And notice that Paul mentions "many witnesses". These were people from Jerusalem, where the events happened. They could have shut down any myths about Jesus by telling what they had seen.

This theory tries to explain facts 1–4 but doesn't succeed.

4. Jesus didn't actually die on the cross. (Swoon theory.)

The Da Vinci Code by Dan Brown dramatized this theory[497], which was popularised by German scholars around 1800. One claimed the physician Luke had drugged Jesus to fake his death. Another version was that members of a secret society dressed in white had heard groaning from the tomb, frightened away the guards, then brought Jesus out and looked after him. Yet another claimed he was in a coma but recovered on his own.[498] Some have argued that crucifixion usually took longer to kill people, and that the authorities handed Jesus' body to his supporters quite quickly, suggesting a fake death.

But could anyone survive a Roman crucifixion? We have only one account of this in all history. Josephus heard three of his friends had been crucified, and tearfully begged General Titus to let them live. As a favour, Titus "immediately commanded them to be taken down, and to have the greatest care taken of them... yet two of them died under the physician's hands, while the third recovered."[499] Those are not great odds—one in three—and it's unlikely that they were flogged and brutalised as Jesus was. We're not even sure they were nailed onto the cross rather than roped, or how long they were on the cross.

And the overwhelming medical evidence we explored last chapter is that Jesus was dead, likely even before the spear thrust to the heart produced blood and water. The Roman soldiers checked very carefully.

But there's another major problem with swoon theory. David Strauss put it well:

> It is impossible that a being who had stolen half dead out of the sepulchre, who crept about weak and ill and wanting medical treatment... could have given the disciples the impression that he was a conqueror over death and the grave, the Prince of Life: an impression that lay at the bottom of their future ministry.[500]

A half-alive human Jesus sneaking out of his grave would not give anyone evidence to believe anything miraculous had happened, or the confidence that he could resurrect anyone who was killed for telling his story. So the various versions of this theory don't explain why the disciples suddenly found such tremendous, long-lasting courage.

It is clear that this theory denies fact 1 (he died) and tries to explain fact 2 (his tomb was empty) but fails. And it doesn't even touch fact 4 (eyewitnesses persisted under threat).

5. Wrong tomb theory

What if Christ's disciples got confused about which tomb he really was buried in?

Jesus and Afterlife: conclusions

This an old theory. Around AD200, the Christian writer Tertullian responds to a claim that the gardener changed the location of Jesus' tomb so that crowds would not step on his lettuces![501]

But it has major problems. The women who saw Jesus die were careful to watch his burial on the Friday, and they returned there on the Sunday morning to anoint his body.[502] And we can safely assume that Joseph of Arimathea, the tomb's owner who brought the body from Pilate, would know his own property.

One variant theory is that Jesus was never buried but was tossed into a common grave.[503] It is true that many crucifixion victims across the Roman Empire were shamed even further by anonymous burial, or left on the cross to be eaten by birds or other wild animals, or allowed to decay up there for maximum public impact.[504] This explains why archaeologists today have so little physical evidence of crucifixion. But in Israel, the Romans almost always respected Jewish burial customs, as noted by historians Josephus and Philo.[505] And there is evidence of victims of crucifixion being given an honoured burial. The Israel Museum in Jerusalem displays the right heel bone of a young man with an 11.5 cm iron nail driven through it. Dated around the time of Jesus, it belonged to Jehohanan son of Hagqol. He suffered Roman crucifixion and had his legs broken, presumably to speed up his death, yet Jehohanan was still buried in his family's ossuary or bonebox. And a dig in a Roman town in Britain has found a young man in a tomb with a nail through his heel. Near the nail is a smaller nail-hole from a previous attempt to nail him to a cross. His skeleton also had six broken ribs and other injuries, suggesting rough treatment. Yet he was buried in a tomb.[506] So victims of crucifixion could still be given a proper burial.

The wrong tomb theory tries to explain Fact 2 (his tomb was empty) but is not convincing, and it does nothing to explain Facts 3 (people reported sightings) and 4 (eyewitnesses persisted under threat).

6. The Lost Tomb of Jesus?

In 1980, demolition workers on an apartment site in the Jerusalem suburb of Talpiot stumbled upon a tomb carved into the rock. It contained burial boxes, also called ossuaries, with names including Yeshua bar Yehoseph (Jesus, son of Joseph), Matya (Matthew), Marya, Mariamenou e Mars (maybe Mary or Miriam) and Yehuda bar Yeshua (Judah, son of Jesus).

Archaeologists dated it somewhere from 515BC to 70AD: they had found about 900 wealthy families' tombs in the area.[507]

If this really was the tomb of Jesus, then he did not die on the cross and was not resurrected—and he left behind a child. A film by *Titanic* director James Cameron and a book claimed this.[508]

However, the vast majority of archaeologists are not convinced, and many have criticised Cameron and the writers for misquoting expert opinion.[509] First, these were very common names in Israel at that time.[510] It would be a bit like finding a tomb in England named for John and Mary Smith and their son Jim. Second, Jesus' family was not from Jerusalem but from Nazareth, up in the North of the country, and 150km was a long way in those days.[511] And third, Jesus' family was unlikely to afford such an expensive tomb.

This theory tries to explain Fact 2 (the empty tomb), but seems to fail. And it does nothing about Facts 3 (people reported sightings) and 4 (witnesses persisted under threat).

7. Delay theory

Gerd Lüdemann and others have claimed that the Jerusalem authorities could have produced Jesus' dead body and showed it to people to disprove the resurrection rumour, but they didn't bother because the disciples didn't claim a resurrection until 50 days later at the Feast of Pentecost.[512]

But that's factually incorrect. Firstly, we've seen that the disciples were reporting an empty tomb and encounters with Jesus long before that, starting on the first Sunday. Second, the chief priests knew on Sunday morning that the tomb was empty, so they made up a cover story. And third, the authorities were worried that Jesus' disciples might pull off a deception, which is why they posted a guard at least by Saturday morning. These reports had been circulating for 50 days by the time Peter stood up to speak on the day of Pentecost, and had laid the foundations for the thousands of people who expressed their faith in Jesus' resurrection that day.[513]

This theory tries to give a non-supernatural explanation for Fact 2 (the empty tomb), but it fails. And it doesn't touch Facts 3 (people reported sightings) and 4 (eyewitnesses persisted under persecution).

8. A Spirit person appeared

Some writers claim Jesus appeared in a spirit form after his death, not as a body.[514]

This view would at least fit with belief in God and some kind of afterlife. But we can do better, because Jesus made it crystal clear he had a body. Luke records that when Jesus first appeared to his disciples on the Sunday night of his resurrection, they were terrified and thought they were seeing a ghost. Jesus showed them his wounded hands and feet, and asked them to touch him: "Handle me and see, for a spirit does not have flesh and bones as you see I have." Then they were so ecsatic that "they still did not believe for joy, and marvelled". (Can you blame them?) So Jesus took a piece of fish and ate it in front of them.[515] This made it very clear to the disciples, and the Christian preacher and apostle Peter later said that King David was dead and buried, but Jesus was not and "we are witnesses".[516]

This theory accepts fact 1 (he died) and could explain fact 2 (the empty tomb) but it doesn't explain the kind of sightings reported in fact 3 and is unlikely to explain fact 4 (witnesses persisted under threat)—would ghost stories really send eyewitnesses to the ends of the earth with confidence in the certainty of bodily resurrection?

Bottom line:

We are left with four facts, which are agreed by the vast majority of experts, both Christian and non-Christian. If none of these rival theories can handle these facts, then we are back to what the eyewitnesses themselves said: their friend and teacher was dead on Friday and alive on Sunday.

What if Jesus's resurrection is a fact of history? What would that mean?[517]

1. There is a God.
2. Death is not the end.
   "Move him into the sun", says Wilfred Owen in a tragic poem about a young soldier lying dead in the snow. The "kind old sun" used to wake him at home, and it brings life to this cold planet—but why did it bother, the poet cries, when death devastates everything? The poem is called "Futility".

But if Jesus resurrected, then death doesn't ruin everything. Life and joy have the last laugh. So Paul the apostle can laugh and jeer at death:

O death, where is your sting?
O grave, where is your victory?[518]

And the Christian poet John Donne can make fun of death, writing in 1609:

> Death be not proud, though some have called thee
> Mighty and dreadfull, for, thou art not soe,
> For, those, whom thou think'st, thou dost overthrow,
> Die not, poore death, nor yet canst thou kill mee. . .
> One short sleepe past, wee wake eternally
> And death shall be no more, death, thou shalt die.[519]

3. There is a real afterlife.
   Jesus told the thief on the next cross that he would be with him "in paradise"[520], and the Bible often describes a place with no death or tears or pain, no emotional baggage, relationships of understanding and kindness, where we can plant vineyards and build houses and be stimulated by fascinating projects, where people from every nation can feast and make music together in peace, where there is no animal suffering, where we can "be glad and rejoice forever", with our greatest happiness coming from knowing the most loveable, fascinating person ever—God.[521]

   I've found that knowing this fills the God-shaped gap.

4. God loves us humans and wants our company in an afterlife of eternal bliss, which is why Jesus died.
   Our failures, selfish mistakes and shameful actions can be forgiven by God, and they don't have to define us any more. Paul writes that Jesus was "handed over to die because of our sins, and he was raised to life to make us right with God."[522]

   At this general resurrection, there is justice and righting of wrongs.

5. We can live in this life with bullet-proof hope. This can help us bounce back from whatever hurtful nonsense might happen to us in this life.

6. Jesus' teachings—love your enemy, turn the other cheek, go the second mile, etc—are confirmed by his resurrection. Could God have given any greater seal of approval than raising Jesus from the dead?
7. We can have a cause greater than ourselves—loving people, and helping others find faith and an eternity of bliss.

A word about belief

Aristotle's *Rhetoric*, written around 330BC, says persuasion happens for three reasons:

1. Logos—the logic of the argument, analysed by the hearer's reasoning
2. Pathos—the emotions and psychology of the hearer
3. Ethos—the trustworthiness of the speaker, which includes *phronesis* (wisdom or practical intelligence), *arete* (excellence and moral virtue) and *eunoia* (goodwill and kindness). (He would later talk about style and delivery, but that is more on the surface.)

Aristotle said a good case should contain a balance of all, rather than emphasising emotion and leaving out key facts or logic. So why do I believe in resurrection?

1. Logos. I'm convinced by the logic of the case for it.
2. Pathos. I find it very emotionally satisfying.
3. Ethos. I trust what I know of the eyewitnesses.

Of course, some argue that emotion is the only reason to believe it. Professor Stephen Hawking once said, "Religion is a fairy tale for those who are afraid of the dark." But I don't want fairy stories—why fool yourself, and bet your eternity on fluffy stories and pixie dust? But just because faith is emotionally satisfying doesn't mean it's untrue—as long as it has logos and ethos. Many people find it satisfying—and find atheism denies all our human intuitions that we matter, that we are loved, that we have a future, that our choices matter. That's an intuitive argument in favour of faith. I like Professor John Lennox's cheeky reply to Hawking, "Atheism is a fairy tale for people who are afraid of the light."

Summary

1. Various theories have purported to explain the facts about Jesus: theft theory, hallucination theory, myth theory, swoon theory, wrong tomb theory, lost tomb theory, delay theory and spirit person theory.
2. Each one of these theories has major problems.
3. The one explanation that fits all the facts is that Jesus was dead on Friday and alive on Sunday.
4. This has huge implications: There is a God. Death is not the end for us. There is a heaven. And all this gives hope and purpose to life.

14

Ruby

A Curious Conclusion

THE CROWD OUTSIDE THE school was screaming and throwing things.

Dr Robert Coles was drawn to the noise, and asked one of the protestors what it was all about. She replied, "She's coming out in half an hour."[523]

"Who?"

Coles heard racial slurs but no name. Then at 2:30, a little black girl walked out of the school, surrounded by four burly Federal police. The mob went feral, shouting abuse, shaking their fists and threatening to kill her. She walked through the melee and got into a car.

Fearing the crowd might turn violent, Coles left too. It was 1960 in New Orleans, America's Deep South, two years before Martin Luther King said he had a dream. The US Supreme Court had ordered that schools must be de-segregated so that all races went to school together. White parents reacted by pulling all their children out of the school, and white teachers refused to teach—except for one, who was from Boston.

Coles was a Harvard-trained child psychiatrist. They called him the Crayon Man because he got children drawing pictures to help him understand their inner lives. A childish drawing of him would appear on the cover of TIME magazine, which called him "the most influential living psychiatrist in the U.S." He would win a Pulitzer Prize for his book series *Children of Crisis*, and a MacArthur Award or "Genius Grant".

But his own inner life was shaky. After confused teenage years, he had struggled through psychiatry and had issues with the work. He was in therapy himself.

He volunteered to support the little girl and her family, thinking this might be an interesting study on children and stress.

The girl's name was Ruby Bridges. Her father Abon was a janitor. Her mother Lucille tucked their five children into bed each night and went out to clean houses, getting down on her knees to scrub floors and coming home well after midnight for some sleep.

Coles introduced himself as a doctor, but the family had never been able to afford a doctor, even at Ruby's birth. No white person had ever been in their home.

Coles asked, "How are you doing, Ruby?"

Ruby replied, "I'm OK."

Coles couldn't believe that a child who was walking through a vicious mob twice a day could be OK. One woman in the crowd every day threatened to poison her. Another waved a coffin with a black doll in it. Coles asked her mother how she really was. She said, "Ruby's doing fine." Eating well? Fine. Sleeping well? Fine. Playing happily after school? Fine. "Ruby doesn't seem too upset."

Coles wondered if Ruby's parents really understood the symptoms. Surely she must be more upset than they realised.

Struggling for answers, Coles spoke to her teacher. Ruby sat alone each day, the only student in her class. The teacher said, "You know, I don't understand this child. She seems so happy. She comes here so cheerfully."

A Federal marshal said, "She didn't whimper. She just marched along like a little soldier, and we're all very, very proud of her."

Still Coles struggled to make sense of a six-year-old girl from a poor, culturally disadvantaged family under terrific stress but not complaining. He compared that to his well-heeled Boston patients, who complained about many things.

"Now how do you explain that?", Coles wrote. "I was accumulating all this information, but I was getting rather frustrated."

One day, Ruby's teacher told Coles she had seen Ruby talking to the people on the street. Ruby told him, "I wasn't talking to them. I was just saying a prayer for them."

"Ruby, you pray for the people here?"

"Oh, yes."

"Really?"

"Yes."

"Why do you do that?"

"Because they need praying for."
"Do they?"
"Oh, yes."
"Ruby, why do you think they need you to pray for them?"
"Because I should."

Ruby's mother came into the room and explained that she and her husband told Ruby it was important to pray for the people. At her Baptist church, the minister prayed for them up front every week.

Ruby also prayed for herself, for strength to overcome fear.

Later, Coles told the parents he thought it was a bit much to ask Ruby to pray for these people, given what she was going through. Mrs Bridges replied that this was not to hurt Ruby but because it was the right thing to do. She said, "Don't you think they need praying for?"

That was a hard question for Coles. He had been raised by a Christian mother and an agnostic Jewish father, a scientist. He would sit in church with his mother while his father sat in the car outside reading the paper. The parents frankly discussed their views in front of the children, and Coles could understand both. He answered Mrs Bridges' question politely, "Yes, but I still think it's a bit much to ask Ruby to pray for them."

Selfless care for enemies was right at the top of his textbook tables of moral development, so how was it possible for a culturally disadvantaged child to know about it, let alone do it?

Coles discussed this with his wife Jane, and imagined what he would do if a mob was screaming racist violence against him as he walked into the Harvard Club. He certainly wouldn't pray for them! He would call the police—but he realised the local police were on the side of the mob, which was why Federal police had been sent to protect Ruby. He would call his lawyer—but Ruby couldn't afford one. Coles would turn on the mob with clever words, calling them psychologically sick and culturally backwards—but Ruby didn't know those words. Coles would write a book to shame them—but Ruby was just learning to write and her parents couldn't even sign their own names.

Ruby's family were made to pay a price. Abon lost his job. The grocery shop refused to serve Lucille. Ruby's grandparents were thrown off a farm where they had share-cropped for 25 years.[524] Other people—some black, some white—supported the family, but Coles wondered how on earth they were coping.

Later, Ruby told Coles she had heard in church that Jesus went through a lot of trouble, and that he prayed for the trouble-makers, "Father, forgive them, because they don't know what they're doing."

Coles thought, "How is someone like me supposed to account for that, psychologically or any other way?"

Should he label her a masochist who enjoyed suffering? Try to grade her moral development on some scale? Conclude that these uneducated people didn't really know what they were saying, because they hadn't learned from some philosopher-theologian saying what Christ really meant? But Coles, with his Jewish heritage, knew all too well that one of the most educated cultures in history had recently been deceived into committing atrocities. Lawyers, doctors, journalists, professors, ministers, theologians—even psychiatrists like him—had worked for Hitler.

Because Ruby mentioned church so often, Coles went to church to observe and research. He sat with the poorest of the poor, analysing hard, on the lookout for the emotional manipulation he expected. Yet each time he went, he saw worn-out people encouraged, pain lessened, hatred softened. Something was happening here that his textbooks could not describe. These people believed Jesus had suffered poverty, harassment and humiliation just like their own, and was "acquainted with grief".

Coles wrote articles about Ruby[525] and other poor children, trying to describe the curiosity, the love, the hope, the spiritual openness he saw in them. They naturally asked the big, deep questions that religion asks: about meaning, truth, what matters, what our purpose is.

Coles spent two decades listening to the psychological, moral and political lives of children around the world, and writing a million words on the topic. His academic colleagues commended his research, but politely ignored any mention of religion. Later, his friend Anna Freud suggested he look back and see if he had missed anything. He was surprised to find his notes had so many spiritual and religious comments from children, which he had cut out of his writing, aiming for academic respectability. His next book was *The Spiritual Lives of Children*. He said, "The spirit of religion I think is what children connect with—the questions, the enquiry, the enormous curiosity about this universe, and the hope that somehow those answers will come about."[526]

Children's curiosity is valued in the Jewish tradition. In the Passover meal, which remembers the Jewish people being freed from slavery, children are encouraged to ask "Why?" questions.[527] Perhaps this open curiosity is part of what Jesus meant by saying, "Unless you become as little children, you will not enter the kingdom of Heaven."[528]

I aspire to a faith that values critical thinking and research, as well as childlike openness and curiosity. That way of thinking lets you enjoy huge mysteries in humble awe and wonder. That faith is the most valuable thing I have, making my life so much more satisfying than it was before.

I hope this book has encouraged you to look into it for yourself.

Endnotes

1. Baggini, "Yes, life without God can be bleak. Atheism is about facing up to that." *The Guardian*, 9 March 2012.
2. Kim Langley, "What Australians Believe About God", *The Good Weekend* (n.d.) 25–32.
3. Phillip Adams, *Adams versus God* (Nelson, 1985) 156–57.
4. Terry Lane, *As The Twig Is Bent: The Childhood Recollections of Sixteen Prominent Australians* (Melbourne: Dove, 1979) 110–13.
5. Luis Buñuel, *My Last Breath* (London: Vintage, 2003) 104.
6. Buñuel, *Last Breath* 170–74.
7. Buñuel, *Last Breath* 15, 29.
8. Buñuel, *Last Breath* 174.
9. Buñuel, *Last Breath* 252.
10. Buñuel, *Last Breath* 255–56.
11. Alain de Botton, *The Consolations of* Philosophy (London: Vintage, 2001) 242.
12. Friedrich Nietzsche, *The Gay Science* (New York: Kaufman, 1974; original 1882) 181–82.
13. Leon Trotsky, *Literature and Revolution* (1924) chapter 8, at Marxists.org.
14. Albert Camus, *The Myth of Sisyphus* (1942). Martin Heidegger, *Being and Time* (1927). Jean-Paul Sartre, *Existentialism* (1946). Friedrich Nietzsche, *Thus Spoke Zarathustra: A Book for All and None* (1883–1885).
15. Howard Mumma, *Albert Camus and the Minister* (Orleans: Paraclete Press, 2001).
16. Bertrand Russell, *Why I Am Not A Christian* (New York: Simon & Schuster, 1957) 107.
17. Paul Johnson, *Intellectuals* (New York: Harper Perennial, 2007).
18. Bertrand Russell, *The Autobiography of Bertrand Russell* (New York: Routledge, 2000) 194.
19. Richard Wurmbrand, *Tortured for Christ* (London: Hodder & Stoughton, 1967) 34.
20. David ben Jesse, c.960 BC, Psalm 16:11.

21. See Stewart Goetz, "The Argument from the Meaning of Life", in Colin Ruloff and Peter Horban, *Contemporary Arguments in Natural Theology: God and Rational Belief* (London: Bloomsbury, 2021).
22. Daniel C. Dennett, *Breaking the Spell: Religion as a Natural Phenomenon* (London: Penguin, 2007) 244.
23. In Henry Margenau and Roy Abraham Varghese (eds) *Cosmos, Bios, Theos: Scientists Reflect on Science, God, and the Origins of the Universe, Life, and Homo Sapiens* (Open Court, 1992) 83.
24. See William Lane Craig, *Reasonable Faith: Christian Truth and Apologetics*, 3rd ed (Wheaton: Crossway, 2008); "The Existence of God, 1" in J.P. Moreland and William Lane Craig, *Philosophical Foundations for a Christian Worldview* (Downers Grove: IVP, 2003) 464–81; *The Kalām Cosmological Argument* (London: Macmillan, 1979); *The Cosmological Argument from Plato to Leibniz* (London: Macmillan, 1980); J.P. Moreland, *The God Question* (Harvest House, 2009); *Scaling the Secular City* (Grand Rapids: Baker, 1997); W. David Beck, "The Cosmological Argument: A Current Bibliographical Appraisal", *Philosophia Christi* 2 (2000) 283–304. Stephen T. Davis, *God, Reason and Theistic Proofs* (Edinburgh University Press, 1997); R. Douglas Geivett, "The Kalam Cosmological Argument", in Francis J. Beckwith, William Lane Craig and J.P. Moreland (eds) *To Everyone an Answer: A Case for the Christian Worldview* (Downers Grove: IVP, 2004) 61–76.
25. Elizabeth Howell, "How Fast is Earth Moving?", www.space.com/33527-how-fast-is-earth-moving.html
26. *Summa contra Gentiles* 1.13.30.
27. W. David Beck, "God's Existence", in R. Douglas Geivett and Gary R. Habermas, *In Defence of Miracles: A Comprehensive Case for God's Action in History* (Leicester: Apollos, 1997) 151.
28. c.f. Stephen Hawking, *A Brief History of Time* (London: Bantam, 1988)
29. Beverley Clack and Brian R. Clack, *The Philosophy of Religion: A Critical Introduction* (Polity, 2008) 25.
30. Peter Atkins, *Creation Revisited* (Harmondsworth: Penguin, 1994) 143.
31. Dennett, *Breaking the Spell*, 244.
32. "I Am The Walrus", from *Magical Mystery Tour* (London: Parlophone, 1967).
33. Dennett, *Breaking the Spell*, 242.
34. See Peter S. Williams, "Cosmological Arguments I" and "II", in *A Faithful Guide to Philosophy* (Milton Keynes: Paternoster, 2013) 69–107.
35. Richard Taylor, *Metaphysics* (Englewood Cliffs: Prentice Hall, 1983) 91.
36. Dean Rickles, "Why There Is Something Rather Than Nothing" www.closertotruth.com
37. David Hume, *Dialogues Concerning Natural Religion*, IX.
38. After Peter S. Williams, *Faithful Guide to Philosophy*, 71, 75.
39. John Leslie, "The Prerequisites of Life in Our Universe", in G.V. Coyne (ed), *Newton and the New Direction in Science* (Vatican City: Speculo Vaticana, 1988) 97–119: 97. This is similar to the "Proof of the Truthful" argument of the Muslim philosopher Ibn Sina, 980–1037, which influenced Thomas Aquinas and the Jewish philosopher Maimonides.

Endnotes

40. Arthur Schopenhauer, *On the Fourfold Root of the Principle of Sufficient Reason* (La Salle: Open Court, 1974; original 1813) 14–15.
41. Thomas Aquinas, *Summa Theologiae*, 1a 2,3.
42. Keith M. Parsons, "Naturalistic Rejoinders to Theistic Arguments", in Brian Davies, *An Introduction to the Philosophy of Religion* (Oxford University Press, 2004) 433.
43. J.L. Mackie, "Cosmological Arguments", in *The Miracle of Theism: Arguments For and Against the Existence of God* (Oxford University Press, 1982).
44. J.C.A. Gaskin, *The Quest for Eternity* (Hammondsworth: Penguin, 1984):66.
45. Craig, *The Kalām Cosmological Argument* (London: Macmillan, 1979): 149.
46. John Barrow and Frank Tipler, *The Anthropic Cosmological Principle* (Oxford: Clarendon, 1986): 442.
47. John Maddox, "Down with the Big Bang", *Nature* 340 (1989): 425.
48. Stephen Hawking, *A Brief History of Time: From the Big Bang to Black Holes* (London: Bantam, 1988) 46
49. Stephen Hawking and Roger Penrose, *The Nature of Space and Time: The Isaac Newton Institute Series of Lectures* (Princeton University Press, 1996): 20.
50. Paul Davies, *Goldilocks Enigma*: 80.
51. Joshua Rasmussen, "The Argument from Contingency", in Ruloff and Horban.
52. Brian Davies, *Philosophy of Religion*, 54.
53. John Noble Wilford, "Sizing Up The Cosmos: An Astronomer's Quest", *The New York Times* 12 March 1991, p.B9.
54. Keith M. Parsons, "Naturalistic Rejoinders to Theistic Arguments", in Davies, *Philosophy of Religion*, 433.
55. Richard Swinburne, *The Existence of God* 2nd edn (Oxford: Clarendon, 2004) 434.
56. Parsons, "Rejoinders", 434.
57. Robert John Russell, "Cosmology: Evidence for God or Partner for Theology?", in John Marks Templeton (ed),*Evidence of Purpose*, (New York: Continuum, 1994).
58. Peter Harrison and Jon H. Roberts, *Science without God? rethinking the history of scientific naturalism.* (Oxford University Press, 2019).
59. Albert Einstein, *Letters to Solovine* (New York: Philosophical Library, 1987) 131.
60. Lawrence Krauss, *A Universe from Nothing: Why There Is Something Rather than Nothing* (New York: Free Press, 2012) xiii, 183, 105, 150, 19, 183, 185.
61. Richard Dawkins, "Afterword", in Krauss, *Universe from Nothing*, 191.
62. John Horgan, "Is Lawrence Krauss a Physicist, or Just a Bad Philosopher?", scientificamerican.com November 20, 2015; Jerry Coyne, "David Albert pans Lawrence Krauss's new book" whyevolutionistrue.com April 2, 2012.
63. Steve Paulson et al, "The origins of the universe: why is there something rather than nothing?", *Annals of the New York Academy of Sciences* 1361 (2015) 1–17:7.
64. David Z. Albert, "On The Origin of Everything", *The New York Times*, 25 Mar 2012.
65. Ross Anderson, "Has Physics Made Philosophy and Religion Obsolete", *The Atlantic,* April 2012.
66. Anderson, "Obsolete?"
67. Albert, "Origin of Everything"

68. in Horgan, "Bad Philosopher?"
69. Sean M. Carroll, "A Universe from Nothing?", *Discover Magazine*, April 29, 2012. See also Alan Guth, *The Inflationary Universe: The Quest for a New Theory of Cosmic Origins* (Reading: Perseus, 1997) 276.
70. Keith Ward, *Why There Almost Certainly Is a God: Doubting Dawkins* (Oxford: Lion, 2008) 51.
71. Daniel C. Dennett, *Breaking the Spell*, 242; Richard Dawkins, *The God Delusion* (London: Bantam, 2006): 77; Sam Harris, *Letter to a Christian Nation* (Transworld Digital, 2009): 72–73.
72. Andrew Ter Ern Loke, "The Kalam Cosmological Argument", in Ruloff and Horban.
73. Paul Davies, "The Birth of the Cosmos", in Jill Gready, *God, Cosmos, Nature and Creativity* (Edinburgh: Scottish Academic Press, 1995) 8–9.
74. Krauss, *Universe From Nothing* 106, 183, 105, 119.
75. Gerald Holton, *Victory and Vexation in Science: Einstein, Bohr, Heisenberg and Others* (London: Harvard University Press, 2005) 32; Abraham Pais, "Einstein and the quantum theory", *Review of Modern Physics* vol 51 no 4, Oct 1979, 910
76. Werner Heisenberg, "Tradition in Science", *Bulletin of Atomic Scientists* 29 (10) 1973: 4.
77. In Henry Margenau and Roy Abraham Varghese (eds) *Cosmos, Bios, Theos: Scientists Reflect on Science, God, and the Origins of the Universe, Life, and Homo Sapiens* (Open Court, 1999) 83.
78. A Scientist Caught Between Two Worlds: Interview With Robert Jastrow", *Christianity Today*, August 6, 1982. Robert Jastrow, *God and the Astronomers* (2nd ed) (New York: Norton, 1992).
79. From an interview with Ken Campbell on the 1995 show Reality on the Rocks: Beyond Our Ken.
80. "The Dawkins Confusion: Naturalism *ad absurdum*", *Christianity Today*, March/April 2007.
81. Erin Blakemore, "Buzz Aldrin Took Holy Communion on the Moon. NASA Kept It Quiet", Sep 6, 2019; Jesse Greenspan, "Remembering the Apollo 8 Christmas Eve Broadcast", Dec 17, 2018; history.com.
82. Transcript at Cosmonaut.ru. Paul Froese, "Forced Secularization in Soviet Russia: Why an Atheistic Monopoly Failed", *Journal for the Scientific Study of Religion* 43/1 (Mar 2004): 35–50. "Gagarin's family celebrated Easter and Christmas, Korolev used to pray and confess". Interfax-religion.com 11 April 2011.
83. See Peter D. Ward and Donald Brownlee, *Rare Earth: Why Complex Life Is Uncommon in the Universe* (New York: Copernicus Books, 2000); Guillermo Gonzalez and Jay W. Richards, *The Privileged Planet: How Our Place in the Cosmos is Designed for Discovery* (Washington: Regnery Publishing, 2004).
84. Ross, 'Fine Tuning', number 38.
85. Tamara Goldin, "Astronauts overexposed", *Nature Geoscience* Vol 7, Dec 2014, 858. M. Lockwood and M. Hapgood, "The rough guide to the Moon and Mars." *Astronomy and Geophysics*, 48 (6) (2007) 6.11- 6.17.
86. John C. Lennox, *God's Undertaker: Has Science Buried God* (Oxford: Lion, 2009) 72.

87. Ross, 'Fine Tuning', numbers 1, 16.
88. Stephen Hawking and Leonard Mlodinow, *The Grand Design: New Answers to the Ultimate Questions of Life* (London: Bantam Press, 2010) 152–53.
89. Michael Allen, "What's the maximum gravity we could survive?", *Astronomy.com*, September 20, 2018. https://astronomy.com/news/2018/09/gravity-to-the-max
90. Kevin Fong, *Extreme Medicine: How Exploration Transformed Medicine in the Twentieth Century* (London: Penguin, 2014).
91. NASA, "Exercise Physiology and Countermeasures Project (ExPC): Keeping Astronauts Healthy in Reduced Gravity".
92. J.M. Acres et al, "The influence of spaceflight and simulated microgravity on bacterial motility and chemotaxis", *Nature Partner Journals Microgravity* (2021) 7:7:1–11. Ed Yong, "Space: Medicine's Final Frontier", *Wired* 5/11:118–27.
93. Kevin Fong, "The Strange, Deadly Effects Mars Would Have on Your Body", *Wired*, Feb 2014.
94. Hawking and Mlodinow, *Grand Design*, 160.
95. Paul Davies, *The Goldilocks Enigma: Why is the Universe Just Right for Life?* (London: Penguin, 2007) 163.
96. Martin Rees, *Just Six Numbers: The Deep Forces that Shape the Universe* (New York: Basic Books, 2001) 4.
97. Stephen Hawking, *A Brief History of Time*, (London: Bantam, 1988) 125.
98. See John Leslie, "The Prerequisites of Life in Our Universe", in G.V. Coyne (ed), *Newton and the New Direction in Science* (Vatican City: Speculo Vaticana, 1988) 97–119.
99. See also John D. Barrow and Frank J. Tipler, *The Anthropic Cosmological Principle* (Oxford University Press, 1986): 166.
100. Hugh Ross, *Why The Universe Is The Way It Is* (Grand Rapids: Baker, 2008); and RTB Design Compendium, https://reasons.org/
101. Jim Holt, in Steve Paulson et al, "The origins of the universe: why is there something rather than nothing?", *Annals of the New York Academy of Sciences* 1361 (2015) 1–17:7, 6
102. See Joshua Rasmussen, "Foundation of Reason", in *How Reason Can Lead to God: A Philosopher's Bridge to Faith* (Downers Grove: Downers Grove: IVP Academic, 2019).
103. Keith Ward, *God, Chance and Necessity* (Oxford: One World Publications, 1996). Further see William Lane Craig, "God and the 'unreasonable effectiveness of mathematics'", www.reasonablefaith.org.
104. Quoted in Keith Devlin, "Do Mathematicians Have Different Brains?" in *The Math Gene: How Mathematical Thinking Evolved And Why Numbers Are Like Gossip* (Basic Books, 2000): 140.
105. Nathalie Sinclair and William Higginson (eds.) *Mathematics and the Aesthetic: New Approaches to an Ancient Affinity* (Springer, 2006): 36.
106. Carola Baumgardt and Jamie Callan, *Johannes Kepler: Life and Letters* (1953) 50
107. See Davies, *Goldilocks*, last chapter. Also Robert J. Spitzer, *New Proofs for the*

Existence of God: Contributions of Contemporary Physics and Philosophy (Grand Rapids: Eerdmans, 2010).

108. In his BBC debate with Frederick C. Copleston, S.J., on the existence of God.
109. Thomas Fink, "A singular mind: Roger Penrose on his Nobel Prize", *The Spectator*, 19 Dec 2020.
110. Interview for the film *A Brief History of Time*, 1991.
111. Hawking and Mlodinow, *Grand Design*, 135.
112. Aka selection bias and observer bias. See Brandon Carter, "Large Number Coincidences and the Anthropic Principle in Cosmology", *IAU Symposium 63* (Dordrecht: Reidel, 1974) 291–98. Nick Bostrom, *Anthropic Bias: Observation Selection Effects in Science and Philosophy* (New York: Routledge, 2002); "Was the Universe Made for Us?" www.anthropic-principle.com
113. Krauss, *Universe from Nothing*, 125.
114. John Leslie, *Universes* (London: Routledge, 1989) 13–15.
115. Krauss, *Universe From Nothing*, 122, but c.f. 136.
116. c.f. Krauss, *Universe From Nothing*, 176.
117. Robin Collins, "Design and the Many-Worlds Hypothesis", in William Lane Craig, *Philosophy of Religion: A Reader's Guide* (Rutgers University Press, 2002) 130–48. Paul Fitzgerald, 'An Interview with John Polkinghorne'. John Polkinghorne, "A Potent Universe", in John Marks Templeton (ed),*Evidence of Purpose: Scientists Discover the Creator* (New York: Continuum, 1996).
118. Fred Hoyle, "The Universe: Past and Present Reflections", *Engineering and Science* November 1981. See also M. Livio et al, "The anthropic significance of the existence of an excited state of 12C", *Nature* 340 (6231):281–84.
119. Quoted in John D. Barrow, *The Constants of Nature* (London: Vintage, 2003) 157.
120. Freeman Dyson, "Energy in the Universe", *Scientific American* 224, 1971, p.50.
121. e.g. Richard Carrier, "Neither Life Nor the Universe Seems Intelligently Designed", in John W. Loftus (ed),*The End of Christianity* (Amherst: Prometheus, 2011).
122. Isaac Newton, *Newton's Principia: The Mathematical Principles of Natural Philosophy*. Translated A. Motte. (New York: Daniel Adee, 1846) 501.
123. Alex Rosenberg, *The Atheist's Guide to Reality: Enjoying Life without Illusions* (London: Norton, 2011), 193.
124. Arie Bos, *Thinking Outside the Brain Box: Why Humans Are Not Biological Computers* (Edinburgh: Floris Books, 2018) 232.
125. Galen Strawson, "The Consciousness Deniers", *New York Review of Books*, 13 Mar 2018.
126. Brian Greene, *Until the End of Time: Mind, Matter, and Our Search for Meaning in an Evolving Universe* (London: Penguin, 2021).
127. For this view see Daniel Dennett, *Consciousness Explained* (Little, Brown & Co 1991); Stephen Pinker, *The Blank Slate: The Modern Denial of Human Nature* (Penguin Putman, 2002); *How the Mind Works* (New York: Norton & Co, 1997).
128. Paul Churchland, *Matter and Consciousness* (Cambridge: MIT Press, 1984) 21.
129. C.E.M. Joad, *Guide To Philosophy* (London: Victor Gollancz, 1946) 496.

Endnotes

130. Paul Kurtz, *The New Skepticism: Inquiry and Reliable Knowledge* (Prometheus Books, 1992)
131. Sarah DeWeerdt, "How to map the brain", *Nature* 571, S6-S8 (2019).
132. Thomas Nagel, *Mind and Cosmos: Why the Materialist Neo-Darwinian Conception of Nature is Almost Certainly False* (Oxford University Press, 2012).
133. Matthew D. Lieberman, "Free Will: Weighing Truth and Experience: Do Our Beliefs Matter?" *Psychology Today*, 22 March 2012. See also Geoffrey Madell, *Mind and Materialism* (Edinburgh University Press, 1988) 141.
134. Jerry Fodor, "The Big Idea: Can There Be a Science of Mind?" *Times Literary Supplement* 3 July 1992, 5.
135. "Philosophy Isn't Dead Yet", *The Guardian*, 27 May 2013.
136. Is Science Killing the Soul?" www.edge.org/documents/archiev/edge53.html
137. Nagel, *Mind and Cosmos*, 16.
138. quoted in Bos 144. See also Dick Swaab, *We Are Our Brains: From the Womb to Alzheimer's*. (London: Allan Lane, 2014).
139. Bert Keizer, *Anyone In There? The Fascinating Domain of Neurosurgery* (Amsterdam: Balans, 2010) translation by Liz Waters, Nederlands Letterenfonds, 12.
140. Colin McGinn, *The Mysterious Flame: conscious minds in a material world* (New York: Basic Books, 1999) 13-15; "Consciousness and cosmology: hyperdualism ventilated." in M. Davies & G.W. Humphreys (eds) *Consciousness*. (Oxford: Blackwell, 1993) 160.
141. David J. Chalmers, *The Character of Consciousness* (Oxford University Press, 2010) xiv.
142. Rosenberg, *Atheist's Guide to Reality*, 172.
143. Rosenberg, *Atheist's Guide to Reality*, 193.
144. Rosenberg, *Atheist's Guide to Reality*, 194.
145. Rosenberg, *Atheist's Guide* to Reality, 2.
146. Rosenberg, *Atheist's Guide to Reality*, 223.
147. Daniel C. Dennett, *Consciousness Explained* (Little, Brown & Co, 1991).
148. Daniel C. Dennett, *Freedom Evolves* (London: Penguin, 2003).
149. Saul Bellow, *Humboldt's Gift* (London: Penguin, 1973).
150. From Bos, *Brain Box*, 215.
151. Alexander Rosenberg, *How History Gets Things Wrong: The Neuroscience of Our Addiction to Stories* (Cambridge: MIT Press, 2018) 206, 231, 160.
152. *Atheist's Guide to Reality*, 16.
153. Sam Harris, *Free Will* (New York: Free Press, 2012).
154. Distinguished Science Lectures Series, 25 March 2012 www.youtube.com/watch?v=pCofmZlC72g
155. Annaka Harris, *Conscious: A Brief Guide to the Fundamental Mystery of the Mind* (New York: Harper Collins, 2019) 34-35.
156. Richard Dawkins, "Let's all stop beating Basil's car", www.edge.org/response-detail/11416
157. Harris, *Free Will*, 45.

158. Harris, *Free Will,* 1–3, 18, 37, emphasis mine.
159. Matthew D. Lieberman, "Free Will: Weighing Truth and Experience: Do Our Beliefs Matter?" *Psychology Today,* 22 March 2012.
160. E.g. Patricia Churchland, *Neurophilosophy: Toward a Unified Science of the Mind/Brain* (Cambridge, MA: MIT Press, 1986); Paul Churchland, *A Neurocomputational Perspective: The Nature of Mind and the Structure of Science* (Cambridge, MA: MIT Press, 1989); Stephen P. Stich, *Deconstructing the Mind* (Oxford University Press, 1996). Also B.F. Skinner, Richard Rorty and Georges Rey https://plato.stanford.edu/entries/materialism-eliminative/
161. Iain McGilchrist, *The Master and His Emissary: The Divided Brain and the Making of the Western World* (Yale University Press, 2009).
162. *The Mysterious Flame: Conscious Minds in a Material World* (New York: Basic Books, 1999).
163. John R. Searle, *The Mystery of Consciousness* (New York Review of Books, 2006). Also William Hasker, *The Emergent Self* (Cornell University Press, 2014). Atheists like Susan Greenfield and Roger Penrose and Christians like Nancey Murphy, Peter van Inwagen, Malcolm Jeeves and John Polkinghorne suggest consciousness is an emergent property of matter.
164. Colin McGinn, "Can we solve the mind-body problem?" *Mind* 98 (391) 1989, 349–66. Uriah Kriegel, "The new mysterianism and the thesis of cognitive closure." *Acta Analytica* 18, 177–91 (2003). Erhan Demircioglun, "Human Cognitive Closure and Mysterianism: Reply to Kriegel", *Acta Analytica* (Mar 2017): 125–32.
165. Williams, *Faithful Guide to Philosophy,* 212.
166. *Philosophy of Mind* (Boulder: Westview Press, 1998) 8.
167. J.P. Moreland, "The Argument from Phenomenological Consciousness", in Ruloff and Horban, 159.
168. Paul M. Churchland, *The Engine of Reason, the Seat of the Soul: A Philosophical Journey Into the Brain* (Cambridge: MIT Press, 1996) 211.
169. D.M Armstrong, *A Materialist Theory of Mind* (London: Routledge, 1968) 30.
170. See J.P. Moreland, "The Argument from Phenomenological Consciousness", in Ruloff and Horban, 159.
171. David Skrbina, *Panpsychism In The West* (University of Notre Dame Press, 2006); David Chalmers, *The Conscious Mind* (Oxford University Press, 1996); Annaka Harris, *Conscious.* Graham Oppy, *Arguing About Gods,* 399; Thomas Nagel, *The View from Nowhere* (Oxford University Press, 1986).
172. David J. Chalmers, "Panpsychism and Panprotopsychism", in Torin Alter and Yugin Nagasawa (eds) *Consciousness in the Physical World: Perspectives on Russellian Monism* (Oxford University Press, 2015)
173. William Jaworski, *Philosophy of Mind: A Comprehensive Introduction* (Wiley-Blackwell, 2011) 231
174. See Grace Huckins, "Minds of machines: The great AI consciousness conundrum", *MIT Technology Review,* October 16, 2023.
175. Madell, *Mind and Materialism,* 3.
176. Bos, *Brain Box,* 143.

177. Andrew Melnyk, "Naturalism, Free Choices, and Conscious Experiences", www.infidels.org 2007.
178. Peter Cave, *Humanism* (Oxford: OneWorld, 2009) 29.
179. Richard Lewontin, "Billions and billions of demons", *The New York Review*, 9 January 1997, 31.
180. Robert C. Koons and George Bealer, *The Waning of Materialism* (Oxford University Press: 2010).
181. John Searle, *Freedom & Neurobiology* (New York: Columbia University Press, 2007) 4–5.
182. See J.P. Moreland, "The Image of God and the Failure of Scientific Atheism", in William Lane Craig and Chad Meister (eds) *God is Great, God is Good* (Nottingham: IVP, 2009) 32–48.
183. See John Searle, *Mind: A Brief Introduction* (Oxford University Press, 2005).
184. Gerald R. Baron, "Darwin's Horrid Doubt: Why Monkey Brains Troubled the Great Man of Science", medium.com Sep 9, 2020.
185. Bos, *Brain* Box, 232.
186. After Peter S. Williams, *C.S. Lewis vs the New Atheists* (Milton Keynes: Paternoster, 2013) 103.
187. J.B.S. Haldane, *Possible Worlds and Other Essays* (London: Chatto & Windus, 1932).
188. Andre Comte-Sponville, *The Book of Atheist Spirituality: An Elegant Argument for Spirituality without God* (London: Bantam, 2008) 82.
189. Arthur Conan Doyle, *The Sign of the Four*, chapter 1: The Science of Deduction.
190. See Victor Reppert, *C.S. Lewis's Dangerous Idea: In Defense of the Argument from Reason* (Downers Grove: IVP, 2003) ch 4.
191. Brian Greene, *Until the End of Time: Mind, Matter, and Our Search for Meaning in an Evolving Universe* (London: Penguin, 2021).
192. There are many kinds of dualism but I don't want to complicate things here. I'm fascinated by integrative dualism, also called wholistic dualism, which emphasises how the physical and non-physical parts of a person are interdependent. Charles Taliaferro, "The Promise and Sensibility of Integrative Dualism", in Andrea Lavazza and Howard Robinson (eds) *Contemporary Dualism: A Defense* (Oxford: Routledge, 2014). John W. Cooper, *Body, Soul and Life Everlasting: Biblical Anthropology and the Monism-Dualism Debate* (Leicester: Apollos, 1989) xvi. "The primary biblical emphasis on the person is as a unified agent", says C. Stephen Evans, *Preserving The Person: A Look at the Human Sciences* (Regent College Publishing, 1985) 148.
193. Karl Popper, *Objective Knowledge: An Evolutionary Approach* (Oxford University Press, 1972) 223.
194. Richard Taylor, *Metaphysics* (Englewood Cliffs: Prentice-Hall, 1992): 111, 114.
195. After C.S. Lewis, *Miracles*, chapter 4. See also Reppert, *Argument from Reason*.
196. Thomas Nagel, *The Last Word* (Oxford University Press, 1997) 129.
197. "[I]f the causal closure of the physical domain is to be respected, it seems *prima facie* that mental causation must be ruled out." Jaegwon Kim, *Philosophy of Mind* (Boulder: Westview, 1996): 131–32.

198. John Searle, *Minds, Brains and Science* (Cambridge: Harvard University Press, 1984) 32–33.
199. Aristotle saw this around 350BC, *Metaphysics* bk 4, ch 4.
200. Joshua Rasmussen, "Foundation of Reason", in *How Reason Can Lead to God*.
201. Bos, *Brain Box*, 65.
202. Karl Popper and Sir John Eccles, *The Self and Its Brain: An Argument for Interactionism* (London: Routledge, 1984).
203. After Victor Reppert, "The Argument from Reason", in William Lane Craig and J.P. Moreland (eds) *The Blackwell Companion to Natural Theology* (Malden: Wiley-Blackwell, 2012) 84.
204. Maria Konnikova, "The Science in Sherlock Holmes", *Nature* 21 Sept 2017, 332–33.
205. Nagel, *Mind and Cosmos*, 52.
206. John Gray, *Straw Gods: Thoughts on Humans and Other Animals* (London: Granta, 2002) 26–27.
207. Charles Darwin, letter to William Graham, 3 July 1881.
208. (London: Penguin, 2020).
209. See Alvin Plantinga, *Warranted Christian Belief* (Oxford University Press, 2000) 227–40; *Where the Conflict Really Lies: Science, Religion, and Naturalism* (Oxford University Press, 2011).
210. Thomas Nagel, "A Philosopher Defends Religion", *The New York Review* September 27, 2012.
211. Nagel, *Mind and Cosmos*, 27.
212. e.g. Dennett, *Consciousness Explained*, 33.
213. "Stress Relief from Laughter? It's No Joke" www.mayoclinic.org/healthy-lifestyle/stress-management/in-depth/stress-relief/art-20044456
214. See Kurt Ackerman and Andrea Dimartini (eds) *Psychosomatic Medicine* (Oxford University Press, 2015).
215. Bos, *Brain Box*, 97, 42.
216. Jon Hamilton, "Orphans' Lonely Beginnings Reveal How Parents Shape A Child's Brain", NPR Feb 24, 2014.
217. Bos, *Brain Box*, 16. See Sue Gerhardt, *Why Love Matters. How Affection Shapes a Baby's Brain* (Oxford: Routledge, 2004); J. Bick et al, "Effect of Early Institutionalization and Foster Care on Long-term White Matter Development. A Randomized Clinical Trial.", *JAMA Pediatrics* 196 (3):211–19, 2015.
218. Joseph LeDoux, *Synaptic Self: How Our Brains Become Who We Are* (Viking Penguin, 2002).
219. Thomas Fuchs, "The Brain: A Mediating Organ", *Journal of Consciousness Studies* 1, 7–8 (2011):196–221.
220. Gary Habermas and J.P. Moreland, *Beyond Death* (Wheaton: Good News, 1998) 49.
221. After Williams, *Faithful Guide to Philosophy*, 218.
222. Cami Rosso, "Tech Interface and AI Enable Stroke Survivor to Communicate", *Psychology Today*, September 12, 2023.

Endnotes

223. Benjamin Libet, "Reflections on the interactions of the mind and brain", *Progress in Neurobiology* 78(2006):322–26.

224. After J.P. Moreland, "Christianity, Neuroscience, and Dualism", in J.B. Stump and Alan G. Padgett, *The Blackwell Companion to Science and Christianity* (London: Blackwell, 2012) 470-471.

225. Uriah Kriegel, *Current Controversies in Philosophy of Mind* (New York: Taylor & Francis, 2014) 201.

226. *The Philosophical Review* 83, No. 4 (Oct, 1974) 435–50.

227. Strawson, "Consciousness Deniers".

228. *Mind and Cosmos*, 41.

229. J. P. Moreland, "The Argument from Consciousness", in J. P. Moreland et al, *Debating Christian Theism* (Oxford University Press, 2013) 122

230. Adapted from J.P. Moreland, "Christianity, Neuroscience, and Dualism", in Stump and Padgett, *Science and Christianity*, 471.

231. Michael Egnor, "A Map of the Soul", *First Things*, 20 June 2017

232. Keith Ward, *Is Religion Irrational?* (Oxford: Lion, 2011) 61

233. Adapted from Moreland, "Christianity, Neuroscience, and Dualism", 470-471.

234. Peter Kreeft and Ronald K. Tacelli, "Twenty Arguments for the Existence of God", https://peterkreeft.com/topics-more/20_arguments-gods-existence.htm#10

235. J.L. Mackie, *Ethics: Inventing Right and Wrong* (London: Viking Press, 1977); *The Miracle of Theism: Arguments For and Against The Existence of God* (Oxford University Press, 1982) 115–16

236. *Atheist's Guide to Reality*, p.2

237. "The Moral Argument for God's Existence", www.namb.net/apologetics/resource/the-moral-argument-for-gods-existence/

238. Ben Rogers, *A.J. Ayer: A Life* (New York: Grove Press, 1999): 344. Vikas Datta, "The philosopher who supplanted God, bested Mike Tyson by words, *The Week*, 29 October 2017.

239. Francis J. Beckwith and Gregory Koukl, *Relativism: Feet Firmly Planted in Mid-Air* (Grand Rapids: Baker Books, 1998)

240. *Modern Philosophy: An Introduction and Survey* (New York: Penguin Books, 1996)

241. Friedrich Nietzsche, *Twilight of the Idols; The Anti-Christ* (1888) (London: Penguin, 1990) 66; *On the Genealogy of Morals* (1887) (New York: Vintage, 1967) 89.

242. *Twilight of the Idols*, 80.

243. (London: Penguin, 1990) 38.

244. Gilbert Harman, *Explaining Value and Other Essays in Moral Philosophy* (Oxford University Press, 2000).

245. Kai Nielsen, *Ethics Without God* (Buffalo: Prometheus Books, 1990): 10–11

246. See Larry Arnhart, *Darwinian natural Right: The Biological Ethics of Human Nature* (New York: State University of New York, 1998). See also E.O. Wilson and Michael Ruse.

247. Randy Thornhill and Craig T. Palmer, *A Natural History of Rape: Biological Bases of Sexual Coercion* (Chicago: MIT Press, 2000).

248. Barbara B. Smuts, "Male Aggression and Sexual Coercion of Females in Nonhuman Primates and Other Mammals: Evidence and Theoretical Implications", *Advances in the Study of Behavior* 22 (1993); C.D. Knott et al, "Female reproductive strategies in orangutans, evidence for female choice and counterstrategies to infanticide in a species with frequent sexual coercion." *Proceedings: Biological Sciences 277*: 105–13 (2010); C.S. Han and P.G. Jablonski, "Male water striders attract predators to intimidate females into copulation." *Nature Communications 1*, 52 (2010). J. Bergsten and K.B. Miller, "Phylogeny of diving beetles reveals a coevolutionary arms race between the sexes." PLOS ONE 2, e522 (2007).

249. Richard Wrangham and Dale Peterson, *Demonic Males: Apes and the Origins of Human Violence* (London: Bloomsbury, 1997) 140.

250. Tatiana Zerjal, et al. 'The Genetic Legacy of the Mongols'. *Am J Hum Genet* v.72(3) Mar 2003.

251. M. C.B. Andrade, "Risky mate search and male self-sacrifice in redback spiders." *Behavioral Ecology* Vol 14/4, July 2003: 531–38.

252. Susan Brownmiller, *Against Our Will: Men, Women and Rape* (New York: Simon & Schuster, 1975) 11–12, 15, 6.

253. Preface to the 2013 edition of *Against Our Will*.

254. Louise Perry, *The Case Against the Sexual Revolution* (Cambridge: Polity Press, 2022).

255. Richard Dawkins, *The Selfish Gene* (Oxford University Press, 1976) v.

256. Richard Dawkins, *The God Delusion* (London: Bantam, 2006) 214.

257. Richard Dawkins, "God's Utility Function," *Scientific American* (vol. 273, Nov 1995) 85.

258. Dawkins, *God Delusion*, 220–221.

259. Richard Dawkins, *A Devil's Chaplain: Reflections on Hope, Lies, Science and Love* (Boston: Houghton Mifflin, 2003).

260. Debate with Archbishop George Pell, www.abc.net.au/qanda/values-of-survival-of-the-fittest/10661438

261. Paul Copan, "The Moral Argument", in Meister and Copan (eds) *The Routledge Companion to Philosophy of Religion* (London: Routledge, 2012) 365–70.

262. Richard Swinburne, *The Existence of God* 2nd edn (Oxford: Clarendon Press, 2004) 216–17.

263. www.catholicnewsagency.com/news/257276/famous-atheist-richard-dawkins-says-he-considers-himself-a-cultural-christian

264. Kai Nielsen, "Why Should I Be Moral?" *American Philosophical Quarterly* 21 (1984) 90.

265. J.L. Mackie, *The Miracle of Theism*, 115.

266. Charles Darwin, *The Voyage of the Beagle* (London: Everyman) 430.

267. Charles Darwin, *The Descent of Man, and Selection in Relation to Sex* (London: John Murray, 1871) 201

268. Darwin, *Beagle*, chapter 19.

269. Nigel Parbury, "A History of Aboriginal education", in Rhonda Craven (ed), *Teaching Aboriginal Studies: A practical resource for primary and secondary teaching*, (London: Routledge, 2020) 133.

Endnotes

270. Raymond M. Nichol, "Aboriginal Education in New South Wales: Nineteenth, twentieth and twenty-first centuries", in *Socialization, land, and citizenship among Aboriginal Australians: Reconciling Indigenous and Western forms of education* (Lampeter: Edwin Mellen Press, 2005) 253–76: 273.
271. Joanna Cruickshank, "Darwin, race and religion in Australia", *ABC Religion and Ethics Report*, 9 Jan 2012.
272. See the classic by John Harris, *One Blood: 200 Years of Aboriginal Encounter with Christianity: A Story of Hope* (Brentfort Square: Australians Together, 2019).
273. Nagel, *Mind and Cosmos*, 27. C.f. Sharon Street, "A Darwinian Dilemma for Realist Theories of Value", *Philosophical Studies* 127.1 (Jan 2006) 109–66.
274. Michael Ruse, "Evolutionary Theory and Christian Ethics", in *The Darwinian Paradigm* (London: Routledge, 1989) 262–69.
275. James Rachels, *Created from Animals* (Oxford University Press, 1990) 171–72.
276. Joel Feinberg, *Social Philosophy* (Englewood Cliffs: Prentice-Hall, 1973) 84–97.
277. Harris, *The End of Faith*, 178–82; "God Debate: Sam Harris Versus Rick Warren", *Newsweek*, April 9, 2007.
278. L.A. Jensen-Campbell et al, "Dominance, prosocial orientation, and female preferences: Do nice guys really finish last?" *Journal of Personality and Social Psychology* 68(3) 1995: 427–40.
279. P. Barclay, "Altruism as a courtship display: Some effects of third-party generosity on audience perceptions", *British Journal of Psychology* 10(1):123–35.
280. W. Iredale et al, "Showing Off in Humans: Male Generosity as a Mating Signal", *Evolutionary Psychology* 6(3) 2008: 159.
281. N.J. Raihani and S. Smith, "Competitive helping in online giving", *Current Biology* 25(9) 2015: 1183–1186.
282. Thomas Hobbes, *Leviathan*, in Richard Tuck (ed), *Cambridge Texts in the History of Political Thought* (Cambridge University Press, 1996) 89.
283. Rachel Jewkes et al *(2011)* "Gender Inequitable Masculinity and Sexual Entitlement in Rape Perpetration South Africa: Findings of a Cross-Sectional Study", *PLOS ONE 6 (12); and (2016)* "Why, when and how men rape: Understanding rape perpetration in South Africa", *South African Crime Quarterly 34*.
284. Vrushali Patil and Bandana Purkayastha (19 May 2017) "The transnational assemblage of Indian rape culture", *Ethnic and Racial Studies. 41 (11)*; "'Everyone Blames Me': Barriers to Justice and Support Services for Sexual Assault Survivors in India", *Human Rights Watch*, 8 November 2017. Kavita Krishnan (3 December 2015) "Rape Culture and Sexism in Globalising India", *Sur International Journal on Human Rights 12 (22): 255–259*.
285. P.A. Ali and M.I. Gavino (April 2008) "Violence against women in Pakistan: a framework for analysis", *The Journal of the Pakistan Medical Association 58 (4): 198–203*. Salman Masood, "Pakistani Woman Who Shattered Stigma of Rape got Married", *The New York Times*, 17 March 2009.
286. See David Gauthier, *Morals by Agreement* (Oxford: Clarendon Press, 1986).
287. Peter Padfield, *Himmler, Reichsführer SS* (London: Papermac, 1990) 444.
288. Albert Speer, *Inside the Third Reich.* (New York: Macmillan, 1971):143

289. Padfield, *Himmler*, 167–68
290. E.g. James 1:27; Isaiah 1:17; Psalm 82:3–4.
291. David Buss, *The Evolution of Desire: Strategies of Human Mating*. (New York: Basic Books, 2016): 256.
292. Dina McMillan, 13 April 2018, https://singjupost.com/unmasking-the-abuser-dina-mcmillan-at-tedxcanberra-full-transcript/
293. Buss, 39.
294. See K.A. Lonsway and L.F. Fitzgerald, "Rape Myths: In Review", *Psychology of Women Quarterly* 18(2) 133–64. Martha R. Burt, "Cultural myths and supports for rape", *Journal of Personality and Social Psychology* 38/2 (1980) 217–30.
295. C.S. Evans and Trinity O'Neill, "The Moral Argument", in Rulof and Horban.
296. Ezekiel 16:27, 47–48, 51; 36:22; c.f. Romans 2:24; Matthew 11:21.
297. Helga Kuhse and Peter Singer, *Should the Baby Live?* (Oxford University Press, 1985) 118–39.
298. J.L. Mackie, *The Miracle of Theism*, 115–16.
299. Elsa J. Marty, *A Dictionary of Philosophy of Religion*, (London: Continuum, 2010) 154.
300. David Hume, *Dialogues Concerning Natural Religion* (Indianapolis: Bobbs-Merrill, 1980) Part X, 198.
301. https://www.independent.co.uk/news/world/europe/stephen-fry-blasphemy-god-ireland-police-investigation-quotes-full-a7722256.html
302. Graham Lawton, "Why almost everyone believes in an afterlife – even atheists", *New Scientist* 20 Nov 2019
303. Jan Westerhoff, "Creation in Buddhism", in Simon Oliver (ed),*The Oxford Handbook of Creation*, (Oxford University Press: 2021).
304. Adams, *Hitchhikers Guide*.
305. J.L. Mackie, "Evil and Omnipotence", *Mind* (64) (1954) 200–212; *The Miracle of Theism: Arguments For and Against the Existence of God* (Oxford: Clarendon, 1982).
306. J.L. Mackie, "Evil and Omnipotence", *Mind* 64 no 254 (1955) 200–212; *The Miracle of Theism: Arguments For and Against the Existence of God* (Oxford: Clarendon 1982) 150.
307. Alvin Plantinga, *God, Freedom and Evil* (Grand Rapids: Eerdmans, 1977): 30.
308. Marilyn McCord Adams, *Horrendous Evils and the Goodness of God* (Melbourne University Press, 1999) 26.
309. See D.Z. Phillips, *The Problem of Evil and the Problem of God* (Minneapolis: Fortress Press, 2005) 106.
310. 1 John 4:8.
311. Hebrews 6:18, 2 Timothy 2:13, James 1:13
312. Plantinga, *God, Freedom and Evil*, 93–94.
313. Alvin Plantinga, *God and Other Minds: A Study of the Rational Justification of Belief in God* (Ithaca: Cornell University Press, 1967); *The Nature of Necessity* (Oxford: Clarendon, 1974); *God, Freedom and Evil; The Nature of Necessity*. Oxford: Clarendon Press. *Warranted Christian Belief* (Oxford University Press. 2000).

314. David Basinger, "Evil as Evidence against God's Existence", in Michael L. Peterson (ed),*The Problem of Evil: Selected Readings* (University of Notre Dame Press, 1992); Kevin Timpe and Daniel Speak, "Introduction", in *Free Will and Theism: Connections, Contingencies, and Concerns* (Oxford University Press, 2016). Chad Meister, *Introducing Philosophy of Religion* (Taylor & Francis, 2009) 134; William P. Alston, "The Inductive Argument from Evil and the Human Cognitive Condition", *Philosophical Perspectives* 5 (1991) 29–67. Matthew A. Benton et al, "Evil and Evidence", *Oxford Studies in Philosophy of Religion* 7(2016) 1–31.

315. William Rowe, "The Problem of Evil and Some Varieties of Atheism". *American Philosophical Quarterly* 16(4) (1979): 335–41.

316. Rowe, "The Problem of Evil and Some Varieties of Atheism", 336–37.

317. Paul Draper "Pain and Pleasure: An Evidential Problem for Theists". *Noûs*. 23 (3) (1989): 331–50.

318. Benton et al, 2.

319. Marie Conn, *C.S. Lewis and Human Suffering: Light Among the Shadows* (Mahwah: HiddenSpring, 2008) 21.

320. C.S. Lewis, *Surprised By Joy: The Shape of My Early Life* (London: Harvest Books, 2008) 115.

321. C.S. Lewis, *Mere Christianity*, 25. http://samizdat.qc.ca/vc/pdfs/MereChristianity_CSL.pdf

322. Mackie, *Miracle of Theism*, 115–16.

323. John Stott, *The Cross of Christ* (IVP, 1986) 335–36, quoting P.T. Forsyth, *Justification of God*, p.32.

324. Mitsuo Fuchida, *For That One Day: The Memoirs of Mitsuo Fuchida, Commander of the Attack on Pearl Harbor*, (Kamuela, HI: eXperience, 2011) 255.

325. Mitsuo Fuchida, "I Led The Attack on Pearl Harbor", *Proceedings of the US Naval Institute*, Sep 1952, Vol 78/9/595.

326. Craig Nelson, *Pearl Harbour: From Infamy to Greatness* (New York: Scribner, 2016).

327. Craig Nelson, *The First Heroes: The Extraordinary Story of the Doolittle Raid – America's First World War II Victory* (New York: Penguin, 2002).

328. Nelson, *Pearl*, 397.

329. Nelson, *Heroes*.

330. Fuchida, *One Day*, 179.

331. Nelson, *Pearl*, 404.

332. Fuchida, *One Day*, 232–34. See Lisa M. Samra, 'Covell, Margaret "Peggy"' in George Thomas Kurian and Mark A. Lanport, eds, *The Encyclopedia of Christianity in the United States* (Rowman and Littlefield).

333. Gordon W. Prange with Donald M. Goldstein and Katherine V. Dillon, *God's Samurai: Lead Pilot at Pearl Harbour* (Washington: Brassey's Inc, 1990) 203.

334. Jacob De Shazer, "I Was A Prisoner of Japan", quoted in Nelson, *Heroes*.

335. Richard Swinburne, *The Existence of God* 2nd edn (Oxford: Clarendon Press, 2004): 244–76. R. Douglas Geivett, "The Evidential Value of Religious Experience", in Paul Copan and Paul Moser (eds) *The Rationality of Theism* (Taylor & Francis, 2003) 175–203. Clack Clack, *Philosophy of Religion*, 43–49. William P. Alston, "Religious

Experience Justifies Religious Belief", in Michael Peterson and Raymond J. VanArragon, *Contemporary Debates in Philosophy of Religion* (Malden: Blackwell Publishers, 2004) 183–90; Mackie, *Miracle of Theism*, 204–10.

336. William P. Alston, "Religious Experience and Religious Belief" *The Journal of Philosophy* 67/14 1970: 471–76; Paul Draper, "The Problem of the Hiddenness of God and the Problem of Evil" *Religious Studies* 35/3, 1999: 331–52; John Hick, *An Interpretation of Religion: Human Responses to the Transcendent* (Yale University Press, 1989); William L. Rowe, "Religious Experience and the Principle of Credulity", *International Journal for Philosophy of Religion*, 16/2, 1984:73–93.

337. Kai-man Kwan, "The Argument from Religious Experience", in Ruloff and Horban.

338. Caroline Franks Davis, "The Devotional Experiment", *Religious Studies* March 1986 Vol 22 No 1, 15–28.

339. Aldous Huxley, *Ends and Means: An Enquiry into the Nature of Ideals*, 1937 (Oxford: Routledge, 2012) ch XIV.

340. Nagel, *Mind and Cosmos*.

341. Thomas Nagel, "A Philosopher Defends Religion", *The New York Review* September 27, 2012.

342. Nagel, *Mind and Cosmos*, 27.

343. Thomas Nagel, *The Last Word* (Oxford University Press, 1996) 130.

344. After Martin Dowson, "A biblical philosophy of education", in Ken Goodlet and John Collier (eds) *Teaching well: insights for educators in Christian schools* (Canberra: Barton Books, 2014) 39–51.

345. Dawkins, *God Delusion*, 97.

346. Sylvester Vierek, "What Life Means to Einstein", *Saturday Evening Post*, Oct 26, 1929.

347. Bart D. Ehrman, *Did Jesus Exist? The Historical Argument for Jesus of Nazareth* (New York: HarperOne, 2012): 37. See also *The New Testament: A Historical Introduction to the Early Christian Writings* (Oxford University Press, 1999).

348. "Christianity", in Simon Hornblower et al (eds) *The Oxford Classical Dictionary* (Oxford University Press, 2012) 325.

349. William David Davies et al (eds) *The Cambridge History of Judaism*, vol 3 (CUP, 2000) 677.

350. John P. Meier, *A Marginal Jew: Rethinking the Historical Jesus,* vol I (London: Doubleday, 1991) 56.

351. That was claimed by writers Apion and Celsus, but denied by the Jewish writer Josephus, *Contra Apion,* and the Christian writer Origen, *Contra Celsum,* Bk VII.

352. N.T. Wright, *What Saint Paul Really Said: Was Paul of Tarsus the Real Founder of Christianity?* (Grand Rapids: Eerdmans, 1997) 46.

353. Marcus Tullius Cicero, *Against Verres*, 2nd pleading, 5th book, section 170, c. 70 BC.

354. Ronald J. Mellor, *Tacitus* (New York: Routledge, 1993) 40.

355. Tacitus, *Annals*. Translated C.H. Moore and J. Jackson. (Cambridge: Harvard University Press, 1962) 283.

356. e.g., Luke 3:1, 23:24.

357. Paul Barnett, *Finding the Historical Christ* (Cambridge: Eerdmans, 2009) 60.

Endnotes

358. Louis H. Feldman, *Jewish Life and Thought among Greeks and Romans* (Edinburgh: T&T Clark, 1996) 332; James D. G. Dunn, *Jesus Remembered* (Grand Rapids: Eerdmans, 2003) 141–43. William L. Lane, "Social Perspectives on Roman Christianity during the Formative Years from Nero to Nerva: Romans, Hebrews, 1 Clement", in Karl Paul Donfried and Peter Richardson (eds) *Judaism and Christianity in First-Century Rome* (Grand Rapids: Eerdmans, 1998) 204–6.
359. Paul Eddy and Gregory Boyd, *The Jesus Legend: A Case for the Historical Reliability of the Synoptic Jesus Tradition* (2007) 166; Craig S. Keener, *The Historical Jesus of the Gospels* (2012) 66. John G. Cook, "Chrestiani, Christiani, Χριστιανοί: A Second Century Anachronism?" *Vigiliae Christianae* (2020) 253–56.
360. Acts 18:2.
361. e.g., Matthew 14:1–12.
362. e.g., Mark 15:1–5; John 18:13.
363. Acts 15:13–29; Galatians 2:11–14. See Barnett, 52.
364. Graham Stanton, *The Gospels and Jesus* (Oxford University Press, 2003) 148.
365. C.f. Galatians 1:19; 2:9; Mark 6:3; Acts 15:13; 21:18.
366. Gerd Theissen and Annette Merz, *The Historical Jesus: A Contemporary Guide* (Minneapolis: Fortress Press, 1998) 65.
367. See Craig A. Evans, "Jesus in Non-Christian Sources", in Bruce Chilton and Craig A. Evans (eds) *Studying the Historical Jesus: Evaluations of the State of Current Research* (Leiden: Brill, 1994) 466–67.
368. See Barnett, *Finding the Historical Christ*, 49.
369. John Dickson, *Investigating Jesus: An Historian's Quest* (Oxford: Lion, 2010) 74.
370. Robert E. Van Voorst, *Jesus Outside the New Testament: an introduction to the ancient evidence* (Grand Rapids: Eerdmans, 2000) 53–55.
371. Lucian, *The Death of Peregrine* 11–13, trans H.W. Fowler and F.G. Fowler, *The Works of Lucian of Samosata* (Oxford: Clarendon Press, 1949) vol. 4.
372. Van Voorst, *Jesus Outside the New Testament*, 58–64.
373. Celsus, *True Doctrine*. His book is quoted in full by Origin, *Against Celsus*. See Henry Chadwick, *Origen: Contra Celsum* (Cambridge: CUP, 1980).
374. e.g., Matthew 27:45.
375. These saying were written around 200, but compiled around 400–500. Van Voorst, *Jesus Outside the New Testament*, 117. See Theissen and Merz, *Historical Jesus*, 75.
376. Justin Martyr, *Dialogue With Trypho*, 69.
377. Theissen and Merz, *Historical Jesus*, 63.
378. Meier, *Marginal Jew*, 87.
379. Christopher Hitchens, *God Is Not Great: How Religion Poisons Everything* (London: Twelve, 2007) 114.
380. Sir Isaac Newton, *Observations upon the prophecies of Daniel, and the Apocalypse of St John* (London, 1733).
381. John 13:19. C.f. John 14:29.
382. Isaiah 46:10.
383. www.un.org/ungifts/replica-edict-cyrus

384. There's a copy in the Bible: Ezra 7:11–26. Previous decrees by Persian kings Cyrus (Ezra 1:1–4; 6:3–5) and Darius (Eza 6:1–12) had dealt with the Jews and the temple, but Artaxerxes' decree was the first to deal with the city of Jerusalem, rebuilding it and restoring it as a civil and legal centre. This was in the seventh year of his reign (Ezra 7:7–8) which was 457 BC.
385. Leviticus 25:3–7.
386. Josh McDowell, *Evidence That Demands a Verdict: Historical Evidence for the Christian Faith*, Vol I (Nashville: Thomas Nelson, Nashville, 1979) 170, 172: "Daniel knew that the Babylonian captivity was based on violation of the Sabbatic year, and since they were in captivity for 70 years, evidently the Sabbatic year was violated 490 years (Leviticus 26:32–35; II Chronicles 36:21 and Daniel 9:24)."
387. John 2:19–20.
388. Chronologies can vary slightly. For example, Stephen Miller argues for 458 BC and sees Jesus anointed in AD 26, in *Daniel* (Broadman & Holman, 1994) 266. McDowell (173) says Jesus died in AD 33.
389. John 4:25–26.
390. Matthew 24:15.
391. John 6:15.
392. Matthew 16:21–23.
393. Isaiah 53:10; John 1:29.
394. Jacques B. Doukhan, *Secrets of Daniel: Wisdom and Dreams of a Jewish Prince in Exile* (Hagerstown: R&H Publishing, 2000) 148–49.
395. The "flood" of Daniel 9:26 is understood this way by Josephus, the Talmud and the great medieval rabbis Rashi, Ibn Ezra and others. Doukhan, *Secrets of Daniel*, 150.
396. Matthew 23:37–39; 24:15.
397. Luke 21:20–24.
398. Yechiel Eckstein, *What Christians Should Know About Jews and Judaism* (Nashville: W Publishing Group, 1984) 262, 261.
399. Luke 24:26.
400. Dan Cohn-Sherbok, *The Jewish Messiah* (Edinburgh: T&T Clark, 1997).
401. Peter de Rosa, *Vicars of Christ* (London: Corgi, 1988) 3–6.
402. Micah 5:2.
403. Matthew 2:17–18; Jeremiah 31:15.
404. Hosea 11:1.
405. Matthew 2:23. He doesn't name the prophet, but he may be referring to predictions of Jesus having humble origins (e.g. Isaiah 53:2) because Nazareth was a despised town (John 1:46). And the name Nazareth may pun on the Hebrew word *netser* (= shoot, branch) since Jesus was called a branch or shoot from David's family (Isaiah 11:1) and a shoot out of dry ground (Isaiah 53:2).
406. Matthew 4:13–16; cf Isaiah 9:1–2, which describes that area in various ways.
407. Psalm 22: 16.
408. Peter W. Stoner and Robert C. Newman, *Science Speaks: Scientific Proof of the Accuracy of the Bible* (Chicago: Moody Press, 1976): 99–112.

ENDNOTES

409. Debate with Philip E. Johnson, *Origins Research* 16/1, 1994:9.
410. Suzanne Carbone & Lawrence Money, "Hold on, Kerry, it seems there is something there", *The Age* 31 August 2009.
411. See Gary R. Habermas & Michael R. Licona, *The Case for the Resurrection of Jesus* (Grand Rapids: Kregel, 2004).
412. Marcus Tullius Cicero, *Against Verres* 2.5.64, 165; *Pro Rabirio* 9–17.
413. Josephus, *Jewish Wars*, Bk 5, Ch 11.
414. Seneca the Younger, *De Consolatione ad Marciam* ("To Marcia on Consolation") c. AD 40.
415. John Dominic Crossan, *Jesus: A Revolutionary Biography* (San Francisco: Harper-Collins, 1991) 145, 154, 196, 201.
416. E.g. Matthew W. Maslen, Piers D. Mitchell, "Medical theories on the cause of death in crucifixion", *Journal of the Royal Society of Medicine* 99(4) 185–88 (April 2006). Gary Habermas, Jonathan Kopel, Benjamin C.F. Shaw, "Medical views on the death by crucifixion of Jesus Christ", *Baylor University Medical Center Proceedings* 34(6): 748–52 (July 30, 2021). Thomas A. Miller, MD, *Did Jesus Really Rise From the Dead? A Surgeon-Scientist Examines the Evidence* (Wheaton: Crossway, 2013). Frederick T. Zugibe, *The Crucifixion of Jesus: A Forensic Inquiry* (Rowman & Littlefield, 2005). William D. Edwards, Wesley J. Gabel & Floyd E. Hosmer, "On the Physical Death of Jesus Christ", *Journal of the American Medical Association* 255 (1986): 1455–1463. W. Reid Litchfield, "The Search for the Physical Cause of Jesus Christ's Death", *Brigham Young University Studies 1997-98*, Vol. 37, No. 4 (1997-98):93–109. Joe E. Holoubek & Alice Baker Holoubek, "A Study of Death by Crucifixion With Attempted Explanation of the Death of Jesus Christ," *The Linacre Quarterly* 61/1 (1994). Pierre Barbet (1953) *A Doctor at Calvary: The Passion of Our Lord Jesus Christ as Described by a Surgeon* (New York: Doubleday Image Books, 1953). C.T. Davis, "The Crucifixion of Jesus. The Passion of Christ From a Medical Point of View", *Arizona Medicine* 22 (1962): 182. Robert Bucklin, MD, JD, "The Legal and Medical Aspects of the Trial and Death of Christ", *Medicine, Science, and the Law* 10 (1970): 14–26. F.V. Mikulicz-Radeeki, "The chest wound in the crucified Christ." *Med News* 1966; 14:30–40. F.P. Retief, L. Cilliers (December 2003) "The history and pathology of crucifixion", *South African Medical Journal* 93 (12): 938–841. B. Brenner (2005) "Did Jesus Christ die of pulmonary embolism?". *J Thromb Haemost.* 3(9): 1–2; J. Zias and J.H. Charlesworth, "Crucifixion: Archaeology, Jesus and the Dead Sea Scrolls,» in: J.H. Charlesworth (ed.) *Jesus and the Dead Sea Scrolls* (The Anchor Yale Bible Reference Library, 1992) 273–89.
417. Luke 22:42-44
418. Frederick T. Zugibe, "Forensic and Clinical Knowledge of the Practice of Crucifixion", Turin Lecture, 2000.
419. John 18:12–14, 19–23; Matthew 26:57–68; Mark 14:53–65; Luke 22:54, 63–64.
420. Matthew 27:11–26; Mark 15:20; Luke 23:13–22; John 18:29—19:1.
421. Miller, *Did Jesus Really Rise*, 70.
422. Bucklin, "Legal and Medical Aspects".
423. Miller, *Did Jesus Really Rise*, 71.
424. Matthew 27:27–30; Mark 15:16–19; John 19:2–5

425. Zugibe, Turin Lecture.
426. Three gospels mention him (Matthew 27:32; Luke 23:26; Mark 15:21) and Mark says his sons were among the Christian community. c.f. Acts 11:20; Romans 16:13.
427. One was found in 2017 in a Roman site in Britain www.cnet.com/science/skeleton-with-nail-in-heel-offers-evidence-of-roman-crucifixion/ Joseph Zias & Eliezer Sekeles, "The Crucified Man from Giv'at ha-Mitvar: A Reappraisal", *Israel Exploration Journal* vol. 35, No.1 (1985): 22–27.
428. Joseph Zias, "Crucifixion in Antiquity: The Anthropological Evidence", 2016. www.academia.edu/588244/Crucifixion_in_Antiquity Edwards et al. Alternately, Zugibe describes nails through the muscle mass near the thumb base.
429. Archaeologists do not have many surviving nails from the period, but two have been found in the tomb of Caiaphas, the High Priest involved in Jesus' execution. See Ariel David, "Are These Nails From Jesus' Crucifixion? New Evidence Emerges, but Experts Are Unconvinced", *Haaretz*, Oct 12, 2020.
430. Miller, *Did Jesus Really Rise*, 76.
431. Edwards et al, "Physical Cause", 1461.
432. Matthew 27:34.
433. Barbet, *Doctor at Calvary.*
434. Edwards et al, "On The Physical Cause"; Davis, " Crucifixion of Jesus", 182.
435. Bucklin, "Legal and Medical Aspects" Mikulicz-Radeeki, "Chest Wound". Davis, "The Crucifixion". Barbet, *Doctor at Calvary*, 12–18, 37–147, 159–75, 187–208.
436. Retief & Cilliers "History and Pathology".
437. Zugibe, 2005.
438. Brenner, "Pulmonary embolism?".
439. Retief et al; Habermas et al; Edwards et al.
440. John 19:31–33; Mark 15:44–45.
441. John 19:34–38.
442. Zugibe, 140.
443. Alfred Edersheim, *The Life and Times of Jesus the Messiah*, vol. 2, (Grand Rapids: Eerdmans, 1962) 617.
444. Matthew 27:55–61; Mark 15:40–41; Luke 23:49.
445. John 3:1–21.
446. John 19:38–42.
447. Matthew 27:62–66.
448. Matthew 28:1–8; Mark 16:1–8; Luke 24:1–10; John 20:1–2.
449. John Andrew Couch, "Woman in Early Roman Law", *Harvard Law Review* 8/1 (1894) pp. 39–50:43
450. *Mishnah Rosh Hashanah*, 1.8.
451. *Antiquities* 4.8.15.
452. Celsus, *On The True Doctrine: A Discourse Against the Christians*, 3.44, c.AD 170.
453. Luke 24:11.
454. Tom Wright, "Appendix B", in Anthony Flew, *There is a God: How the World's Most*

ENDNOTES

Notorious Atheist Changed His Mind (2007) with Roy Abraham Varghese (San Francisco: Harper One) 207. See also Lisa Fields jude3project.org.

455. Matthew 28:11–15.
456. Justin Martyr, Trypho 108; Tertullian, *De Spectaculis* 30.
457. Gerd Lüdemann, *What Really Happened to Jesus? A Historical Approach to the Resurrection* (Louisville: Westminster John Knox, 1995): 80.
458. Bart D. Ehrman, *The New Testament: A Historical Introduction to the Early Christian Writings*. 3rd edn. (Oxford University Press, 2004): 276.
459. He had either older half-siblings from Joseph's first marriage or younger siblings from Joseph and Mary's marriage, or both. Matthew 13:55–57; Mark 6:3.
460. John 7:3–5; Matthew 12:46–50; Mark 3:21, 31–35; 6:3–4.
461. 1 Corinthians 15:7.
462. James 1:1.
463. Galatians 1:18–19.
464. Acts 1:12–13; 15:1–29.
465. Josephus, *Antiquities* vol 20, 9.1. The 2nd-century historian Hegesippus and Clement of Alexander also describe James' martyrdom, as recorded by Eusebius, *Ecclesiastical History* 2.23. See C. Bernard Ruffin, *The Twelve: The Lives of the Apostles After Calvary* (Our Sunday Visitor, 1998) 84–86.
466. John 20:28.
467. George Menachery (ed), *Apostle Thomas, Kerala, Malabar Christianity*. The St. Thomas Christian Encyclopaedia of India. Vol. II. (Trichur, 1973); Orpa Slapak (ed.) *The Jews of India: A Story of Three Communities*. (Muzeon Yisrael, 1995).
468. See Sean McDowell, *The Fate of the Apostles: Examining the Martyrdom Accounts of the Closest Followers of Jesus*, 2nd edn, (Routledge, 2024).
469. J.M. Farquhar and G. Garitte, *The Apostle Thomas in India, According to the Acts of Thomas* (Kerala: Syrian Church Series, 1972).
470. Acts 7:54–60; 1 Corinthians 15:9–10, Galatians 1:13–16, 22–23; Philippians 3:6–7.
471. Acts 9:26–28; Gal 1:18–24.
472. 2 Corinthians 11:23–26; 2 Corinthians 12:10.
473. Matthew 12:38–40; 16:1–4, 21; 17:22–23; 20:17–19; Mark 8:31–32; 9:31; 10:33; 14:58; Luke 9:22; 11:29–30; John 2:18–22.
474. Matthew 16:22–25; Mark 8:31–33; 9:31–32; 14:27–31; Luke 24:13–24.
475. John 20:2, 9, 13–15.
476. Luke 24:10–12.
477. William David Davies, Louis Finkelstein, William Horbury, John Sturdy (eds) *The Cambridge History of Judaism, vol 3* (Cambridge University Press) 677.
478. You Ask The Questions Special, *The Independent* 4 December 2006.
479. Sir James N.D. Anderson, QC, "A Dialogue on Christ's Resurrection", *Christianity Today* 12 April 1968.
480. Matthew 28:11–15.
481. Polybius, *The Rise of the Roman Empire*, c.110BC.

482. Matthew 28:11–15.
483. Mark 14:50; John 20:19.
484. Luke 24:41; Matthew 28:17; Acts 1:6.
485. Charles Colson, *Born Again*. www.prisonfellowship.org/
486. John 20:8.
487. Gerd Lüdemann, *What Really Happened to Jesus? A Historical Approach to the Resurrection* (Louisville: Westminster John Knox, 1995): 80.
488. See Gary Habermas, "Explaining Away Jesus' Resurrection: The Recent Revival of Hallucination Theories" (2001) *LBTS Faculty Publications and Presentations*: 107.
489. See Acts 9:1–19; 22:6–16; 26:12–23.
490. Acts 22:17–21.
491. Galatians 1:18–19; 2:1–10.
492. See Bart D. Ehrman, *How Jesus Became God: The Exaltation of a Jewish Preacher from Galilee* (San Francisco: HarperOne, 2014); and Michael F. Bird et al, *How God Became Jesus: The Real Origins of a Belief in Jesus Divine Nature – A Response to Bart Ehrman* (Grand Rapids: Zondervan, 2014).
493. F.F. Bruce, *The New Testament Documents: Are They Reliable?* (Grand Rapids: Eerdmans, 1981):42–43.
494. Acts 7:54–60.
495. 1 Corinthians 15:3–8.
496. Galatians 1:18—2:16.
497. See Grenville Kent and Philip Rodionoff, *The Da Vinci Decode* www.thedavincidecode.net
498. Google Karl Friedrich Bahrdt, Karl Venturini or Heinrich Paulus.
499. *The Life of Flavius Josephus*, 75.
500. David Strauss, *the Life of Jesus for the People*, vol 1 (London: Williams and Norgate, 1879): 412.
501. *De Spectaculis*, ch.30.
502. Matthew 27:61; Mark 15:47; Luke 23:55.
503. John Dominic Crossan, *Who Killed Jesus? Exposing the Roots of Anti-Semitism in the Gospel Story of the Death of Jesus* (San Francisco: HarperCollins, 1995) 160–88. John Shelby Spong, *Resurrection: Myth of Reality?* (San Francisco: HarperCollins, 2001) 230–270.
504. Joseph Zias (1998). "Crucifixion in Antiquity: The Evidence". www.mercaba.org
505. Craig A. Evans, *Jewish Burial Traditions and the Resurrection of Jesus*. B.R. McCane, *Roll Back the Stone: Death and Burial in the World of Jesus* (Harrisburg: Trinity Press International, 2003) 89–108.
506. David Ingham and Corinne Duhig, "Crucifixion in the Fens: life and death in Roman Fenstanton", *British Archaeology* Jan-Feb 2022, 18–29.
507. Mati Milstein, "Jesus Tomb Claim Slammed By Scholars", *National Geographic News*.
508. Simcha Jacobovici and Charles Pellegrino, *The Jesus Family Tomb: The Discover, the Investigation, and the Evidence That Could Change History* (San Francisco: Harper,

2007).

509. Amos Kloner and Shimon Gibson, "The Talpiot Tomb Reconsidered: The Archaeological Facts", in James H. Charlesworth (ed),*The Tomb of Jesus and His Family? Exploring Ancient Jewish Tombs Near Jerusalem's Walls* (Grand Rapids: Eerdmans, 2013) 29-75. Michael Heiser, "Evidence Real and Imagined: Thinking Clearly About The 'Jesus Family Tomb'" https;??drmsh.com/michaelsheiser.

510. Richard Bauckham, *Jesus and the Eyewitnesses* (Grand Rapids: Eerdmans, 2008).

511. See Dillon Burroughs, *The Jesus Family Tomb Controversy: How the Evidence Falls Short* (Ann Arbor: Nimble Books, 2007); Thomas F. Madden, *Not Dead Yet: The Lost Tomb of Jesus One Year Later* online.

512. Copan, *Fact or Figment*, 153.

513. Acts 2.

514. John Shelby Spong, *Why Christianity Must change or Die* (New York: Harper Collins, 1999): 116-17. John Dominic Crossan, *Jesus: A Revolutionary Biography* (San Francisco: Harper, 1994).

515. Luke 24:36-44.

516. Acts 2:14-39.

517. Further see Ross Clifford and Philip Johnson, *The Cross Is Not Enough: Living as Witnesses to the Resurrection* (Grand Rapids: Baker, 2012) 43-61.

518. 1 Corinthians 15:55-57

519. Holy Sonnet X, *The Complete English Poems* (London: Everyman's Library, 1985), 440-441.

520. Luke 23:43.

521. Revelation 21:1-4, 22-27; 22:1-5; Psalm 16:9-11; Isaiah 65:17-25; Luke 13:29.

522. Romans 4:25.

523. This chapter is based on Robert Coles' words in "The Inexplicable Prayers of Ruby Bridges", *Christianity Today*, August 9, 1985; his radio interview with Krista Tippett for On Being, "The Inner Lives of Children"; Philip Yancey, "The Crayon Man", *Christianity Today* February 6, 1987; Ruby Bridges, *Through My Eyes* (New York: Scholastic Press, 1999); *Ruby Bridges Goes to School: My True Story* (Scholastic Press, 2009); *I Am Ruby Bridges: How One Six-Year-Old Girl's March to School Changed the World* (New York: Orchard Books, 2022).

524. Debra Michals, "Ruby Bridges", National Women's History Museum, 2015.

525. Robert Coles, "In The South These Children Prophesy", *The Atlantic* March 1, 1963.

526. Interview with Krista Tippet.

527. Exodus 12:26-27; 13:14; Deuteronomy 6:20-21.

528. Matthew 18:3.

www.ingramcontent.com/pod-product-compliance
Lightning Source LLC
Chambersburg PA
CBHW071439150426
43191CB00008B/1175